The Deeper the Sorrow, The Stronger the Spirit

A tribute to those who've found solace in their spirituality

ALEXANDRA LEVIN

You will be awed and inspired by the true personal stories of the men and women who invite you into the moments where their lives were intrinsically changed, making them who they are today.

The Deeper the Sorrow, the Stronger the Spirit is a must for anyone truly interested in the power of adversity and its ability to alter the course of one's life, to start on a new path, and to open and release the ties that bind, so that the soul may soar.

Alexandra Levin has drawn out of her interviewees, affirmations of hope, healing and boundless joy for the thirsting souls of our age.

Aliya B Haeri
Integral Life Psychologist & Coach

AUTHOR BIOGRAPHY

Alexandra Levin was born in Johannesburg South Africa and graduated from the University of Cape Town with a Bachelor of Arts Degree, majoring in Drama. A successful writing career followed, first as a fashion journalist and later as a multiple award winning advertising copywriter in leading agencies, mainly Grey, BBDO, Ogilvy-Mather and Young & Rubicam.

In 1997 Penguin (South Africa) published Alexandra's first novel **If Advertising's The Most Fun You Can Have With Your Pants On, How Come My Knickers Are Always In A Knot?**

Adversity in her personal life set Alexandra on a quest for esoteric enlightenment and her first spiritual work of non-fiction **Out of this World** – *The Alternative South African Spiritual Experience* was published by Penguin South Africa in 2003.

In 2011 Pegasus Elliot Mackenzie published Alexandra's humorous novel **Sexty** – *How to Keep Your Spirits Up When the Rest of You is Falling Down*. Her highly controversial spiritual autobiography **Marie Antoinette, Diana & Alexandra** – *The Third I* was published in London in 2012.

Alexandra is divorced. She has two married daughters and is a proud grandmother.

Published by
Heartspace Publications
PO Box 1085
Daylesford
Victoria 34660
Australia

Tel: +61 450260348
www. heartspacebooks.com
pat@heartspacebooks.com

Copyright © 2016 Alexandra Levin

All rights reserved under international copyright conventions. No part of this book may be reproduced, stored in a retrieval system, or transmitted in any form or by any means electronic, mechanical, photocopying, recorded or otherwise without written permission from Heartspace Publications.

Whilst every care has been taken to check the accuracy of the information in this book, the publisher cannot be held responsible for any errors, omissions or originality.

ISBN: 978-0-9924338-2-6 (Print)
ISBN: 978-0-9924338-3-3 (ePub)

A portion of the proceeds from the sale of this book will be donated to CHOC — Childhood Cancer Foundation of South Africa in recognition of the inspiring work they are doing with children suffering from life threatening diseases as well as to the Credo Vusamazulu Mutwa AIDS Hospital in Kuruman in the Northern Cape. Founded by the great healer, prophet, artist, sculptor and author, Credo Mutwa and his wife Virginia, this small hospital treats not only AIDS sufferers but also abused children in this impoverished community.

CONTENTS

Introduction vii
Blessings xiii

Alexander Shani Krebs   1
Drug Dealer, Prisoner, Poet, Artist, Motivational Speaker, Author

Bianca Van Der Schyff   17
Near-Fatal Car Crash Survivor

Mandy Young   32
Psychotherapist/Eco-Therapist

Maja Abramowitch   44
Wife, Mother, Grandmother, Lecturer, Holocaust Survivor

Diana Cooper   55
Therapist, Healer & International Author

Karen Tocknell   63
Mother, Author, Motivational Speaker

Rainbow Heart Flower   73
By Lara Edmonds

Dan Sefudi Rakgoathe   89
Blind Poet, Artist & Mystic

Micki Pistorius   102
Serial Killer Profiler & Writer

The Reverend Olive Izaaks   112
Spiritual Psychic

Jason Light Wing *Sound Engineer, Conservationist, Psychic,* *Recovered Drug Addict, Healer*	123
Brandon Bays *International Spiritual Teacher & Counsellor*	133
Victor Vermeulen *Former Champion Cricketer, Motivational Speaker & Quadriplegic*	143
Maureen Wigoder *Mother & Grandmother*	154
Cari-Ann *Channel, Spiritual Counsellor, Epidermolysis Bullosa Sufferer*	166
Stephen Loeb *Husband, Father, ALS Sufferer*	178
Johan Calitz *Husband, Father, Big Game Hunter*	181
Joanne, Andrew & Frankie Brown *Tsunami Survivors*	194
René Coetzee *Wife, Mother, School Principal, Cancer Survivor*	207
Peter Feldman *Journalist, Movie Critic, Hijack Survivor*	221
Rodney & Heila Downey *Zen Buddhists*	232
Sanette Boulton *Leukaemia Sufferer*	243
Aliya B Haeri *Integral Life Psychologist & Coach*	254

INTRODUCTION

When my life of wealth and privilege disintegrated before my astonished eyes, in an effort to discover why I was suddenly faced with so much adversity and financial hardship, I began to follow a more spiritual path.

This led to the publication of my book **Out of this World** – The Alternative South African Spiritual Experience — a series of richly illustrated in-depth interviews with a wide variety of esoteric practitioners ranging from psychics to sangomas; Aura Soma therapists to astrologers; hypnotists to spiritual healers, amongst others. To get a more balanced view, I also interviewed people who had visited these practitioners.

For me one story in particular stood out: Intuitive Spiritual Counsellor Colleen-Joy Page told me the story of Bronwen, a counselling psychologist who was feeling unfulfilled in her career and who consequently consulted with her. Two months later, Bronwen's twenty-one year sister Bianca was involved in a serious car accident. Intuitively Colleen-Joy knew that as Bianca hovered between life and death, her soul was making the decision whether to stay on earth or to return 'home.'

By four o'clock that day, Colleen-Joy realised that Bianca's soul had elected to stay on this earth in order for Bianca to meet life as a physically challenged person. Some months later I visited Talisker, a healing centre, which was hosting an esoteric fair at which various spiritual speakers were talking. Amongst the speakers was Bianca, blind and in a wheelchair, who, despite the fact that her impaired speech was dysthartic, was both motivational and inspiring.

Looking at Bianca with her damaged body and listening to her speak in somewhat broken tones, I was deeply moved: "How is it that some people handle adversity with such grace and courage whilst others sink into deep depression, even to the point of committing suicide?"

Thanks to Bianca's magnificent example, this book T**he Deeper the Sorrow, the Stronger the Spirit** was born. I interviewed people who had gone through tremendous sorrow and adversity in their lives. Especially moving is the testimony of mothers who have lost a beloved child. The beautiful story written by Lara Edmonds in memory of her young son, baby James Edmonds is especially inspiring — she and her husband Andrew discovered that rainbows have no end because of the eternal faithfulness of God.

When Maureen Wigoder lost her teenage son Alan, following a period of darkness and despair, Maureen told me: "I could choose to be bitter or twisted and become a professional mourner or I could chose to turn my suffering into something positive to be used to help others. I chose the latter."

To the sorrow of her parents, when much longed for child Sanette Boulton was diagnosed with leukaemia, such was the little girl's spirit and faith, even as she was being airlifted to hospital, Sanette, much to the surprise and admiration of the emergency crew, sang songs of praise to her beloved Lord.

Not that this book is only about sorrow. From the incomparable author, spiritual teacher and angel lady Diana Cooper we learn of the healing power of angels; a sentiment echoed by journalist Peter Feldman, whose life was saved not once, but twice by his guardian angels.

Integral Life Psychologist and Coach, Aliya B Haeri, brings to our attention an old Sufi saying:

> *You presume you are an insignificant entity,*
> *Yet within you is enfolded*
> *The entire universe.*

International spiritual teacher and counsellor, Brandon Bays, author of *The Journey*, overcame adversity in her own life by becoming aware of the following wisdom: *"Know whatever comes to you unexpected, to be a gift from God, that will surely serve you if you use it to the fullest."*

Can one go through the ultimate hell of this earth and still emerge with the belief that God is our Saviour? For Jewish Holocaust survivor, Maja Abramowitch, this question is debatable, yet she bowed down to the faith of her childhood nurse Petronella Vilmans, who felt that by 'converting' her beloved charge to Catholicism, young Maja would be spared by the Angel of Death.

For Alexander Shani Krebs, his personal hell on earth was his drug addiction and the fact that he was caught smuggling heroin, was forced to endure eighteen years of imprisonment, under unspeakably harsh conditions, in jail in Thailand. Ultimately, it was his faith in Hashem, his Jewish God, which released him from the grip of the drugs that had held him in his sway and opened the bars of his prison doors.

Today, Shani is recognised as an artist, an author and as an motivational speaker — proving that the deeper you sink, the more you turn your life over to a Higher Power, the greater your chance of salvation.

Can dangerous prisoners be successfully rehabilitated? Buddhists Rodney and Heila Downey certainly think so. Abandoning their lives in the fashion industry, they established the Dharma Centre in Somerset West in 1998. Requested by Poep Am, a maximum security criminal in Malmesbury Correctional Centre in the Western Cape, to help uplift prisoners spiritually, they introduced their MAIA programme (Mindful Awareness in Action) to the Malmesbury inmates.

Undoubtedly, one of my most moving experiences in writing this book was spending time with Robert and Heila in the prison and observing how a group of so-called social outcasts were being converted to the gentleness of living life as Buddhists.

Is there any greater sadness we have to endure in this life than the death of a loved one? What happens when someone dies? For the magnificent and totally humble spiritual psychic, The Reverend Olive Izaaks, death is not the end of life but simply the beginning of a new existence of life in another dimension. Thus her work on this earth is all about comforting the living by connecting with the dead.

For the people I interviewed who believe in reincarnation, they all held the similar view that according to the suffering you have inflicted on others in a previous life, so will your lot in this life be proportioned.

Thus for Micki Pistorius, serial killer profiler, psychologist, author and the aunt of Paralympian Oscar Pistorius, has the uncanny ability to connect with the psyche of violent murderers. She attributes this to the fact that in a previous life she herself was connected to the energy of her ancestor Tancrede II, a soldier and killer in the time of the Crusades.

Former school principal, René Coetzee feels that her gift of getting into the minds — and hearts — of underprivileged Black school children is because in a former life she was Dingaan, the cruel Zulu chief who became king after the brutal assassination of his half-brother, Shaka. In order to redress the wrongdoings of the past, René maintains that her current life is her pay-back time.

Epidermolysys Bullosa is a rare genetic skin disease which causes the painful blistering and shearing of the skin. Psychic artist, channel and spiritual counsellor Cari-Ann believes that, because in the time of Lemuria, she was responsible for genetic experiments which resulted in the creation of human monsters, she is now condemned to her present life of constant pain.

Through writing this book I have come to learn that the deeper the sorrow, the greater the healing power of nature. Recovered drug addict, psychic and healer, Jason Light Wing, had almost hit rock-bottom when he decided to clean up his life by working with wild birds of prey. He regained his equilibrium by becoming involved with Wattled Cranes, Cape Vultures, Goliath Herons, Macaw Parrots as well as with his much loved falcons.

Following her troubled childhood, when she sought the solace and comfort of her beloved bush, psychotherapist and eco-therapist Mandy Young, now takes groups into nature. She has come to realise that the human species can learn so much, particularly about kinship and mothering skills by observing wild dogs, meerkats and elephants in their natural habitat. On a more playful note, Mandy also facilitates swimming with dolphin excursions to the untouched stretches of the white Mozambican shoreline.

Gored by a wild and injured buffalo, professional game hunter, Johan Calitz, realised that he faced certain death. He prayed to God to save him. In agony, he looked up at the sky and beheld a soft triangular white light shining down on him and he knew that God had heard — and had answered — his prayers.

How small and insignificant we humans are when confronted with the unshackled power of Mother Nature. In September 2005 experienced yachtsman, Neil Tocknell and the crew of the yacht Moquini went missing off the Southern tip of Madagascar during the Mauritius to Durban Yacht Race.

Buoyed up only by her strong Christian faith, his widow Karen, mother of three young children, managed to rise above the waves of despair, which battered the family, to emerge as a successful business woman, motivational speaker and author.

What chance of survival did the toddler, Frankie Brown have against the all-encompassing Tsunami when visiting Thailand with her parents Joanne and Andrew Brown and her child minder Vicki Nwayo?

As the enormous wave, the size of a three-storey building hit the beach of Hong Island, her panic stricken father Andrew rushed up and down the beach looking for his little daughter while reciting the Shema – the most sacred of all Hebrew prayers. In the midst of all the mayhem, the Jewish God, Hashem must have heard Andrew's prayers for little Frankie was miraculously saved.

Of all the people I was privileged to interview for this book, who gave so generously of their time and who opened their hearts and their souls to me, few are more courageous than Victor Vermuelen and his devoted mother, Isabella, who cares for him twenty-four hours a day, three hundred and sixty five days of the year.

A promising cricketer, Victor became a quadriplegic as the result of a diving accident. Now a motivational speaker, Victor says: "Regardless of the fact that my physical body is confined to a wheelchair, I encourage my spirit to soar, so that I can help those in need through my ability to motivate and inspire."

One of the deepest regrets I have about the completion of this book is that blind poet, artist and mystic Dan Sefudi Rakgoathe, the most fervent and ardent supporter of my writing, did not live to see its publication. Dear Dan, I am sure that you are watching the progress of **The Deeper the Sorrow, the Stronger the Spirit** from the prime position you so richly deserve in heaven.

This book embraces the spirituality of the major religions as well as the faith and courage required to carry one through the many trials and tribulations that we as human beings will almost certainly experience during our time on earth.

The people I interviewed, through the strength of their spirit and through their refusal to sink into the quagmire of depression and despair, have somehow managed to transcend their difficulties. Instead of cursing their adversity, they have seen it as a learning curve along life's uneven path.

For me, interviewing these subjects was inspirational and I thank each and every one of them for giving so generously of their time and for allowing me to write about their painful journey through their personal grief.

I hope that reading about these inspirational beings will help those in pain to move through the hurt into the comforting arena of acceptance; from all-encompassing darkness to all-embracing Light.

In conclusion, I would like to end this introduction with the wise and unspeakably beautiful words of the late and much loved Stephen Loeb, Motor Neuron Disease sufferer:

Let your faith carry you. Remember everything in life is based on either love or fear and there is NOTHING to fear except fear itself. Love yourself and love life. Just be, and try to discover the beauty of the inner you, the bigger you, the real you, the person within, which is perfect and has no flaws. You do not need any part of your physicality to be truly happy. Your beauty and happiness are within yourself. You don't need anybody to make you feel special. You are all special. You are all a spark of The Divine. Use this time to ignite this spark and discover the light within you and you will find out that life is beautiful.

Amen.

BLESSINGS!

To those of you who know suffering and pain, know that you are not alone. God, the Divine Self, is within you. When your heart is troubled and you do not know which way to turn, go within. The Divine spark is in all of us equally but only those who realise it, are awakened. When the realisation comes, the veil drops away. God is always there, like the sun shining through a curtain.

Open the curtain and let the light of God shine in. With God walking beside you, no matter how many times you stumble and fall, you will be able to pick yourself up and walk with your head held high once more.

My blessings to you all!

Sri Swami Vishwananda

Sri Swami Vishwananda, or Visham, as he was previously known to his followers throughout the world, had divine visitations from the age of four, when Shirdibaba healed him after he had eaten poisonous seeds.

Able to help and uplift people spiritually from the age of fourteen, Swami Vishwananda is also able to materialise vhibuti (holy ash) and small gifts.

Mother Mary appears to him weekly in visions and gives him vital messages for the benefit of mankind. Every Easter the stigmata appear on Sri Swami Vishwananda's hands, feet, brow and crown and he goes into retreat.

Talking of Jesus, Sri Swami Vishwananda says that after his Resurrection, he continues to do his work around the world and also on other planets and galaxies, not limiting himself to the body, as the body merged, becoming one with the Father.

"Jesus teaches us the way of life and the joy of it. Through his Word go deeper into it and rediscover the true meaning of what he really taught his disciples. Apply it in your daily life and you will surely experience life in a different way. Forgive and move on with love in your heart."

When asked how he knew this, Sri Swami Vishawananda replied with a shy smile: "Because Jesus told me so!"

www.bhaktimarga.org

ALEXANDER SHANI KREBS

DRUG DEALER, PRISONER, POET, ARTIST, MOTIVATIONAL SPEAKER, AUTHOR

FROM HEROIN TO HASHEM

LET THE STORY FLOW

The rain falls the river flows.
It's time to get up as the sun glows.
What's it going to be?
What will the rain bring?
The water is not clear.
My destination is near.
I don't want the rain no more.
I don't want to see the river flow.
I want to go home.
Before the next downpour.

Alexander Shani Krebs

The fifty two year old, Shani Krebs I meet, in his sister Joan's house in Orange Grove in Johannesburg, a room filled with Shani's work-in-progress art projects, is a very different person from the drug addict and trafficker who spent eighteen years of his life incarcerated in almost sub-human conditions in various prisons in Thailand.

Balding Shani appears relaxed and welcoming. Casually dressed in chinos and a T-shirt, a necklace chain around his neck, liberally tattooed, his eyes twinkle as his talks and he smiles readily. He recalls the events in his life with an astonishing clarity and takes a certain pride in recounting the misdemeanours of his eventful youth. Growing up in an orphanage, without the benefit of any parental supervision for a large part of his formative years, once senses that his rebellious behaviour gained him a certain admiration amongst his less adventurous peers.

Shani returned to South Africa on the 28th of April 2012, when he was met at O.R. Tambo International Airport by his aged mother Katlina, his sister Joan and other members of his family and friends, all wearing black t-shirts emblazoned with the word *Welcome Home Shani,* as well as a sizeable press contingent.

"How did you feel when saw all your family and friends again after such a long separation?"

"I was totally overwhelmed by all the love and support. Also seeing the press there was incredible. In isolation in prison, I hadn't realised the depth of interest in my story."

"How have you been spending your time since your return?"

"I've been incredibly busy ... there don't seem to be enough hours in the day. Not only have I held a number of art exhibitions of the works which I created whilst in jail — all highly successful, thank God — I have also written my biography *Dragons and Butterflies* — my publishers are really excited about the book and they are even talking about selling the movie rights. I have also become a motivational speaker teaching young children and teenagers about the evils of drugs."

Alexander Shani Krebs was not born with a silver spoon in his mouth. His mother Katlina, together with his father Fritz, emigrated from Hungary to South Africa in 1956. Shani was born in Mafeking in 1959.

His parents divorced when Shani was one year old and his mother remarried another Hungarian, Janos Horvath, whom young Shani believed to be his real father.

Both Shani and his sister Joan were strictly disciplined — Katlina used a wooden spoon to this end while Janos, who worked on the mines, was physically abusive both to his wife and children.

Jewish by birth, Katlina's parents had been killed by the Nazis and not wishing to see her children persecuted for their religion, she had her children baptised as Roman Catholics.

When Shani was eleven, Katlina left her second husband and began working in the canteen in the Iscor Steel Works. This menial work was poorly paid and Katlina, finding it difficult to make ends meet, decided to return to Hungary. Because of their Jewish roots, Shani and Joan were placed in Arcadia, the

Jewish orphanage, which embraced Jewish culture and traditions. Shani was circumcised and given a barmitzvah.

"How did you feel about Judaism at this stage?"

"Cool. I have always been proud to be a Jew."

Shani was sent to the Jewish Day School King David in Victory Park, where while he excelled on the sports field, and showed a natural inclination for art, he was somewhat wild and rebellious. In his final year before graduating school, Shani stole a car and as a punishment he was sent to Norman House School, a reformatory in Edenvale.

Jeffrey Wolf, headmaster of King David Victory Park at the time, and Sydney Klevansky, the vice-head of Parktown Boys, head of the school's Latin department as well as the principal of Arcadia orphanage, successfully pleaded Shani's case.

A popular boarder at Arcadia, where he was head boy for two years, Shani returned from Norman House to the Jewish orphanage.

Back at King David In his final school year, Shani began experimenting with marijuana or dagga — the start of his drug addiction — a habit which he only managed to kick many years later when he was sentenced to life imprisonment in a Bangkok prison for drug trafficking.

****

The Angolan Bush War in South Africa was a conflict that took place from 1966 to 1989 in South West Africa (now Namibia) and Angola between South Africa and its allied forces (mainly the National Union for the Total Independence of Angola (UNITA) on the one side and the Angolan Government South-West African People's Organisation Swapo and their allies (mainly Cuba) on the other.

After leaving school, Shani Krebs was to spend two years in the South African army, firstly joining the 4 SAI Battalion in Middelburg, between the capital Pretoria and the gold mining town of Lydenburg.

Shani soon joined up with his Jewish comrades and the complaints started coming in thick and fast. "Why was there no kosher food in this battalion?"

"How did the authorities react to your insubordination?"

"Frankly, I think that they couldn't wait to get us guys out of their unit," he laughed.

Shani and his friends were then transferred to the 3 SAI Battalion in Potchestroom in South Africa's North-West Province, which had kosher food for the Jewish soldiers. Basic army training was of twelve weeks duration and the apprentice soldiers were taught counter-insurgency training methods; they learnt about mortar bombs and sniper rifles. All this was a bit above Shani's head and he decided to go AWOL — resulting in twenty-one days detention in barracks.

Shani and five of his friends then decided that the army unit to which they were best suited was playing in the army band. It did not matter to them that not one of them knew how to play a musical instrument.

The 'band' was duly moved to military headquarters and told by Staff Sergeant Meintjies to polish up their playing. Unfortunately, the only playing that these guys knew was how to smoke weed and get stoned.

When the band was required to perform, Shani grabbed a trumpet. Too bad that he didn't know anything about trumpet playing … hard as he blew on the instrument, not a single note came out.

"Hey," said Shani, 'Can't I rather play the cymbals?"

"Was your cymbal playing any more competent?"

"At the first parade I was stoned — what's new? — and I banged the cymbals so loudly and with such discord that the Staff Sergeant begged me: 'Don't play. Just pretend that you're playing.' "

After a couple of months, the Jewish members were slowly thrown out of the band. Next, Shani served in the army as a regimental policeman and armed with an R1 rifle, his job entailed searching cars and checking who came in and out of the camp.

One day, when Shani was (as usual) stoned, assisted by one of his army band mates, he pointed his R1 rifle through the open window of a car, which happened to belong one of the top army brass — a Lieutenant Colonel from Pretoria.

Once again, he was in trouble and having been severely reprimanded, he managed to toe the line for a short period before deciding that he was suffering from severe boredom. Putting down his rifle, declaring that he had had enough, Shani hitchhiked to the coastal town of Durban to purchase a sack of weed.

On his return to the Potchestroom army base, Shani spent his time jolling (South African slang for celebrating in a lively way) and selling weed. With a bent for business, his dagga sales proved so successful that he and his friends were able to buy the Cadillac that had once belonged to Apartheid Prime Minister B.J.Vorster.

Going AWOL once again, a nationwide manhunt was instituted for Private Krebs, who, once he was found, was subject to detention for ninety days.

"This was physically much harder," recalled Shani ruefully. "We guys in detention had to do exercise for four hours a day and we were was woken at 3.30 am."

Two guys, to their peril, tried to rape Shani. As a member of King David's first school rugby team and playing for the army's football team, as well as being accomplished in the martial arts, Shani is not a guy to be trifled with ... especially as, despite trying to keep his temper in control, he will be the first to admit that he has a short fuse when his anger is aroused.

"Detention might have been hard, but things really came to a head on my twentieth birthday," recalled Shani, who when it comes to remembering his escapades, appears to have a photographic memory.

"What happened then?" I asked intrigued.

"On my twentieth birthday, I went AWOL yet again. Meeting up with my old mates from Arcadia, I smoked weed and when one of my friends offered me some tablets, I randomly took a red pill. I then borrowed a motorbike from one of my friends. We kids from Arcadia were wild, really wild," Shani recalled with a certain degree of pride.

Not surprisingly, this ride resulted in a multiple accident when a car in front of him attempted to turn right and Shani, travelling at speed, collided with the vehicle in Oxford Road in Johannesburg, just outside Temple Emmanuel Synagogue.

The impact of the crash sent Shani flying into the wall of the convent. Lying injured on the ground, with severe injuries including a broken leg and a severed finger, Shani's last thought before being rushed by ambulance to Hillbrow hospital, was, "I must be dead."

His release from hospital also meant his release from the army — army officials had no idea where Shani was and he had no intention of enlightening them about his whereabouts.

What now followed was a depraved period of sex, drugs and rock 'n roll. Taking drugs — no longer content with merely smoking weed, Shani went on to smoking mandrax and snorting cocaine, taking LSD, as well as dealing in mainline drugs. To cover up the fact that his earnings came from drug dealing, he also appeared to have more conventional work, such as selling and designing clothes. For a time he was a taxi driver for the prostitutes who worked at The Romance Escort Agency in Johannesburg's city centre.

"What are you saying? You actually chauffeured prostitutes?" I asked incredulously.

"Sure. I developed a special relationship with the girls. Not only did I supply them with drugs, but when any of their clients got abusive, I protected them. I've never been afraid of getting into a fight."

At this stage, Shani's place of residence changed with alarming frequency and his relations with the opposite sex were, to put it mildly, unstable. Sometimes, without a roof over his head, Shani walked the streets, homeless.

He was also involved in skirmishes with the police. One New Year's Eve, when both Shani and his friends, as well as the police had been drinking, Shani shot a beer bottle off the roof of a car with a maverick 9 gauge shot gun, the ammunition used by the police when on a raid. The cops who happened to be at the nearby traffic lights, demanded to know what the shooting was about.

Shani immediately threw the gun under the car, but he had another gun strapped to his waist — "I always carried two guns," he said matter-of-factly.

"After witnessing the shooting of the beer bottle, one of the cops came towards me and I pulled out the second gun." As the policeman grabbed the weapon from Shani's hand, he lost his footing, falling to the ground. He lay there screaming. Another cop came to see what was going on. Pointing to the policeman lying on the ground, Shani asked: "Is he drunk or something?"

Fortunately, the policeman did not sustain any real injuries and eventually the cops let Shani and his friends go.

Following a night of revelry, boozing and taking LSD, the guys returned to Shani's apartment, where before falling asleep on the couch, he gave his friends money to buy more liquor from the bottle store.

His friends took the shotgun Shani kept under his mattress and when he woke up a few hours later, he was alarmed to find that his friends had not yet returned. Not sure how to react, Shani decided to wait an hour before reporting to the police that his shotgun had been stolen.

Driving recklessly, Shani's friends had jumped a red traffic light. They were immediately pulled over by the police who found Shani's shotgun. The cops, who were on the look-out for these hoodlums, followed the car back to Shani's abode.

"Were you able to get away from the cops?"

"Next thing I knew the cops were jumping over his wall. Telling me not to move, the cops searched the residence. I broke out into a cold sweat — a valuable stash of cocaine was hidden in the Jacuzzi."

"Did the cops find the cocaine?"

"No, the cocaine remained undetected. However, I was arrested and charged with the attempted murder of the policeman and for firing a weapon in a built-up area."

Living dangerously on the edge, Shani was gambling with his life. Following one near-fatal seizure, he was later to suffer another severe seizure. Nobody was more surprised than Shani that he hadn't yet killed himself.

"God must love me," he decided.

****

On the 26th of April 1994, a day before South Africa's first democratic elections, Shani was arrested at Bangkok's international airport for trying to smuggle 2.7 kilo of heroin out of the country.

"The drug was hidden in a secret compartment in a largish leather satchel — unless you knew it was there, you would never have detected it," said Shani.

His orders were to pick up the heroin in Bangkok and take it to Kenya where he would meet a contact who would take it to New York.

His instincts told Shani that he was being watched while he was in the hotel in Bangkok. Uneasy, he contacted his drug connection in South Africa and said that he thought that he should abandon ship. To which the contact replied, "Don't worry. The heroin is so well concealed, the airport police will never find it."

As Shani walked through the departure lounge at the airport, his heart sank.

Putting the bag with the heroin through the X-ray machine he said a prayer, making a pact with his Jewish God. "Hashem, if they don't find the heroin stash, I promise you that I will no longer take drugs or deal in drugs. You have never abandoned me through all my troubles … please, Hashem, don't desert me now."

There was no problem getting the leather satchel through the X-ray machine, but as Shani handed in his passport in the International Departure lounge, he knew something was seriously wrong — he was the only passenger there. Out of the corner of his eye he noticed that there was a lot of movement … soon he was surrounded by armed Thai police with Walkie-talkies.

"Does that leather satchel belong to you?" demanded one of the policemen.

"Can you see anyone else here?" enquired Shani.

The policemen led him to a small security room at the back of the airport. Cutting open the satchel, they pulled out the heroin, which they weighed and tested.

"They found that it was indeed pure heroin. They had been waiting for me. Someone had snitched on me."

"Was this your first conviction for drug trafficking?"

"In the 80's I was given a suspended sentence for being in possession of Mandrax. This sentence had expired by the time I was arrested in Bangkok."

Shani's arrest was the lead story on every one of Bangkok's local news channels. Interrogated by the Thai police, who had been thoroughly trained by the United States Drug Enforcement Administration — the USA had been conducting international counter-narcotics training since 1969 — Shani was questioned and tortured. He was told that he would be given a lesser sentence if he gave the police the names of his accomplices.

"Were you prepared to give them the names of your connections?"

"I had grown up in the Arcadia orphanage and I was street-wise. To rat on somebody was considered to be the worst crime that one could commit in the underworld. There is a certain honour amongst thieves ... informers deserve to be killed," Shani remarked solemnly.

The court case was a nightmare for Shani. Not able to speak Thai, he had no idea what was being said in the court. His government-appointed lawyer spoke no English. In Thailand the law states that if you are caught committing a crime, you are guilty until proven innocent.

"If you are found to be in possession of drugs, there is no chance of bail and the penalty for being found guilty is the death sentence."

"How did you plead?"

"I initially pleaded innocent."

Shani was sentenced to death by the Thai court, a sentence which was then reduced to life imprisonment when he changed his plea to one of guilty of drug trafficking.

Together with about a hundred men, Shani landed in the notorious Bombat Prison. Shackled and thrown into an over-crowded cell with a hundred other men, conditions for the prisoners were abominable — the ill-kept, manually flushed toilets were communal, a small two foot wall separating the cubicles. With many of the prisoners being bi-sexual, rape, as in Western prisons was common, and sleeping arrangements were primitive in the extreme. Shani slept in a cardboard box with a beach towel as his mattress. His wardrobe consisted of two T-shirts, two pairs of shorts, a couple of pairs of underpants and some slippers.

Shani was angry, in fact he was furious with his God. "Hashem, no matter what I've done you have always protected me. Remember my motorbike accident. I should have been dead. Through all the bad things I've done, you have looked after me and let me get away with murder. Why have you abandoned me now?"

"How did you manage your anger?"

"It was at this time that I began painting. Taking the bristles from my toothbrush and attaching them to a bamboo stick I fashioned these paint brushes and by diluting coffee I was able to sketch birthday cards for my fellow prisoners."

Always popular, firstly with his schoolmates, later with his army mates, his 'work' colleagues and then with most of the other prisoners, Shani's cards were well received by inmates who had very little to look forward to.

During his stay in Bombat, Rabbi Kantor, an orthodox Jewish rabbi, came to visit Shani to offer him comfort. Through all his trials, Shani never lost respect for his Jewish roots. Now, seeing this rabbi standing before him, with his glowing cheeks and long ginger beard, Shani could not believe that there was a rabbi who was caring and compassionate enough to visit a Jewish prisoner in this ghastly prison, with inmates suffering from TB and AIDS and sufficiently dirty for insects and bugs to crawl all over the prisoners bodies as they tried to cat-nap on the floor.

"It was like seeing an angel. The Rabbi offered me moral and spiritual support at this low ebb in my life. He offered to contact my family on my behalf. This link with the outside world helped me overcome my depression, to see that suicide was not a viable option. He gave me the strength to see that despite the harshness of my sentence, with the help of Hashem, I would one day walk free."

****

A prisoner was about to be beaten by one of the guards. Hot headed and a champion of the underdog, Shani grabbed a baton and threatened the guard.

Now considered 'dangerous', Shani was transferred to Klong Prem prison in August 1994. The cells here all measured approximately 1.5 metres x 3.5 metres and held three to four prisoners. There were no chairs or beds and prisoners slept side by side on the hard concrete floor.

"The conditions sound totally inhuman. How did you and the other prisoners pass the time?"

"Many of the prisoners had intricate body art or tattoos — it gave the guys something to do to pass the long, boring hours. I had a tattoo of a ferocious dragon on my back and bands of butterflies on my arms — hence the title of my memoirs — *Dragons and Butterflies.*"

With some of the Thai prisoners being delicate, slight and feminine in appearance, in the absence of any female company, certain of the prisoners chose to enter into relationships with these 'lady boys'. Transvestites are part of Thai culture and the guards never prevented these relationships

In the course of his eighteen years of incarceration, Shani was to spend time in five prisons. He was next moved to Bang Kwang Central Prison in Nonthaburi Province, about seven miles north of Bangkok. The prison houses many foreign prisoners who have either received long to life sentences or the death sentence.

Known to mete out extremely harsh treatment to its inmates, all prisoners are required to wear leg irons for the first three months of their imprisonment, while death row prisoners have their leg irons permanently welded on.

During his incarceration in Bang Kwang, Shani continued developing his artistic talents. He drew with a pencil and whatever paper he was able to obtain.

There was a Burmese junkie in the prison who was an artist. As cash transactions were forbidden, he would paint portraits of the other prisoners in order to support his drug habit.

"Were you still taking drugs?"

"I had kicked my drug habit, but not my craving for drugs ... I saw my own art, not only as a need of satisfying my soul, I also saw the remuneration it bought as a way of escaping my reality."

Shani got the Burmese artist to paint portraits of his sister and his niece. He signed them with his own name and sent them back to South Africa. Soon requests came in for him to draw other family members.

He quickly realised that his dishonesty had cost him dearly. "Teach me how to do a portrait," he pleaded with the Burmese artist.

In possession of an A4 sketch pad, a sharpener and a pencil and a rubber, Shani began perfecting his artistic craft by drawing between six to thirteen hours a day. He then graduated to drawing with a Bic ballpoint. As his artistic ability grew, so Shani realised that he was evolving both spiritually and as a person. He felt that Hashem was giving him a second chance.

Amongst the many women who wrote to Shani, whilst he was in prison, Edna Ralph, a very religious Jewish woman from Manchester, England, began writing to him, enlightening him on many aspects of Judaism.

Following his periods of dark depression, Shani's mood seemed to be lifting and with his burgeoning spirituality, he was able to transcend his reality, feeling that he left his body and entered into the spiritual realm, where he maintains that he was 'touched by angels'.

"So you were now able to control your angry outbursts?"

"Not exactly," replied Shani shaking his head ruefully.

Despite his uplifted state of mind, in 1999 Shani still got into a prison fight. "About forty Nigerian prisoners turned on me. I felt that I was honour bound to attack their leader. You see, many of the prisoners had now come to respect me and regard me as their leader."

"Was it a fight between two rival groups?"

"Yes. The Nigerian leader was bigger than me … it was sort of a David and Goliath fight … we had a fist fight and I gave him a good hiding."

Shani was immediately shackled by the prison guards and thrown into solitary confinement. He was obliged to sleep on a concrete floor, with no ventilation, and in darkness, except for a trickle of light filtering in from the passage.

"How did you cope? Did you sink into depression?"

"Surprisingly enough, no. In these stark conditions, where I stayed for six months, I reconnected with Hashem. For the first time in my life, I actually never felt more free. It was a liberating experience. I finally realised that God had given me a second chance. Coming to prison was my destiny; a blessing in disguise."

"I had been taking and selling drugs for sixteen years and I knew that if I had not been imprisoned I would not ever have been free of my addiction — I would never have reached forty years of age."

"I began davening — reciting Jewish liturgical prayers — three times a day. Basically, I was locked up in solitary confinement for one month, for twenty-four hours a day. I finally managed to pay the guards to let me out of the cell from eight until two pm every day.

"For the first time, I wanted to paint in colour. I managed to obtain basic water colours and I worked tirelessly to broaden and refine my technique. My solitary confinement was to give me a freedom of spirit that I had never known before."

****

Shani had not been truthful to his family about his arrest. He was too ashamed to admit that he knew that he was carrying a stash of heroin for he felt certain that the family would abandon him. In addition, believing that he had been set up, he wanted to protect his family in the event of their being repercussions. He had lied about his innocence.

His family, and in particular, his sister Joan never stopped attempting to get him released. He found that he had support from all over the world and he sometimes felt ashamed that he was South African. Whilst other countries have treaties with Thailand so that prisoners can go home and serve their sentences in their home country, the South African Government has no such treaty.

A few family members did in fact visit Shani in prison, but he asked them not to come as it made him too emotional and he felt that the money they spent on the trip could be put to better use if they sent him the money for food.

"What was the prison food like?" I asked.

"Prisoners were given a plastic bag filled with rice and another filled with an inedible stew made from a couple of vegetables, pork fat or chicken bones. This was our only meal of the day and not only was it insufficient, it was also inedible and I suffered severe hunger pains. You simply had to have the means to buy food from the prison canteen or else from an outside source."

"Did you manage to stay reasonably healthy in spite of your poor diet?"

"Baruch Hashem, I would look in the mirror and thank God for my good health, but then in September 2008 I had what I thought was a mild heart attack. I was diagnosed with the condition known as atrial fibrillation, which means that I had an irregular heartbeat caused because my arterial blood flow was blocked and that I was at severe risk of having a stroke.

"Following an electro-cardiogram test I was placed in hospital for two nights and one and a half days. I prayed to Hashem with tears in my eyes. I told him that this is not where I wanted to die as my death would have devastated my family. More than likely it would have caused the death of my mother, who every night of her life since my arrest, got down on her hands and knees begging God to give her only son his freedom.

"I also prayed ... reciting the Shema, the most sacred and powerful of Jewish prayers, over and over again, my right hand covering my eyes, begging Hashem to release me."

Refusing to take medication, Shani embarked on a vigorous exercise programme, changing his diet to salads and vegetables and, because of the poor quality of the prison food, ordering his sustenance from an outside grocery store.

He was already observing the Jewish Sabbath to the best of his ability, declining to draw or paint on that day and not handling any money. What more did God desire of him?

****

In 2008 one of Shani's ex-girlfriends — as he talks one gets the impression that his number of ex-girlfriends and the women who wrote to him while he was in prison is certainly sizeable in number — came to visit him, together with her husband-to-be.

Penelope and Ivan, a prominent businessman, decided to make it their mission to work towards Shani's release. With the assistance of a top Israel attorney, Shani was the first foreign prisoner to whom the Israeli government granted citizenship. The procedure was long and drawn out — Shani only got his Israeli citizenship on the 18th of October 2010 because of the controversy surrounding his citizenship.

The Israeli government was well aware that in 2011 the Thai monarch, King Bhumibol Adulyadei, the world's longest serving monarch, would be celebrating his 7th 12th cycle birthday, when he turned 84, on the 5th of December. Amongst the celebrations earmarked to commemorate this milestone eighty-fourth birthday, the king would be granting a general amnesty to prisoners.

****

Following his long incarceration in Bang Kwang, Shani had become a leader amongst the prisoners, and just as his peers in Arcadia had once looked up to him, so he had earned the respect of both guards and inmates alike.

In late October 2010, Shani became involved in a series of fights, one being with his fellow Israel inmates and he attacked one of them. Ever a firebrand, Shani stabbed one of the Chinese prisoners with a screwdriver.

This incident was followed by more fighting between the Thai and Chinese prisoners. To avoid the problem between Shani's Thai friends and the Chinese prisoners from escalating into a riot, Shani was removed from Building 2 and placed in a holding cell with twenty Thai prisoners in Building 6. Over the next couple of days, he was once again relocated to a cell with only eight foreign prisoners.

At this stage Shani was the longest serving Western prisoner in Bang Kwang.

During his long incarceration he had petitioned governments and human rights organisations around the world, not only for his freedom, but also for conditions that would improve the lot of prisoners in Thai jails — through his petitions he managed to alleviate the overcrowding in cells; improve the quality of both the drinking and the water used in the prison ablution facilities; the standard of the prison food was raised and public telephones were installed for the use of the prisoners. In Thai prisons, nothing is for free and Shani was able to buy a private cell and a studio where he could paint at his leisure.

After making himself comfortable, speaking to Shani in South Africa, one senses that in spite of all the hardships he was forced to endure — there are certain things, such as the camaraderie and the respect of his fellow prisoners that he misses — six months down the line in the early hours of the morning, Shani was ruthlessly removed from his cell by members of the police force and the correctional services.

He was only permitted to take his toiletries and a couple of items of clothing including his tefillin* and his Siddur, a Jewish prayer book containing a set order of daily prayers.

Shackled and placed in a prison transport vehicle with twenty other prisoners, Shani was moved to an isolated, high security prison 300 kilometres outside of Bangkok. This event occurred on the eve of Pesach, coinciding with the exodus of the Israelites from Egypt.

Shani managed to get a note to his girlfriend at the time, Elisabeth, telling her that he had been forcibly removed from Bang Kwang prison. She contacted the

---

* tefillin — A set of small black leather boxes containing scrolls of parchment inscribed with verses from the Torah, which are worn by observant Jews during weekday morning prayers.

South African Embassy and informed them of this. Following the intervention of the South African Consular Officer, Shani was moved back to Bangkok and taken to another prison and placed back into solitary confinement. With only a single towel for a bed, Shani used his Siddur for a pillow.

Shani was, once again, to remain in solitary confinement for six months. For him, it was a time of immense spiritual growth. He laid tefillin each morning and davened* repeating the Scharit or morning prayers, Mincha, the afternoon prayers, and the Maariv or evening prayers five times each day.

With plenty of time for introspection, Shani realised that his freedom was imminent and that Hashem in all his glory had been preparing him for this day. He went from being a powerful prisoner, to a guest in another prison building, and now in solitary confinement he had been reduced to nothing. With this realisation Shani had finally gained what he had so desperately searched for-his spiritual release.

On the 8th November 2011 he was released from solitary confinement and in January 2012 he was given his official release date of the 22nd April of that year. The fact that he had survived many years of substance abuse followed by eighteen years in prison with his health intact, was in itself a miracle.

On the 22nd of April Alexander Shani Krebs, under police escort, walked out of prison, a free man. Free not only in spirit, but free of all the temptations that had held his mind and body prisoner for so much of his life.

"What was it like to finally be released? Despite your faith, surely there must have been times when you thought that you would die in prison?"

"One cannot describe my euphoria when I walked out of the prison gates. Eighteen years in itself was a lifetime, yet it felt like I had just got into prison the other day ... I had lost all concept of time," reflected Shani.

"I had evolved on so many levels — artistically, spiritually and as a person. I was very different from the man who had entered those prison gates. I now know that Hashem had a purpose for me. I had no illusions about fitting into society ... in fact, I didn't want to fit into society. I wanted to make a difference. If I can save just one young life from a life of drugs, then I will know that I am headed in the right direction towards fulfilling that purpose."

www.shanikrebs.com

BIANCA VAN DER SCHYFF

NEAR-FATAL CAR CRASH SURVIVOR

SEEING MORE THAN THE SIGHTED

TAPESTRIES

(Dedicated to and inspired by my sister)

A life born,
But not lived.
Till my tender soul did call,
And whereupon you answered …
Our bond of flesh
Encapsulates our joint spirits,
As our tapestries become unveiled.
As my soul weeps your tears of pain
Your heart embraces my soul's disdain
Joyous moments shared in time
While our dreams intertwine;
The Courage of one to the
Wisdom of the other
Near or far, our eyes penetrate
The windows of joint souls
Unmasking a deep understanding
With a love unconditional
Ever pending ….
Destiny
The Brutal tapestry calls,
That each soul
May walk its path …
Amid darkness
Enlightening the awakening
Of your flickering soul.
Oh …Twin of light

*There within the
Darkness of your mind
Search no more,
I lurk within your shadows
Fear not ...
For I am ever present
Enfolding you in a realm
Of love and light
Heed ...Precious Soul
Take Courage,
Within the finesse of a
TAPESTRY, lies
each painfully woven
Stitch
Twin of light upon your journey
Re-member
Your candle of light
To the flames of
the Son.*

*Bronwen Van der Schyff
(Bronwen wrote this while Bianca was fighting for her life
in the early days of her coma)*

"Mom, I don't want all these dolls you keep giving me," pouted young Bronwen Van der Schyff. "In this family we still need to have another skin baby... I feel that a little girl baby wants to join us here."

Her mother Louise bit her lip and tried not to cry. The doctors had told her that she couldn't have another child, so it seemed unlikely that Bronwen would ever have this much longed for sibling. "I know we're going to have another baby. I know it," the little girl insisted.

Bronwen was seven and a half years old when her beloved baby sister, Bianca, was born. The pregnancy had not gone to its full term, but right from the start Bianca made her fighting spirit known. Her soul needed to be here in this family with her father Bryan, her mother Louise and her sister Bronwen.

"Without Bianca, I didn't have the essence of me," said Bronwen, as I sat chatting with the three remarkable Van der Schyff women in their delightful, light-filled studio. "Bianca and I are what I have always referred to as 'Twins of Light.'

I believe that we have a very deep Soul connection. We guide and support each other and we are simply best friends. As Twin Sister souls we have a very deep intuitive kindred connection. My mom says that even before Bianca's birth we were like two united souls. It was as if Bianca's infant soul was calling me, with me frequently asking Bianca's soul to join me here on this Earth journey," explained Bronwen.

With Bianca's birth the family was finally whole; the four elements had come together. "My mom Louise is a Libran — the air sign; my father Bryan is a Cancerian — water; I am earth for my star sign is Taurus The Bull and Bianca is a Leo and consequently a fire sign." From the time of her first pregnancy, Louise had wanted a little girl.

Jokingly she told her gynaecologist, "If the baby is a boy, you must please swop it." Likewise, it was important to that the new baby was a girl. "I prayed. I wanted another little girl so badly," smiled Louise.

Once Bianca was born, the sisters were so close that Bronwen used to tell her mother to wake her up if she was doing a night feed. She couldn't do enough to help her mother care for her baby sister. Bronwen wanted a part in everything that Bianca was doing. "We have a far more intense commitment and involvement than I have observed in other families," remarked Bronwen thoughtfully. "Consequently, Bianca's accident shaped my life, my career and all the subsequent decisions I made."

The two girls, although seven years apart, looked very much alike, a resemblance which continued even after Bianca's almost fatal accident.

Tall, slender and beautiful, the sisters did not appear quite as if they came from this planet — with their long, flowing hair they resembled fairies, or mermaids or heavenly angels without wings.

There is a much cherished picture of Bianca in the studio. She is wearing a headdress and a gossamer-like dress. This is more than simply a lovely portrait of a young girl on the brink of womanhood going to an important dance — it has the quality of an ethereal spirit, who like some exotic butterfly, has simply alighted on this world for a brief visit.

When I mention this to the family, Bianca, now visually impaired and physically challenged since the accident, doesn't seem at all surprised.

Speaking softly, in a voice altered by the crash, but with a mind still razor sharp, she giggled: "I look like Spirit for I am Spirit."

I cannot help noticing how, despite the tragedy of the accident that nearly claimed Bianca's youthful life, there is so much laughter between the three women. If it is possible, the accident has brought the trio even closer together. With the realization that life is ephemeral and can be snuffed out at any moment as quickly as a candle flame, they have learned what many of the great sages teach ... to live in and to cherish the moment.

Louise as a young mother — with two grown-up daughters, still looks remarkably youthful — without consciously knowing it, instilled a sense of spirituality in her daughters, teaching them to have enquiring minds; to be creative and, above all, to celebrate life.

"See those Canterbury Bell flowers growing outside your windows," she told her young daughters, "Watch them carefully. For that is where the fairies live. Perhaps, if you're lucky one night, you might even catch one."

****

Bianca believed in living life to the full. In a moving essay she was to write some time after the accident she said: "As a really enthusiastic and ambitious youth, I set out to dazzle the world with my talent and brilliance.

"I had enrolled myself in poetry eisteddfods, public debates, dancing classes, guitar lessons and displaying my acting skills on stage. I made sure that when I left school that my hours were filled with friends who needed a bit of mutual life coaching.

"Holding down two jobs, being a fulltime law student, doing secretarial work, getting an elementary qualification in ballet, then meeting my friends for squash and clubbing ensured that I was living my life to the ultimate — Viva la Vida — which to Bianca means 'Live life.'

"After a relatively ordinary day, in my estimation, I took my friends off to see my new boyfriend at a restaurant where we both worked — I was waitressing at the time. It was raining heavily and I remember that I had to draw the blinds of the smoking area in the restaurant to ensure that the rain didn't bother the patrons. At 1.30 am my friends left the restaurant.

"At 2.00 am, I was finally satisfied that my day was complete. I made my way home, humming a tune in jovial spirit as I loved to sing in the privacy of my car.

"Everything changed that evening. Some would say that the change was a tragedy."

In December 1999, during the time of the floods in Mozambique, particularly heavy rains were falling in South Africa, as Bianca drove home in her beloved red City Golf, a car she had christened Flubber, she had an accident, the details of which are still unclear.

As Bianca lay motionless within the vehicle, six or seven young girls who had enjoyed a night on the town, were also returning home in two cars. Having taken a wrong turn, they were lost and so, instead of being almost at their destination, they landed up at the scene of Bianca's crash.

One of these girls, Jay,* had lost her sister, Collette,* in a car crash about two months previously. Collette, like Bianca, was just twenty-one and the physical resemblance between these two young women apparently was quite remarkable. Even their interests and hobbies were similar.

Jay heard the voice of her sister saying that they must pull up to the side of the road because someone needed help. The other girls argued that it was unsafe, but Jay was adamant. Guided by two apparent 'flash lights', she found a distraught Bianca in the wrecked car, she immediately began to try and calm her down. Jay recalls that she amazingly phoned an emergency number, a number she didn't know — "Perhaps I was assisted by my beloved dead sister and the paramedics quickly arrived on the scene."

When the paramedics arrived, Jay asked her friends: "What happened to the two policemen with the flashlights?"

"There were no policemen here. Only we were here," replied the girls.

"You know, those policemen could only have been angels," murmured Louise.

"We are indebted to all the people involved that night whom we never really had the chance to thank properly. As collective souls we joined together in the roles we played at the time. Jay and her friends even accompanied Bianca to the hospital. Somehow our families are connected. I think it's more than mere

---
* Not their real names

coincidence that Jay's little daughter was born on Bianca's birthday," remarked Bronwen.

As she lay in the crumpled wreck of her car, Bianca had two near death experiences and had to be resuscitated and brought back to life twice. During these near death experiences, Bianca recalls that two angels came to her assistance.

"What happened, Bianca?" I asked.

"During the accident there were two angels present — Percucious and Michelle. Percucious had red hair, red eyebrows, icy blue eyes and these l-o-o-ng eyelashes," recalled Bianca, demonstrating the length of the eyelashes with a deep swoop of her slender hand. "I remember that Michelle had dark hair in a bob and an olive complexion.

"I couldn't breathe at all and Percucious and Michelle were basically coaxing me, helping me to breathe. In and out. In and out. It was all very strange, then I died."

"You died?"

"Yes. In the time that elapsed after the accident and the time it took to get me to hospital, I was aware of dying twice."

"It took forty-five minutes to get Bianca from the scene of the accident to the hospital," explained Bronwen. "Bianca, you might like to explain that this was not the first time that you met Percucious."

"Hmmm. Yes. One day before the accident, I was distraught. I had run up my cell phone bill way too high. I didn't know how I was going to pay it. I could not stop crying. I was with a friend of mine who was very spiritual. He offered to do a relaxation technique with me.

"During this relaxation, I closed my eyes and I saw Percucious as a pixie. I saw him painting vivid colours like blue, green, yellow, gold in a spiral circling effect. I saw a city silhouetted and stars were shooting up from this city. It seemed as if Percucious was showing me this magical place, although at the time I couldn't quite grasp the symbolism, I found his presence and the process calming.

"So yes," Bianca reflected, "I had met him before and I associated him with a relaxing energy, and therefore, when I met him again I knew him and was able to listen to him as he talked to me. When I met him again I knew him and I was able to listen as he coaxed me to breathe shortly after the accident occurred."

"Let's go back to the scene of the accident. What happened when you died the second time?"

"I saw myself in the tunnel with the clinical white tiles. From there I intuitively went into a place which I instinctively knew was called The Hall of Wisdom. It was like a huge auditorium inside.

"Scenes from my life were flashed before my eyes and from there I was somehow transported to a place where I was told to get back into my body."

"So you had left your body?"

"Yes. I was above my body and looking down at the sorry, crumpled mess that my body had become. No wonder I didn't want to get back in there.

"But then I thought that if I got back in, I'd somehow survive the accident. The next thing that I can remember is that I was fighting off whales and sharks. Perhaps these were the doctors and nurses in the hospital stabilising me medically with pipes and monitors."

Ever since Bianca was born, Louise had had disturbing recurring dreams. In these dreams Bianca was always a small toddler. Even though something terrible always happened to the child, she didn't die.

"Would you like to elaborate on these dreams?"

"One of the dreams had to do with swimming pools. Bianca was drowning and I couldn't get to her, although in the end she survived.

"Then I had this other frequent nightmare. I got home from work and Bianca was lying hanging over a door — the doors of our house are arched — and she was pale. The carpet was dark brown and where I stepped I could see the blood coming up between my toes. I walked to my husband and asked him why he hadn't taken her to a hospital," Louise said, her face clouding over with anxiety at the memory.

"It was as if, over the years, I was being prepared for Bianca's accident. For, after her crash, these nightmares finally stopped."

The week before the accident, Bronwen was also experiencing vague feelings of uneasiness. " With Bianca and I being well connected souls there were definite moments where I recall that it seemed as if Bianca's energy was gently dissipating, as if in some way it was fading in and out."

A few days before the accident Louise gazed at her daughter who was always rushing here, there and everywhere and she said to her younger daughter: "What is your urgency, my girl? You have your whole life ahead of you."

Then without really knowing why, Louise broke down and cried. "At that stage none of the family was aware of the extent of the changes that were to follow," recalled Louise, slowly shaking her head.

Bronwen adds: "The night of Bianca's accident was particularly distressing and I remember experiencing a sense of uneasiness and misplaced anxiety. I was totally distraught ... I went to bed but I couldn't sleep. Sometime in the early hours of 3rd December 1999, I must have drifted off into a restless sleep as I was startled by a knock on my door at about 3.30 am. It was my dad who informed me that Bianca had been in a very bad car accident."

Sitting in the studio, the light was beginning to fade, casting a shadow over Bronwen's face.

"It felt as though I had been hit by a bolt of lightning. I knew my world had been changed forever. In grave silence my dad and I headed for the hospital but somehow I within my core I felt a slow unfolding, which held a deeper sense of knowing what could be done to facilitate my sister on her path as a soul. Even though I didn't know the outcome of the accident, it was as if I was being guided through the process as it unfolded.

"In the dark hours and days that followed I sat beside her hospital bed and I spoke to her, heart to heart and soul to soul, encouraging her on her own journey as a soul and assuring her that if it was time for her to go and if her soul wished to depart this earth, that we as a family all loved her enough to let her go. Yet I also knew that no matter how severe her injuries were, Bianca's spirit was strong and courageous enough to thrive should she decide to continue her life journey with us on earth."

****

The prognosis from the doctors attending to Bianca was not favourable. "I give her thirty-six hours to live," declared the attending physician, "and if she does survive, I do not believe that she will have any reasonable quality of life."

There was every reason for his pessimism. Bianca had sustained a severe head injury, a right orbital blow-out, her right arm was broken and there was apparent major internal bleeding. This bleeding baffled the doctors who performed scan after scan in their effort to determine its cause.

As with Acquired Brain Injuries the doctors made the decision to sedate Bianca to the point of coma as the more agitated she became, the greater the swelling on her brain would be.

The Glascow Coma Scale is a numerical system used to estimate a patient's level of consciousness after sustaining a head injury. Each of the following are numerically graded: eye opening (4) motor response (6) and verbal response (5). The higher the score, the greater the level of consciousness: a score of 7 indicates a coma. Bianca's score was only 3 and she was considered to be at the point of death.

Unbeknown to the family, Bianca's optic nerves had been severed and that is where the bleeding stemmed from. When the doctors looked into her eyes, her pupils would not constrict or dilate. Unable to move or to speak or to give any kind of response, her death or irreparable damage seemed to be inevitable.

Despite the grave prognosis — no matter what each moment held (be it a sign of miniscule progress or of devastating decline) as a close unit, the family held each moment for the gift it brought. At times they noticed subtle nuances in Bianca's limited reactions to their conversations and visitations and they engaged with her as meaningfully as they could during her 'window of light' periods. Somehow the family sensed that Bianca's enduring spirit was in there. Beyond the dark silence of her body, her 'Being' shone its light, its love, its truth and the depth of her courage. "Those around us, be they therapists, staff or doctors did not see what we saw ... the light of Bianca's soul," said Bronwen.

A trained psychologist, Bronwen felt certain that within her sister's immobile and lifeless body, that Bianca's essence was still aflame. She enlisted the help and love and support of Bianca's many friends and of dearest family members, who all came to visit her daily.

In her anguish, Bianca's mother asked God for proof that there were angels and when Louise read the Bible, every page she opened had a reference to angelic beings. In acknowledgement of this faith, Louise endeavoured to spray paint the windows of the ward where Bianca lay with angels and the doctors attending to Bianca were all given angel pins to wear. Bronwen and her family instinctively knew what to do to ground Bianca and to stabilise her, during her difficult journey.

Colleen-Joy Page, an intuitive spiritual counsellor and a family friend, sent Bianca healing energy during the critical time when Bianca's soul was making the momentous decision whether to leave earth or to remain as a physically challenged person.

Tirelessly, Bronwen worked with Bianca, telling her stories, assuring her that the family believed in her, singing her their favourite childhood nursery rhythms and their favourite songs. "Did you sing me The Mamas and The Papas 'All The Leaves are Brown?' " questioned Bianca. "You know how much I love it."

"Of course I did," replied Bronwen. "Do you remember when I sang the Phil Collins song 'You'll Be in My Heart?'"

Bianca nodded. "Well," said Bronwen, "that's when I knew that the essence of you was still alright. Even though you didn't shed a tear, I saw you cry when I sang this to you. I saw it in your face and I knew that despite what the Glasgow Coma Scale said or what the doctors or my colleagues said, you were still here with us." According to her attending therapists, it appeared that Bianca lay within a low graded classification on the RANCVHO scale for several weeks, and that was mostly assessed on her considerably limited physical movements and her inability to communicate in a consistent way.

Bianca's lack of readiness to enter into a rehabilitation unit was distressing. However, as soon as Bianca was given the opportunity to enter a neuro and physical rehabilitation unit her progress was visible. Over the course of rehabilitation in the weeks and months that followed, Bianca made steady but painfully slow progress. Various forms of therapy were introduced to facilitate her recovery process, such as occupational therapy, physiotherapy and speech therapy.

Finally, to the delight of her family and her friends and to the doctors and the ward sisters, who wept openly when Bianca showed meaningful signs of recovery, it was decided that Bianca was strong enough to return home for weekends.

On the 25th of February 2000 in her speech therapy session Bronwen watched in amazement and cried silently as Bianca started vocalising for the first time in three months — overwhelmed with joy, the sisters laughed and cried together as the silence between them slowly fell away.

In the course of the evening, Bianca, still filled with immense achievement, had been 'chatting' non-stop all day, catching up and joking with all her visitors in her severely dysarthric words.

Only when everyone had left the ward, with only Louise and Bryan at her bedside, Bianca spoke quietly and solemnly, addressing her dad first. Barely moving, her slender hands tried to reach for Bryan's hand.

Louise motioned to Bryan to hold Bianca's hand. Then, as if to comfort her father, Bianca said softly, "Dad I am well. You must not worry about me and I love you very much."

Then turning her head towards Louise, Bianca said "I love you very much too, Mom." In the emotional silence that followed, Bianca added these unforgettable words, "Dad, I am blind."

Bianca's words caused Bryan immeasurable sorrow. His face distorted and his body shook as tears ran down his face like buckets of water. As if to comfort her distraught father, Bianca said: "Don't be troubled, Dad. I will work harder."

****

Later as Louise, Bryan and Bronwen stood around Bianca's bed, they held each other and sang through their tears the song which happened to be playing on the radio 'Don't worry, be happy.'

"It will be okay," said Bronwen softly. "It will be okay. Together, we will be okay."

Quietly, Bryan and Louise added, "Yes, it will be okay."

Bronwen said: "As a family, if there is anything that can be done, it will be done and if it can't be done, then learning to be different will be our adventure together."

****

When I met with Louise, Bronwen and Bianca, some years had passed since the accident. For two years following the accident, Bronwen, who was supported financially by the help of kind-hearted, empathetic and generous family members, took a sabbatical from her work as a psychologist in private practice to work with Bianca fulltime on her rehabilitation.

Bronwen was able to nurture Bianca to a level where, despite her physical limitations, Bianca has become an example of incredible bravery, courage and inspiration to all who meet her. During this time the focus was on reintegrating Bianca meaningfully into her life again — she had lost her world as she had known it ... her identity, her hopes and dreams had been shattered.

Together, Bronwen helped Bianca to build a different life — with a transformed identity, combining her old hopes and dreams with new ones.

By employing her abilities and focusing on her strengths, a new sense of self started to evolve.

Overcoming the fact that her speech is severely dysarthric and that she had lost a lot of confidence in her ability to communicate clearly with others, Bianca still graciously accepted invitations to tell her story in public. On these occasions, she touched the lives of many with her moving courage and silent strength.

****

For a period of time, Louise and her two daughters worked together, celebrating the gifts and lessons that they had learned from Bianca's life-changing experience.

Working in a Health Centre alongside other health practitioners, the three women called themselves 'The Binding Cord', a name derived from the realisation that not only is the family connected on a spiritual level, but the greater family of mankind are all connected, not only to each other, but also to the Divine Source.

Not content with only doing this work, and despite all her physical challenges, Bianca worked alongside Bronwen and a team of doctors and the therapists at the rehabilitation unit. Her input and insights were invaluable to both the medical team and to the patients.

Bianca did what she calls 'Aroma-rei', which is working on the patient's feet to determine their man ailment.

"Bianca, what is Aroma-rei?"

"Aroma-rei is my own invention, which I developed according to spiritual and angelic guidance. While practising Aroma-rei, I would determine which aromatherapy oils would encourage a person to better themselves on the spiritual plain, which would in turn effect their mental, and hence their physical state. I worked in conjunction with psychologists to achieve this result."

In the early days following her accident, Bianca also developed a range of healing oils and creams and with her heightened sensitivity she was able to develop products to suit the individual needs of her clients.

Although her eyes may be sightless, Bianca's insight into the human body and her innate knowledge of the colours that calm and heal, has transformed Bianca into a formidable healer, able to combine aromatherapy with Reiki and reflexology.

****

In the intervening years since I first interviewed Bianca in 2004, much has changed in the lives of the Van der Schyff family.

A bookkeeper by training, when Bianca had reached a reasonable stage of recovery, Louise began to study a range of healing techniques with holistic healer, Keith McFarlane.

Her daughters say of her: "Mom is our 'mother flame', our personal earth Angel who quietly serves and loves us unconditionally. In all that she does for us and for others she is an example of true dedication and devotion. She brings us laughter, spontaneity and an innocent reverence of the simple joyful things in life."

Dad Bryan is seen by his daughters as the strong, silent guide who held the family together and who steadfastly walked the path with his family; a strong support through the darkest of days. He taught his family to stand tall with brave compassionate hearts in the face of adversity and to persevere despite the many obstacles that the family has had to face. Bryan is the family's pillar of strength, who walked behind the family as they tried to find their way forward.

****

Bronwen currently lives and works in Western Australia. She remains truly inspired by the courage, determination and inner strength of her sister and acknowledges that this deep, personal journey shared with Bianca and her family, has changed the way she connects guides and facilitates the lives of others.

"It has been a humbling experience and a deep honour to walk alongside her and my parents on this often still very difficult, life-altering journey. Our lives will never be the same again because we have seen deeper than the eyes can see. It is in this sacred place that we truly saw the essence of each other in a loving, compassionate and respectful way.

"This sacred space of authentic connection was also evident and carried over to those special souls who offered unending support, unwavering love and devotion, and who, without hesitation, walked this journey with us in those first trying days. Your kindness and benevolence will never be forgotten and we hold you all deep in our hearts with humble gratitude.

"Bianca has come much further than anyone could believe. Still blind and in a wheelchair, she has regained a difficult but significant life. As my teacher, she has not only taught me that one only truly 'sees' through our spiritual eyes, she has also removed the illusions of worldly perfection and she has humbly shown the true concept of 'wholeness' in what many would call a 'broken' body.

"Words cannot convey my gratitude and appreciation to her. Once you have met her, you are completely thrown by her immense soul presence —you almost wonder how it is possible to fit all that soul in such a small body. With Divine Honour and Respect, I thank her immensely courageous soul for an awesome and unforgettable spiritual journey, which changed my life dramatically."

The last words in this inspirational story must rest with Bianca.

"Since you first interviewed me, I have developed the nutritional knowledge to support my body in anything that may happen to it; I have a basic understanding of the mind; I also still have Percucious to guide me through life's challenges.

"All these things represent the balance of body, mind and soul. Just as my family functioned as a unit to accomplish my independence, the body, mind and soul need to come together to function as a unit. I would not have been able to come to this realisation if it was not for the spiritual adversity my family encountered.

"In addition to the courses, I have studied to help me understand how to maintain health, I have also done complementary arts. I have done biokinetics to increase my psychical strength. In hydrotherapy, I learned to walk independently in water.

"I have learnt to ride horses and found that horses have a healing effect on people. The main aim of this exercise was to train the horse to take the lead and to take me where I needed to be. I have also studied Tai Chi to learn about the vital balance of body, mind and soul."

"I believe that your interest in the martial arts did not stop with Tai Chi.

"In 2011, I enrolled at the Tai Chi Chuan Institute in the south of Johannesburg. Craig Boden, the instructor was brave enough to take on my physical challenges. Tai Chi Chuan is a form of martial arts that assists with balance, movement and co-ordination as well as mental well-being.

"Tai Chi is not only for the disabled or blind as it has phenomenal positive effects on other ailments of the body and the mind. Tai Chi Chuan methods helped me to dramatically improve my static balance, my co-ordination and my movements to the point of me living in my own apartment with greater agility and ease.

"More than Tai Chi assisting my physical body immensely, it has benefitted my mind and changed my way of perceiving things. Spiritually, Tai Chi allows and accepts what you are capable of giving to the art at that point in time and, when it all comes together, it makes a beautiful tapestry. Craig often says: 'Don't look for it, it will find you.' "

With a wry smile, Bianca concludes: "And when it finds you, be prepared and take it as it comes."

MANDY YOUNG

PSYCHOTHERAPIST/ECO-THERAPIST

TAMING MAN'S INNER BEASTS BY CONNECTING WITH THE WILD

"Who we are inside — how worthwhile we feel and how we perceive ourselves — affects how we relate in the world. Observing wild animals helps us to re-connect with our intuitive, creative, passionate selves; with the ancient wisdom of our predecessors; and reminds us how to relate in ways that are God-created and species-specific."

Mandy Young

Ever since she was a small child, the bush has always been a source of great stimulation and comfort to psychotherapist Mandy Young.

"For various reasons I did not have a very close, loving relationship with my parents and I was forever wandering off into the bush looking for the affection I craved.

"I wish that my parents had understood who I was and had not tried to make me as they would like me to be. Such parents come from a complete, happy-with-who-they-are kind of place," explained Mandy.

"Surely your parents loved you in their own way?" I asked.

"Most parents try their best to love their children with the resources they have at their disposal but they too can be hampered by painful pasts and the unintentional, less conscious, neglectful action of their parents," she replied thoughtfully.

Mandy grew up on a plot ten kilometres outside the small town of Garneton in Zambia — "And there in the bosom of Mother Nature, I communicated with God and sought solace in the wild perfection of these unspoilt spaces. In particular, I felt drawn to the bird life, as well as to the flowing waters of the Kafue River."

"Describe your family situation."

"I think that living in this isolated spot, my mother felt quite abandoned. She has a good heart and honourable intentions but she was frustrated as a young girl.

"She was intelligent, came first in class and played hockey for a provincial side — an all-rounder, in fact, but it was bad luck that at fourteen her father became bankrupt, could not afford to pay her school fees for a while and try and help her family from starving by selling vegetables on the street corner. When her friends came out from school at the end of the day, she hid in embarrassment.

"It is difficult to be emotionally intimate with your children when you have not found your own potential, so my mother found bonding with my two sisters and I a challenge. Physical closeness and doing practical things for us was much easier than really understanding our hearts and our unique likes and dislikes."

"How did you get on with your siblings?"

"I was always jealous of my younger sister who arrived three years after I was born, because she had severe croup and received the care and attention that I craved.

"While she nestled in my mother's arms, feeling excluded, I headed for my nurturing place — the bush at the end of our long driveway, or I searched for my friend, Rosie, the daughter of a Black lady who cleaned our house. Rosie played with me, giving me the nurturing and love I longed for.

"My mother recently reminded me of a 'Rosie' incident. I was three years old, running gleefully after a headless chicken. I burnt the undersides of my tiny feet on the glowing embers of a smouldering rubbish heap. In a Mary Magdalene like gesture, Rosie swept me into her arms and wiped my blistered soles with her tender tears. Such was the nature of her love! In those early years, she became a substitute mother, and within me grew a deep love and respect for traditional Black people which continues to this day."

"Distanced from your parents, did you feel close to God?" I asked.

"From an early age I believed in a God who cared, something my parents taught me."

From a mere three years old, Mandy, searching for the affection and nurturing she craved, used to run away from home, seeking solace in nature — the high grass, the thorny trees, the endless blue skies, which she felt to be as much as the same as spending times with God.

When she was just five years old, Mandy's parents were attending a church service led by Christian missionary friends. "I wanted to respond to an altar call when the priest invited the children to stand at the altar, so my parents tell me. I guess that is where the initial yearnings to know a God of love begun!"

At ten years of age, the emotional separation she had always felt with her parents became a physical reality. This happened when the family left Zambia and moved to Zimbabwe. His father, an analytical chemist, was given the retrenchment package of an overseas trip.

Accompanied by his wife, Mandy's mother, they holidayed for three weeks overseas, leaving Mandy's youngest sister, who was only ten weeks old with an aunt, and her second oldest sister, who had now outgrown her croup with family friends. Both younger sisters were separated from their holidaying parents for a few weeks.

Mandy, however, considered to be 'too clever for local schools' was sent to boarding school for a year and did not see her parents for several months. "The school was in a different country and in a strange place. Not even the friends of my parents or my grandparents visited, even though they lived nearby.

"With no available parent, in order to comfort myself, I used to go to the school chapel and talk to God. He became my greatest friend and confidant, always available to listen and understand."

Several months after seeing her parents, on her first ten day holiday, Mandy was sent to visit with her father's sister. For Mandy, this visit was traumatic.

"Why was that?" I asked.

"My aunt was an austere, unfeeling woman," explained Mandy, adding "My uncle drank too much and my older cousin kept chasing me and wanting me to kiss me. I used to run away, lock myself in my bedroom and sit stunned in confusion at the end of the bed wondering where my mother was.

"I never really went home again after that, except for my last year at Junior School, but by then I had become very independent. I learnt that to survive I had to rely on myself.

"I felt an outsider within my own family, like the ugly duckling in the swan family, and from then onwards I was always on the outskirts of any group with whom I associated.

"At high school, back in Zimbabwe, I was sent to boarding school again, and the friendship-faith with God that had begun during my boarding school experience continued.

"Knowing God gave me a sense of purpose, a reason for living. Life made sense to me when He was around. I became a spiritual leader at school and ran the Scripture Union meetings. At a very young age, I found myself organising break-time get-togethers and outreaches. I was fervent about telling people about a God who cared and give them the life He intended if they choose to be 'born again.'"

"What does being 'born again' mean to you?"

"Being 'born again'" replied Mandy thoughtfully, "is a choice that we need to make if we want a relationship with God. It is essential if we want to experience our rightful connection with our Creator.

"In the Garden of Eden, whether you believe that to be a historical reality or Biblical metaphor, was where mankind made their first choice to be like God. The consequence is that we now know the difference between right and wrong, and have to take responsibility for which we chose and whether we want to do things God's way or our own."

"What about animals who are unable to differentiate between right and wrong?"

"Animals are fortunate in that they did not have to make that choice, so I believe that they instinctively live in their God intended species specific way."

"What about mankind? What if we decide to have a relationship with God?"

"Choosing to have a relationship with God through being 'born again' is just the starting point. The chosen re-connection initialises a new lifestyle with different values and a more loving filter, God's filter, through which we see the world and our relationships."

"How then would you define sin?"

"The word 'sin' with all its various interpretations, often gets bandied about and I understand it to be any non-loving or anti-creative thought or behaviour we inflict on ourselves, others and the God-created world that sustains us.

"Do you believe that Christ died on the cross to save us from our sins?"

"I feel that he knew the torturous guilt and self-destructive consequences we would experience day-by-day through our unloving, anti-creative thoughts and actions if we did not have a way of experiencing forgiveness and a way of clearing the 'sin'-clogged connection channels between us and God."

"So you feel that Christ is our direct connection to God?"

"Yes. He died on the cross on our behalf, paid the price because we could not be re-connected with a loving but 'sinless' God in any other way — definitely not through our own efforts.

"Many people think that if they are good enough they will gain this relationship, but it is not about us, it is about God's mercy. He wanted to provide a way for us to experience the depths, breadths and heights of His love and wisdom, but we need to choose that this is what we want. God is a Gentle-man. He does not impose this on us … we have a free choice."

"You found you own spirituality very early. Perhaps you would like to expand on this …"

"One of my most remembered spiritual experiences was at a teenage camp." replied Mandy. "Here, for the duration of a week, I took it upon myself to fast. When I should have been at meals with the other teenagers, I went off by myself and began to pray.

"One day, while I was praying, I heard someone else praying nearby. Looking up on the hill outside our chalet, I saw it was a man and that he was talking in a strange language.

"I approached him and asked him about the strange words he was using. He explained that when we want to deepen our devotion to God we can asked for what he called the Baptism in the Holy Spirit, and the consequence, he explained, is an ability to 'speak in tongues' — to pray with a spiritual language that is beyond our deepest comprehension.

"With all my heart, I longed for all I could get of God, so I too prayed for this experience."

****

In 1 Corinthians 13: 1-3 NIV Paul says: *If I speak in the tongues of men and of angels, but I have not love, I am only a resounding gong or a clanging cymbal. If I have the gift of prophecy and can fathom all mysteries and all knowledge, and if I have a faith that can move mountains, but have not love, I am nothing. If I give all I possess to the poor and surrender my body to the flames, but have not love, I gain nothing.*

"What do you think Paul meant by this?"

"This biblical reference to angelic tongues implies that they are exceptional, a miraculous demonstration of the power of the Holy Spirit — a phenomenon believed to be true within the pentecostal and charismatic churches."

"Did you acquire this much longed-for gift of being able to 'speak in tongues?' "

"Yes, I do 'speak in tongues.' It is a prayer language used in earnest for certain people and situations that enables us to communicate deep into our or into others' lives, way beyond human words or comprehension. It is a language I also use to praise God, because, let's be honest, who has the words to describe His magnificent presence and being?

"Whilst some of your relationships with your fellow human beings have not been entirely satisfactory, you relationship with God is on-going and enduring?"

"Nowadays, I am not one to label things, rather to describe them. If I was to describe what happened on that day, it was as if I was walking and conversing with God, we were already friends, and then He picked me up, gave me this very tight hug and whispered in my ear just how much He loved me.

"Our walk together from then on has been much deeper, very secure and more intimate. No matter what I have experienced in life subsequently, my love of God and trust in Him has never been shaken. It is a deep, precious and long-standing relationship."

"How do you express this relationship with God?"

"I usually start the day by reading The Bible, journaling and praying, a daily renewing walk and talk with God. I don't go to church anymore since my divorce. Neither God nor the church is responsible for that life happening ... it was the result of my own, rather inadequate, attempts to sustain bonds and attachments. Nevertheless I was very hurt by the way those in the church handled the breakdown in my marriage."

"Yet you are a healer. How do you express this gift if not through the church?"

"I have gifts of discernment and healing, which I would like to implement in the church, but I have lost my credibility there, so instead I use these gifts by taking people into wilderness places where, by looking at the mountains, the rivers, the trees and bushes, the magnificent sunsets, not to mention the incredible array of animals He has created, they can experience the beauty and character of God, and where I can be instrumental in facilitating healing, self-discovery and self-care."

"May I take it that you are disenchanted with the church?"

"A fundamental Biblical concept is to love others as you love yourself. If you do not even know yourself, how can you practise self-love or the authentic love and service of others?

"Do you feel that the church has failed in its teachings?"

"There is too much dishonesty in the church when wounded people chose not to be aware, and healers and counsellors are inadequately trained, so they offer only partial support. When people's lives are not fundamentally changed, they become discouraged and disillusioned. There is a difference between emotional healing and spiritual maturity, although they are so inter-linked."

"Do you think that the fundamentals of the church have kept pace with our modern lifestyles?"

"I believe in the concept of church, a place of meeting where those who have the same beliefs meet together to encourage love and be accountable to one another, but the church is too often a place of control instead of love, where beautiful Biblical truths are carried out with a westernised mindset, and instead of celebrating difference, it becomes divisive, intolerant and judgemental of much that it does not understand. I do not expect people in the church to be perfect, no-one is, and I respect their courage, compassion and desire to follow after truths that honour the God they love, but they just need to be encouraged to be more honest and aware."

****

With her schooling complete, Mandy went on to study Social Work Honours at UCT, Psychology Honours through correspondence at UNISA, and later she completed a Masters Degree in Psychology back at The University of Cape

Town. She married an accountant who later studied to be a Minister within the Church. This union produced two children; a daughter and a son.

Both children were deeply hurt by their parents' subsequent divorce but together with Mandy, they have worked hard at defining themselves and healing. Today they are both married and have children of their own. They contribute significantly into church and their community, and as a tribute to Mandy's conscientious mothering, her offspring are described by most people who know them as above average in their love, wisdom, compassion and maturity.

When her marriage ended in divorce, Mandy, now a qualified psychotherapist, looked for a way of healing both her broken spirit and that of others.

She thought back to the place where she had been happiest as a child — her beloved bush. She thought of the animals in the wild — they did not seem to experience the problems humans did in bonding, both with their offspring and with other members of their herd. Mandy began to observe the behaviour of animals in the wild — initially wild dogs, which she observed over a period of five years both in South Africa and Zimbabwe.

She then went on to study the behavioural patterns of other animals — elephants, meerkats, white lions, mountain gorillas and finally dolphins. She realised that we often suffer with the stresses and strains of city life, and that time spent in the wild, communicating with God, the animals and nature can restore our equilibrium. We have also lost the comfort of spending more time in communities as clans. Mandy validated this understanding when she spent time with the Bushmen in Botswana.

What Mandy was learning through her observation of the social behaviour of animals and tribal people, through her experience as a psychotherapist and a mother, was the desire of both adults and children to reconnect with nature; to de-stress; to rediscover our playful inner child and to be nurtured and to heal.

"How does your eco therapy work?"

"I take people into the wildness of nature, with its different seasons and cycles, where things are always in harmony, to a place where there is total acceptance and unconditional love. It is a place where emotional healing is facilitated ... a place where one can reconnect with one's body, mind and spirit. For me, and, hopefully, for many of those who accompany me on my trips, it is a where one can truly re-connect with and experience God.

"In his important book *Ecotherapy: Healing Yourself: Healing the Earth,* Howard Clinebell writes:

People's heart-level religious beliefs and functional ethical commitments, in contrast to their head-level beliefs and values, influence profoundly how they relate to themselves, other people, their natural environment and the divine spirit.

Religious and ethical dynamics are powerful influences in determining whether individuals and groups will change their behaviour enough to save the biosphere in the years ahead. Spiritual and value dynamics are keys to embrace earth-caring behaviours ... to being nurtured by nature.

"I believe that God created each species with special ways of belonging to and relating with their fellow creatures. If we can live within these behavioural paradigms and processes, our chances of successfully adapting to our own circumstances are so much greater," explained Mandy.

"Tell me firstly about the expeditions when you observe the behavioural patterns of wild dogs."

'This is definitely not for the fainthearted, but for the passionate and courageous,' laughed Mandy. 'We stay in the rustic surrounds of the Mosetlha Bushcamp in the heart of the Madikwe Game Reserve."

"Where exactly is Madikwe?"

"Madikwe is currently the fifth largest game reserve, yet it is one of the lesser known parks in South Africa. Situated in the Kalahari Desert, in the north-west corner of South Africa, eighty kilometres south of Gabarone, the park comprises of wide expanses of grasslands, woodlands and rocky outcrops and is bordered in the south by the Dwarsberg Mountains. One is spellbound by its beauty.

"Through watching these creatures in their natural environment we learnt about the nurturing of kinship bonds. I believe that we are meant to be part of a tribe or clan, as was the case in primitive societies.

"I do not believe that any man should be an island — yet this social integration is hard to achieve in a society where self-sufficiency is the norm and so many families are broken or sad."

"Incidentally watching the wild dogs taught me about being a Wild Woman, not drunken and carousing, but more in touch with my feminine wisdom and attributes — keen sensing, having a playful spirit, a heightened capacity for direction, relational by nature, inquiring, endurance and strength, deeply intuitive, intensely concerned with my young, my mate and my pack, experienced in adapting to constantly changing circumstances, stalwart and very brave."

Mandy also takes groups into the Pongola Game Reserve into a wilderness space that stretches along the Jozini Dam with the backdrop of the Lebombo Mountains to study the timeless wisdom of the fifty-two elephants that reside there.

"To watch these gentle giants in the wild is a moving experience. They are intelligent, highly social animals with an intricate system of communication. Led by the oldest female, the matriarch, they are an example of good mothering, great loyalty and affection.

"Elephant mothers teach us about being child-focused with constant reflective physical and emotional responsiveness to the calf at hand."

"Am I correct in assuming that for you there is no more important job than mothering?"

"Unfortunately, because of the economic demands and social pressures and sometimes career ambition and choices, it is no longer fashionable to stay at home and just be a housewife — mothers are coerced back into the workplace when the baby is just a few months old, when, in truth, both long for each other across the city divide.

"I always like to quote Joanne Fedler, former well-known business woman and feminist. These were her words after giving birth to her first child:

"I have learned that feminism is right, motherhood is possibly the most underrated and undervalued profession, and the state should pay mothers a wage to go bring up kids. When someone tells me, they're just a mother and a housewife, I now pay them homage, as I might have done pre-motherhood to a high-powered businesswoman or politician ... Women with children are the unsung heroes of our world – something feminism taught me in theory, and which I only understood later on in practise (with the advent of her first child). And I have learnt that it is both unfair and magical that women are biologically the chosen people to bear children. I have lost a lot of my theory in the process and found a humility that reminds me that despite what I thought I knew, I

really don't know much about anything anymore, except that teletubbies - Tinky Winky, Dipsy, Laa-Laa and Po, all love each other very much."

This theme of family unity runs through much of Mandy's work, particularly as many children experience parental separation and divorce. Outside of Oudtshoorn in the Western Cape, she takes groups of both adults and teenagers to view the gregarious, cute and sometimes comical, Ungulungu wild meerkat family at the Meerkat Magic Valley.

"By watching these small comical animals as they play and forage for food, one can learn so much about trust, patience, taking care of oneself as well as how to be altruistic towards others.

"For example, when the meerkats go out foraging for food, one meerkat needs to be on guard so that the others can forage in safety from predators such as jackals and raptors in the sky. Science has shown that the wild meerkat on guard is the one who is in the best physical condition and who is therefore able to altruistically go without food to look out for the safety of the others while they forage."

"Am I correct in assuming that we can also learn a great deal about mothering from the small meerkat?"

"Yes indeed." agreed Mandy. "When new meerkat pups are born, wild meerkat adults and sub-adults also sometimes go without food for a whole day while their teammates leave to forage. They stay behind to take care of the immobile young. Again, they remind us that motherhood at certain times necessitates sacrifices when children are young, dependent and without the resources to take care of themselves."

Mandy has reached a stage in her life where after much persevering inner work and healing, she feels comfortable with the work she facilitates and the people she loves, and is at ease with, and with her all-important, all-embracing relationship with God. "So, now I just want to play a bit!"

"In the warm crystal-clear blue water seas, off the untouched white stretches of the Mozambican shoreline, there are surf pods of up to 200 dolphins. I have recently started taking people here to swim with these magical creatures, so full of endearing playfulness and teasing. With their dancing eyes and mischievous grins, these caring, intuitive, responsive mammals teach us about faith and hope, about just being, instead of living with ongoing fears and insecurities."

"You believe that we can learn so much about healing from dolphins?"

"Indeed. I have begun to research whether people with depression, cancer, those dealing with loss and adjusting to divorce, amputees adapting back to life and special needs children will also benefit from the tremendous healing power of dolphins."

Today Mandy is in an ideal space. Happily remarried, a mother and a grandmother, not only does she have a special relationship with God, she is also able to spend time in her beloved bush and show people how much we can learn from observing animal behaviour — for are we not all children of the same God?"

www.peace-of-eden.co.za

MAJA ABRAMOWITCH

WIFE, MOTHER, GRANDMOTHER, LECTURER, HOLOCAUST SURVIVOR

DARK NIGHT; WHITE LIGHT

DISCOVERY

I have found God

In the sulphurous darkness of absolute negation.
An endless brick wall, close-packed and blank
Are his eyes.
I hear his mindless inscrutable voice in
Shapeless silence.
When my brothers walk through the gas-chambers of Auschwitz
I know his sanctuary
In their boots blithely kicking the screaming infant
Helpless to evil
Far beyond frontiers of man's imagining football games
Of judgement-making.
The total absence of love is God
Whose presence
No clearer moments of rapture could stamp in the
Grain of my heart.
Yet his wings of meaning beat impotently patient
Against the opaque
Of my racked
Rejection. I wait in the dense air of living
for the lightning
conductor
of death.

Hilda Schiff

Maja Zarch was born on the 1st of May 1929 in Dvinsk, now known as Daugavpils, an important centre in Latvia, one of the three countries situated on the eastern shore of the Baltic Sea between Poland and the Gulf of Finland.

As the only child of successful businessman David Zarch and his wife Rebecca, who had studied music at the Berlin Conservatory before her marriage in 1927, Maja seemed destined to lead a charmed life.

She was loved and cherished by both her parents and by her adored Catholic Nanny, Petronella Vilmans, who came into the family's life when Maja was a toddler of two. At this stage the family moved from the double-storey brick house, which they shared with David's brother Isaac and his family, into a new house of their own across town.

In her book *To Forgive ... But Not Forget,* Maja wrote:

My room was heaven to me. I shared it with my devoutly Catholic Nanny. There, during the days, I did my homework, I played with my dolls and entertained my friends. At night, Nanny would sit by my bed and tell me stories of the First World War, or read from my fairy-tale books that held me spellbound for hours. She taught me moral standards; 'Christian doctrine' as she called it.

On the quiet, she taught me to say a prayer and cross myself, and always added: 'It will do your Jewish religion no harm!' God was her shining light and she believed in Him implicitly. She admired my father for his deep belief in God and respected all the Jewish customs. The two of them would often set out in the early mornings together to attend their respective houses of worship.

Such was her Nanny's devotion to her young charge, that during the thunderstorms that petrified young Maja, Petronella used to sleep on the floor next to her bed to comfort her. Maja attended the local ballet school, which was run by Madame Mirtzeva. She still has fond memories of the annual concert that took place at the Railway Theatre. She loved the daily rehearsals, the sleepless nights before the performance and finally appearing on stage before the hushed audience.

By some miracle, a couple of photos of Maja and her friends dressed in their pink ballet clothes still remain in her cherished box of Dvinsk souvenirs, but it is heart breaking to look at their innocent faces and realise that almost none of them survived Hitler's onslaught. Likewise, there is a poignant photo of Maja's Hebrew school class taken in 1938. Of the more than forty children in the picture, only three of them survived the Holocaust.

Her birthday parties were highlights of Maja's early youth. The table would be laden to breaking point with beautifully decorated cakes and cookies, lovingly made by her mother and her nanny. Her friends would arrive dressed in white stockings with patent leather or white shoes — white socks if the weather was warmer — and their best party dresses.

Maja would eagerly pounce on their offered gifts, while her father laboured in the kitchen, turning the handle of the ice-cream machine, diligently seeing to it that the proportions of sugar, cream and milk were just right, so that the final result would delight the palates of his daughter's demanding visitors.

The young girl and her family spent the summer months, from May to August at their dacha or holiday home at the popular holiday resort on Lake Stropi.

Idyllic days filled with laughter, swimming, boat rides and volleyball, walks in the nearby forests, where the children picked berries and mushrooms, well aware, even at their tender age, which mushrooms were for eating and which were poisonous.

Alas, for Maja and her friends, the joys of childhood were but short-lived. Following Kristallnacht (The Night of the Broken Glass) on 9th of November 1938 when the Germans destroyed 101 synagogues by fire, demolished a further 76 and destroyed 7500 shops, Jewish refugees from Berlin began flooding into Dvinsk, penniless and with nowhere to go.

It was not long after this, with German consent, that Russian soldiers crossed the Latvian border. Maja's parents, having had the experience of the First World War, anticipated food shortages and began to stockpile big bags of sugar and flour as well as various tinned foods. Maja was taken to the angros (wholesaler) where her parents bought her a coat three sizes too big as well as a pair of tangerine shoes, two sizes too large.

Almost to the year of the Russian occupation, on 22nd of June 1941, Dvinsk was shattered by the news that Germany had declared war on Russia and that German troops had already crossed the Latvian border. With a sense of foreboding, Petronella Vilmans went and stood at the window and looked out on the still peaceful street.

Holding Maja's hand, she said quietly: "I see a white light in the sky. This light predicts that there will be war and many problems. One nation will be almost destroyed by another nation, but finally, after much bloodshed and carnage, everything will come right."

When the sirens sounded and the German planes flew into Latvia and over Dvinsk, Maja and her family — apart from her father who said that whatever happened would be the will of God — rushed to hide in the cellar beneath the kitchen stairs. The sirens continued to wail and bombs exploded. The corner of the Zarch's family house was hit, ripping away the side of the dining room.

With the continual bombing, the major part of Dvinsk was soon in flames. Forsaking the cellar, the Zarch family ran upstairs. Jersey upon jersey was put on Maja, who then grabbed her beloved little dog and ran out into the street, only to see her house engulfed in flames.

"Everyone ran towards the river. It was June, the middle of summer, and in addition to the burning city, everyone was encased in layer upon layer of jerseys and dresses," she recalled. "Sweat was pouring from our faces, we were dry-mouthed and panting, too exhausted and shocked to speak."

Much of the city was burned and charred corpses lay all over the street. The German soldiers arrived in full force and at first they seemed friendly, setting up field kitchens at various points.

Abruptly, the German soldiers' attitude changed. Obersturmführer SS Günter Talbert, the German officer in charge of the city, issued an order for all Jewish men aged between sixteen and sixty to report to the market place.

The men were divided into groups and each group was taken to a different part of the town to help with the cleaning up of the city. These men were not allowed to return home and rumours started surfacing that they had been shot.

One evening when Rebecca could not find her husband in the town, she found him in the prison, with swollen eyes and tears streaming down his face — the Germans had shot and killed his brother Isaac.

The next morning, the prison was emptied and the news came through that its occupants had been taken to the outskirts of town. In a frantic state, Rebecca made her way there, only to find horse drawn carts piled full of men's clothing. She knew then that the Germans had killed her husband. Her grief and that of her young daughter Maja knew no bounds.

****

Shortly after this 30 000 Jews, wearing the yellow Star of David on the back and front of their clothing were taken to the ghetto, a medieval military stronghold in the suburb of Griva.

In the heat of summer, thousands of people were crowded together with hardly any sanitary facilities, no food and only one or two rusty taps for water. Amongst these unfortunate souls were Rebecca and Maja Zarch.

The overcrowding did not last long. The Germans firstly removed the old and sick, saying that they would be moved to a place where they would be taken care of. Shortly after this, the offer was extended to parents with small children.

Rumours began to surface amongst the remaining ghetto inhabitants that these people had all been shot. "These stories … they can't be true," twelve year old Maja told her mother. "How can anyone shoot a young child?"

Poverty and hunger in the ghetto were rife. The only available food was sour cabbage soup, consisting of water and rotten leaves. Maja and her mother were forced to sleep on the floor.

One day, a contingent of high ranking German officials arrived at the ghetto. Using rifles they prodded the inmates who were outside in the yard with guns. "Get inside," they ordered. Once everyone was inside, the selection began. "You … you go to the left. You … you go to the right."

Everyone soon realised that one column of people was meant for survivors; the other column was designated for those committed to death. But no-one knew which column was which.

Rebecca and Maja miraculously survived this selection. Rebecca was sent out to work away from the ghetto. Maja became very ill with severe appendicitis, coupled with jaundice. No medication was available, but somehow she survived.

Every Sunday, Maja used to wait to see her mother at the ghetto gate.

One Sunday her mother failed to arrive and Maja was filled with anxious foreboding. Finally, one week later, a figure arrived at the gate, bent with a shawl covering her head. Her face was swollen from being beaten, her eyes were black hollows.

Accused of being a traitor because the parcel she was carrying contained a letter to one of the ghetto inmates, Rebecca had been beaten and tortured and then placed in a cell with walls covered with ice and rats the size of cats. When a guard finally came to fetch her, Rebecca was certain that he was going to shoot her as soon as she reached the open field.

Surprisingly, the guard let her go free and she returned to nurse. Maja, who was suffering from malnutrition and eczema and was covered in boils and lice. Cleaning her daughter's wounds with sauerkraut soup or coffee, scratching her gently through the night, Rebecca managed to delouse Maja everywhere but her head. It is abundantly evident that without her mother, Maja would not have survived.

When the inhabitants of the ghetto went walking the many miles to their work, Maja's Nanny would stand in the fields, watching anxiously until Rebecca and Maja returned.

In her book *To Forgive ... But Not Forget Maja's Story,* Maja wrote as follows: "One day, on our return to the ghetto, we found my Nanny was waiting for us, upset and agitated. She told us she had heard that graves were being dug. Her fervent plea was that we should convert to Christianity, for she felt that because we were Jews and she a devout Christian, it would be impossible for us to meet in heaven. This deeply religious Catholic woman risked her life every time she met us but, despite this, she never failed to arrive.

We agreed to be sprinkled with her holy water. The following evening she was there in the field waiting for us with a little bottle of liquid to anoint us. She baptized my mother and me, said a prayer and gave us both a medallion of the holy Mother and Child. There in the field at night, under the lonely stars, she was convinced that we had become Christians."

Now, nearly seven decades later, as I sat talking to Maja in her luxurious suburban apartment, immaculately coiffed and elegantly dressed, she seemed light years away from the frightened young girl who had survived not only the ghetto, but also the unspeakable nightmare of the concentration camps of Kaiserwald, Stutthof and Sophienwald.

I asked her if she thought her 'conversion' had anything to do with her and her mother surviving the Holocaust.

"Who knows?" she smiled wryly and shrugged her shoulders.

****

Kaiserwald, on the edge of the forest at Riga, the first concentration camp in which Maja and her mother were incarcerated, was a living hell. Six days of the week, the women worked from dawn to dusk, stopping only to queue for watery soup and ersatz coffee. Sunday was their day of rest and they passed the time delousing themselves.

Included in the arduous work the women were expected to perform, was working at the harbour, off-loading cargo from the ships. It was about an hour's walk to the harbour and this was often done in the rain and cold. Thirteen year old Maja became very ill, but afraid that leaving her in the camp would result in her certain death, either Rebecca or one of her fellow prisoners would carry her to the harbour on their backs.

On Sunday 6th August 1944, all the survivors of Kaiserwald were taken to the Riga docks and loaded into a boat — at least ten times the number of people the boat was meant to carry. No food was provided — only a mouthful of water. Many people did not survive the journey to Stutthof, a concentration camp about thirty-five kilometres east of Danzig.

On both sides of the entrance were huge mounds of shoes, spectacles and some artificial limbs … silent testimony to just how many people had died there.

One day there was a selection by the SS officers of the women at Stutthof and five hundred women were called out to work. Divided into groups of twenty or thirty, the women were first forced to undergo a medical inspection. Parading in front of a long table at which sat about five SS officers, women with no scars on their body, who looked as if they could still work, were selected for duty.

Rebecca was stamped as being fit for work, but young Maja was rejected. Dressing as quickly as she could, the teenager went and hid herself under a bunk.

"I saw my mother's feet and I heard her wailing. I tried to get out, but I could not move because the space between the bunk and the floor was too tight. I started calling her softly as I was afraid one of the Germans would hear me. At last, my mother heard my cry. She tried to locate my voice, so I told her where to bend down as I could not get out. She asked the other women to help her lift the bunk. My mother's quick action saved me.

"The number of the last woman stamped was still wet and she managed to transfer it onto my arm. My mother removed her panties and stuffed these into my clothes to give me a bosom and I walked out with the others.

"The Almighty must have answered my devoted Nanny's prayers for our survival, for in the next group rejects were not allowed to mix with the stamped people. I had miraculously cheated death once more," recalled Maja.

Rebecca and Maja were transferred from Stutthof to Sophienwald, a place so remote that even today Maja has difficulty locating it on a map. In this camp, Maja fulfilled her creative urge. By using an empty toothpaste tube, which she cut in half up to the hard nozzle, she twisted a few strands of thread from the linen interfacing of her coat and pulled these through the nozzle. The remainder of the thread formed a wick, which rested on a jar lid that contained a small piece of margarine, the size of a thumbnail. This had been painstakingly collected by the other inmates.

"When I lit the wick for the first time, it felt as if the Almighty had once again brought light to the dark earth. Until that moment, we had lived in complete darkness from evening until morning."

The war was finally ending and the Germans were facing defeat on all fronts. As living victims of German cruelty, evil so extreme that even the Germans were afraid to admit to their maltreatment of concentration camp victims. Thus, before the Russian soldiers arrived at Sophienwald, on the 9th of March 1945, the women prisoners were rounded up and sent on a nightmare march to Gottendorf, a German military camp near the Baltic Sea in Western Poland.

Resting in a barn that night, terrified and exhausted, Maja and her mother heard shots being fired. "Was it the end for them?" they wondered. Suddenly, the barn gates were flung open by Russian soldiers with fixed bayonets. These men were their rescuers. Rebecca and Maja stood there dumbfounded. This was a miracle beyond credibility.

After the war, Petronella Vilmans first letter to Maja and her mother began: *My dear Christian friends, my prayers were answered ...*

****

From the beginning of the war, Maja's mother told her to memorise the contact numbers of her two uncles, David and Leon, who lived in South Africa.

She even sewed this number into the hem of Maja's dress "In case something happens to me and you survive," she said.

The number was safe with Maja until her clothes were removed from her, but even so, after the war, in 1947, Rebecca and Maja having re-established contact with their South African relatives, travelled on the Durban Castle to Cape Town to rejoin what remained of their sadly depleted family.

In Johannesburg, assisted by David and Leon, Rebecca and Maja set up home in a small, but comfortable flat and Maja went to Damelin College to complete her education.

Maja was soon to meet up with Sidney Abramowitch, a successful young architect, and the two were later married. The union was blessed with four children — two girls, Diana and Karen, and two boys, Roy and David. Maja and Sidney have seven grandchildren and are greatly looking forward to becoming great grand-parents.

Maja's life in South Africa has been rich and full. An accomplished linguist, a warm and welcoming hostess with a wealth of culinary expertise, a successful business woman with a flourishing business in cultured pearls, it is difficult, on meeting this sophisticated and cosmopolitan woman to believe the hardships she was forced to endure as a young girl.

The Holocaust, however, is something she will never forget. Nor does she want young South Africans ever to forget the horrors that certain peoples, most particularly the Jews, endured at the hands of their German torturers. Thus, under the auspices of the Foundation for Tolerance in Education, Maja was often to be found lecturing in schools about her personal experiences during the war.

Judging by the heart-warming letters of appreciation, she received from many of the scholars who were privileged to hear her talk, her talks obviously struck home.

This is one such letter:

Dear Maja,

Thank you is just not enough. I could think of many words to represent that little phrase but none of them could describe how grateful I am for the talk you gave us. The bravery you showed while talking was amazing — you didn't even shed a tear. I'm sure you and your nanny will meet one day in heaven before the Lord's throne. Your mom must be a wonderful and strong woman to keep her and yourself fighting for a brighter day. Congratulations you have won much more than a gold medal in a race. You have won freedom and the right to say: 'I am a survivor.'

You have taught me that age doesn't matter — you can always make a difference and the sun will keep rising so we should keep fighting. Even though the clouds stand in the sun's way it doesn't stop trying or give up and neither should we.

If we don't stand for what we believe in then who will? Even though this word is not enough I'm going to say it all the same, '"thank you,' from the bottom of my heart.

Yours sincerely,

Khanya Radebe.

"The children often asked me a question at the end of my talk. Maja, after all that you have been through, do you still believe in God?"

"What did you reply?"

"I am not a spiritual person. I take things as they are. Yet in my life, things happened that were miraculous. Why, for example was I saved during The Selection? Why was I even part of this process? Rabbis and children were invariably put straight to death. This in itself is a miracle. Their suffering was mercifully short. 'You to the left. You to the right'. Why was I told to go to the right? The line for the survivors. There must be a greater power, a grand and charitable person, who could notice me in that endless queue of humanity."

One of the many miracles of Maja's life, was that her mother, Rebecca, who undoubtedly saved her only child's life during the Nazi occupation, was spared for many years in good health. Rebecca Zarch, a wise and lively matriarch, who developed a wide circle of adoring friends throughout South Africa, died in 1993, aged 98 years.

Petronella Vilmans, Maja's devout Catholic nanny, is honoured by Yad-Vashem, the Martyrs' and Heroes' Remembrance Authority in Jerusalem in Israel, as a righteous Gentile. She died at 94 years of age.

DIANA COOPER

THERAPIST, HEALER & INTERNATIONAL AUTHOR

BRINGING ANGELS DOWN TO EARTH

*I am the angel of the Moon, darkened to be rekindled soon
beneath the azure cope.
Nearest to earth, it is my ray that best illumines the midnight way.
I bring the gift of Hope.*

The Golden Legend — Gabriel, Henry Wadsworth Longfellow

The shadows outside are lengthening as we sit in the conservatory of Diana's comfortable Dorset home on a cool late November evening, gazing out into her garden. "Dorset," she said, "is a portal for angels. So much so that when I organised World Angel Day, I awoke to find my garden awash with white feathers."

On this particular evening, all I can see, however, is the clear lawn under the spreading trees. Diana sees more than I do. "There are unicorns outside on the grass. I see them often. They are part of my new consciousness. For the angels with whom I work, have told me that my core work is changing.

"While I will still lecture and give workshops on the angels, the archangels and the Ascended Masters, I have been told by my guide Kumeka that my new path will involve instruction about the ancient civilisation of Atlantis during its purest years from 20 000 to 10 000 BC before it was destroyed by floods, and the preceding civilisation of Lemuria, when the light beings placed their awesome crystals in the Earth, specifically to help us with the twenty year transition to the New Golden Age starting in 2032.

"At the height of its glory, Atlantis had the highest level of spiritual consciousness that the world has ever known. Now this energy is being returned to us, with spiritual teachings for the higher good of the planet and I have become aware that it is only in honouring the best of Lemuria and the golden era of Atlantis that this planet can come into balance and harmony," she explained.

Diana's early life gave little indication that she would one day be an internationally acclaimed spiritual teacher. "I was born in the Himalayas — I still feel a particularly strong connection to India and its centuries-old spiritual energy — to materialistic parents who derided religion, psychic phenomena and spirituality. My father, a lieutenant-colonel in the army, was very authoritarian and powerful. He demanded that people conform. My mother, a nurse, was deeply compassionate, but also extremely unhappy, masking her discontent with criticism and sarcasm."

With her acquired wisdom and insight, Diana knows that she chose her parents before she made her decision to come to Earth. As she wrote in her bestselling book *A Little Light on the Spiritual Laws* 'Your Higher Self makes certain decisions before you come to Earth. Your soul makes these choices based on the experiences you need for your progress. You may choose to be born to difficult parents because they embody the challenge your soul needs. While you may reject this as ludicrous your soul views life from a greater perspective.'

Consequently, after her parents' death in 2003 her attitude towards her parents healed. Able to see their souls and their beautiful golden energy shining down, Diana realised that her problematic upbringing taught her many invaluable lessons.

Married by the time she was twenty-one to an executive who worked for Shell, Diana became an expatriate wife living in Holland and the West Indies. With three children — Dawn, Lauren and Justin — to bring up, she did not work but devoted herself to being a fulltime mother and housewife.

When she was forty-two, the family returned to England. Faced with a difficult divorce, with no skills and her self- esteem and confidence at zero, Diana was in such an anxious state that she could not see a future for herself. Only blackness loomed.

"It was in this dark state of mind that I threw myself into a chair and asked for help from 'anything out there.' Immediately a 6ft angel came in, took me out of my body and we flew together. Several times the angel took me to a mountain top and pushed me off.

"Each time I fell I was held by hands of light. Finally the golden being flew with me over a hall full of people with rainbow auras. I asked if I was in the audience and she told me that I was on a platform, where beings with rays of light shining through them stood. She telepathically imparted to me that she was showing me my future and I must prepare for it. When I returned to my body I had an awareness that I did not previously possess."

"Diana, when are angels willing to help you if you call out to them in dark despair?"

"Angels come to us in three circumstances. The first is when you send out a cry from the depth of your soul. They can help you on the ray of compassion under The Law of Grace. This is what happened to me when I cried out for help when I was at the bottom of an emotional pit. My angel appeared and showed me my destiny. I then had to work tirelessly to achieve it.

"When the soul is calling, the person is ready to change his or her life. The angels can then intervene. However, if you cry out from neediness and frustration, your plea comes from your ego. Were the angels to rescue your ego, you would not change your ways. Therefore they cannot help.

"Secondly, if it is not your time to die or be injured, your angel will step in and save you. If you are about to undergo a traumatic experience, which your soul does not need, your angel will intervene.

"Angels cannot interfere with the blueprint of your life, so if your contract is to die as a child or young adult, they must let it happen. Your angel must also bow to the dictates of your higher self. This means that if your soul wants you to have a wake-up call such as an illness, accident or financial disaster, your angel has to stand by with love and compassion and allow you to experience it."*

After this angelic visitation, Diana's struggle to find a new home and a way of earning a living continued. One day, while she was in a bookstore, a book on spiritual healing fell from the shelf and after reading it, Diana felt an immediate excitement. After deciding to train as a hypnotherapist and healer, her life changed. Filled with an immediate desire to help and heal people, Diana, working mainly through her spirit guides rather than angelic help, was able to bring guidance, comfort, health and happiness to those who sought her services.

---

* Reference for this conversation *Angel Inspiration* by Diana Cooper

After a few years of working as a healer, her guiding angels persuaded her to begin writing books. Her first book *Light Up Your Life* was birthed, based on her experiences and those of her clients and friends and on her heaven-sent spiritual understanding. A book a year was to follow and Diana felt herself to be well content with the path she was following.

Then came another move of home and the angels returned. Diana was lying in the bath, quietly asking for guidance for the classes that she ran. A golden angelic voice said into her head, "We want you to introduce people to angels." Diana responded that she knew nothing about angels and that she was not sure that she wanted to do this anyway.

Whereupon the angel said to her 'Who is teaching your classes? Your ego or your Higher Self?"

"Point taken," replied Diana, in her charming, matter-of-fact manner. Going downstairs in her dressing gown, Diana informed her surprised daughter, "I've just had a visitation from these heavenly beings. I think I'm going to teach about angels. My daughter and I looked at each other in horror, fearing that my credibility would be questioned."

It is a story that Diana has told many times before, both to the media and to her enthralled audiences. Yet the corners of her eyes crinkle and a wide smile lights up her face as she recalls that the numbers attending her classes immediately doubled.

"I have been talking about angels ever since," she concluded with a modest smile.

****

Diana has many angel stories to tell. In her book *A Little Light on Angels* she tells how three golden angels appeared before her and gave her a lot of information, telling her that, by Divine Decree, angels were now pouring into the planet, more than at any other time, in order to help with a shift in the higher evolutionary consciousness of the planet.

"These angels confirmed that everyone has a guardian angel to protect us, encourage us and to act as our voice of conscience," explained Diana.

"If we have a guardian angel, where does our spirit guide fit into the bigger picture?"

"Everyone also has a spirit guide, who has lived on Earth and volunteered after their death to train as a guide to help those who are still here. Your spirit guide is attracted to you according to the light you radiate and different guides come to you as you change. An evolved person will attract greater guides."

"Tell us something of your guide Kumeka."

"The most amazing thing happened. It was New Year's Eve, around 1997, and I had several people coming around to my house. One by one, for varying reasons, they all fell away. Until only one person, Shaaron, was left. At this time I didn't know her very well. We decided that we would both spend the evening meditating together and tuning in for guidance.

"During our meditation we both connected with Kumeka and what we learned is that Shaaron and I both come from the same monad — the same original divine spark — and that we are like soul cousins.

"Lord Kumeka is the Master of Light and Chohan or Lord of the eighth ray of cleansing, which is aquamarine and he is very powerful when evoked.
He has never had a physical body nor been on earth, but he really wanted to bring in transformation to this planet and he could only do this when Shaaron and I were together.

"Now Shaaron is psychic and so I was thrilled when she received the same message as I did. In fact I was to learn that Kumeka had originally connected with my energy when I still lived in the West Indies and before I had had any spiritual thoughts. Since then, he had worked tirelessly to bring Shaaron and I together.

"One year Kumeka asked Shaaron and I to bring him a Christmas gift. What on earth can you give a spirit as a gift? Shaaron brought him a present of some music and I, knowing that he was on this blue ray, brought him a beautiful blue crystal.

"However, wherever I walked, a bit of the crystal fell off. Walking alone on the beach on Skiros one morning, I went to wash the crystal in the sea and another piece of it fell off. Kumeka, I said, In future I won't be carrying this crystal any more. I will rather leave it at home. I then went to the village to look for something to eat.

"A powerful force led me in the direction of the jewellery shop. The last thing I wanted was a piece of jewellery but the pull towards the store was irresistible.

In the shop was this blue topaz ring shining at me, pulsing is the word. I thought to myself that I certainly didn't want the ring. In fact, I had recently got rid of all my jewellery. But there was this ring beckoning to me. I went to try it on. It won't fit I told myself. However it fitted me perfectly. I left the shop and spent a restless night with the blue energy of the ring shining clearly in my Third Eye. The following morning I went and bought the ring.

"Yes Diana," said Kumeka, "your angel and I kept leading you towards that shop." (Here Diana burst out laughing.)

"Kumeka has given me another blue ring now, a bigger one than the first. If someone is sending negative energy towards me, black spots will appear in the ring which Kumeka will clean away until it is completely clear. When I am teaching I wear blue nail polish to complement the colour of the rings.

"After I moved to this home in Dorset I called it Kumeka House. Kumeka said to me that if I gave it that name, I would be his servant. I replied that I was humbled and honoured to be in this amazing position. His energy is truly mind blowing. It never ceases to amaze me."

"Diana you are obviously very connected to your angels and your guides. What advice would you give to those of us who long to make this connection?"

"This is what I wrote in *Angel Inspiration*. I hope that it will prove helpful to those seeking guidance.

Meditation to connect with your angel and find his name

1. Make sure that you are in a place where you will be undisturbed.
2. If possible, raise the energy with flowers, a candle, incense, angelic music if you like it and beautiful objects or books.
3. Sit or lie with your back straight.
4. Ground yourself by imagining roots reaching down from your feet into the Earth.
5. Place an egg of golden light around you for protection. Take a few seconds to breathe the colour gold into it, relaxing your body as you do it.
6. Mentally ask your Guardian Angel to step into your aura and touch you. Expect a physical sensation, or a fragrance or a feeling of great love.

7. Ask your angel to put his wings around you and hold you. Relax into this.

8. Ask your Guardian Angel's name. Accept the first name that comes to you.

9. Calmly ask for any help that you need.

10. Thank your Guardian Angel.

11. Open your eyes and stretch.

****

It was while writing her first spiritual novel *The Silent Stones*, a book which involved extensive research in such far-flung places as the Himalayas and Machu Picchu, that Diana was once again visited by the angels.

Although she was desperate to finish *The Silent Stones* before taking a well-earned six months sabbatical in Australia, the angels had other plans for her. She was awakened one night by a host of angels who surrounded her bed, telling her that they wanted another book from her and that they wanted it *immediately*.

This book was *Angel Inspiration*, a guide not only to the angelic realms, but also to the importance of angels in our lives. While Diana laboured at this task, writing fourteen hours a day, she felt that she was being held and supported by the angels so that miraculously, the book was finished in just three short weeks.

Angel Inspiration has touched thousands of readers throughout the world and has brought to light testimony from people who have been helped through their adversity by these heavenly beings.

Susan Anthony, Diana writes, *was rescued from death on several occasions by no less than Archangel Michael himself. A crack cocaine addict, her first near death experience resulted from a seventy-two-day binge on a cocktail of class A drugs. As she died she felt her spirit leave her body and was approached by an immense shining pillar of royal sapphire blue light, which identified itself simply as 'Michael.' Later she discovered it was the Archangel.*

In death Susie was cocooned in peace, love and compassion beyond human comprehension as she was gently guided through her life review. Michael revealed to her that her personality self was filled with such deep self-loathing and despair that no mere mortal could have reached her. Yet she made a sacred life contract before being born to bring great life to the darkness of Earth. She learnt that her soul carried enormous wisdom and healing power.

Her choice was to remain in the peace of the other side or to return and fulfil her contract on Earth, with new gifts and keys bestowed on her by Archangel Michael.

She returned and totally healed her physical body, which had been ravaged and destroyed by her addiction to drugs. Susie has written a book about her awesome meeting with Michael in the hope that it will bring comfort to those who feel overwhelmed by darkness and despair.

****

Despite her international reputation as a spiritual teacher, Diana remains incredibly modest. I recall that when I went to Dorset to interview her, I asked Diana how I would recognise her when I met her at the busy station, adding that I would be carrying a copy of her book *Angel Inspiration*.

She laughed. "Well, I will be carrying a copy of your book **Out of this World** — *The Alternative South African Spiritual Experience*," she replied. A gesture which touched me deeply for it demonstrated to me that Diana still retains her sense of equality, humility and her astonishing generosity of spirit.

www.dianacooper.com

KAREN TOCKNELL

MOTHER, AUTHOR, MOTIVATIONAL SPEAKER

RISING FROM THE DEPTHS OF DARKNESS AND DESPAIR

MAY ANGELS YOU SAFELY KEEP

Howling winds, waves creep,
White foamed blue deep
Rise and fall, rise and fall …
Be at peace, sleep.
They be knights upon their steed
God speed, God speed
See the darkness swarming in …
Be at peace, sleep.
Fear not the sea, fear not the deep,
Fear not the creatures way beneath,
In His hands you'll safely keep,
Sleep my love, sleep.
Flaming lights like stars do streak
Up high of hoping help will seek …
Alas the silence closes in.
The angels will you seek.
Viciously the sea will leap,
The darkness lurking between your feet.
Smash, crashing, sinking, bashing,
The angels will you seek.
A new light does your wide eyes meet
Awaiting you is heaven's seat.
Be not angered, forgive life, please …
Sleep my love, sleep.
Beauty does your new eyes meet
As the silence around you slowly creeps
In from a life way beneath.

> *Be at peace, sleep.*
> *In his hands God does you keep*
> *Away from death so as to be*
> *Of evil's grasp, out of reach ...*
> *Be at peace, sleep.*
> *My Prayer to God is for him to keep*
> *You my father in Heaven's sheets*
> *Keep him safe God, in your arms ...*
> *May angels you safely keep.*

A poem by Terry-Sue Cochrane written for her father, Graham

In early July 2005 Neil Tocknell, an experienced yachtsman who had been sailing since he was a boy, mentioned to his wife Karen that he would be participating in the Mauritius to Durban Ocean Yacht Race. Neil and the other six members of the crew would be sailing on the Moquini, named after the African black Oystercatcher Wader bird. This fast state-of-the-art forty-two foot yacht had been manufactured by Fast Yachts in Durban where Neil had been working at the time.

The Moquini was owned by Graham Cochrane, who, being well aware of the difference between the haves and the have-nots in South African society, had founded *I Care,* a non-profit organization, designed to give street children the opportunity to learn sailing skills in order to secure jobs in the yachting and allied industries.

Eighteen year old Michael Goolam and twenty-four year old Sifiso Buthelezi, both development sailors with the *I Care* programme, were selected from the trainees to join the crew of the Moquini. Sheldon Dickerson, who worked in the *I Care* Sailing School was logged in as skipper for the race and it was decided that he, together with Neil Tocknell, would make all the tactical decisions in the race. Making up the crew of seven was Sheldon's cousin, Mark Dickerson and Kurt Ostendorf, both experienced sailors in their forties who were well regarded by the racing fraternity.

Initially Karen thought that she should fly to Mauritius to be with Neil for the start of the race, but with three young children — their daughters Jenna and Sarah were seven and four respectively and their son Ryan would be celebrating his first birthday on the 19th of September, she decided to stay home with the children, making Neil promise that he would be home in time for Ryan's birthday celebration.

Sailing was an integral part of the Tocknell family's life, with their children sailing on their two yachts Flyer and later B2G2, from the time that they were only a few weeks old. Despite this, Karen didn't know why but she had a sense of foreboding about the Moquini's journey from Mauritius to Durban.

The yacht's voyage across to Mauritius had been anything but plain sailing. The vessel had been caught up in an extremely fast moving current south of Madagascar and had been battered by fifty knot winds and extremely high seas for three consecutive days before managing to break free of the current. In response to advice from race headquarters in Durban, a new course was plotted and the Moquini would now sail in a south-easterly direction. In addition, electrical problems had been encountered en route and the steering mechanism had jammed.

All these problems had been sorted out, but as they were packing Neil's bags for the trip, a deep sense of anxiety came over Karen. "I don't think you're coming back," she said softly "and I don't know what to do."

Neil comforted his wife as best he could but still Karen's feelings of unease would not go away. "I think your dad is going to die too," she whispered. "What will I do? How will I run the business and provide for the kids?"

"You will be okay, Karen," Neil said, taking her into his arms.

The next day, even Jenna the oldest of the Tocknell children, turned to her father as he drove her through Hillcrest en route to her school. "Daddy, don't go," Jenna whispered as she hugged her father outside the classroom door. "Something is wrong, please stay."

"Everything will be alright," Neil reassured his daughter. "If anything happens to me, look after your mom, sister and brother for me. I know that you will be a brave little girl."

As the oldest child, these words left Jenna with an overwhelming sense of responsibility. A few miles away, Cari Dickerson lay in bed with her dad, Mark, crying as if her heart would break. She did not know why she was sobbing. Her father had been on many sailing trips before and Cari had never been anxious about him going away.

Dropping Neil off at the Fast Yachts factory, Karen felt a feeling of total despair. She sobbed uncontrollably all the way home — unable to reconcile her deep-rooted fears with her trust in a God who had always cared for those she loved.

Before he left his workplace, Neil, perhaps sensing that something might go wrong on this trip, said to Andreas, his work colleague and friend, "Please take care of Karen while I am gone."

Despite having sailed in so many yacht races and having been away from home so often, it was the first time Neil had ever felt the inclination to ask anybody to look after his wife.

****

The Moquini's journey from Durban to Port Louis had not progressed smoothly. The trip should have taken ten days, but had taken eighteen. On arrival, the five crewmen were exhausted, bedraggled and withdrawn. The yacht had taken on water and everything on board, including the crew were soaked.

One of the boat's fuse boxes had blown and all the instruments needed to be reconnected. Neil, Dick and Sheldon scrubbed and cleaned the boat, keeping their spirits high, despite the enormous task with which they were confronted.

On Friday 9th of September, the Moquini underwent a compulsory inspection by David Cox, one of South Africa's most highly regarded and reputable yachtsmen. David gave the boat a 'Cat A' certificate, saying that it was 'good to go'. This meant that the yacht's construction met legal standards and that safety equipment, such as life rafts, jackets, flares, harnesses, torches, tools, blankets, water and food were in place. A Sailor EPIRB — an emergency position indicating radio beacon, which signals maritime distress was on board.

Nevertheless, some of the crew members felt a sense of unease. Sifiso vanished from the boat. When he was eventually located he said that he was afraid that if he remained on board, he would die. Neil decided that Sifiso could return home and that the Moquini would sail with one crew member short. "Sifiso," said Neil, "It takes a brave man to go against what is expected of him. You have made the right decision."

Sifiso Buthelezi, aged twenty-four was a reformed criminal and a born-again Christian. He changed his way of life after a stint in jail for an armed robbery when he was sixteen. Sailing gave him a sense of comfort and so his decision to quit the Monquini's crew could not have been taken lightly.

For crew member Michael Goolam, sailing offered him escape from his life as a street child. The son of an Indian mother and an African father, Michael, until he found sailing, had never fitted in. When his father abandoned the family, his mother, embarrassed by her son's African appearance, shunned him. Michael lived on the streets and found his only comfort in sniffing glue.

The Moquini set sail from Grand Baie on the 10th of September 2005 — its destination was Durban, which was 1600 nautical miles away. On Tuesday 13th September at 22.45, Denise Cochrane spoke to her husband via satellite phone. Graham assured her that everything was fine ... the crew had enjoyed a light meal of tinned beef. A storm had apparently started building late in the afternoon. The wind had increased from about twenty-five knots to between forty and fifty knots and for most of the night there were huge swells and troughs, providing little chance of controlled sailing.

Shortly after midnight, in the early hours of Wednesday morning 14th September, the Moquini transmitted her position for the last time. The Maritime Rescue Co-ordination Centre (MRCC) reported that the Moquini's Star Track satellite tracking system had failed giving its last positional report at 25°50'25S and 47° 44'01E at 01.17. This put the Moquini some sixty nautical miles off the South-eastern tip of Madagascar. This was to be the last message received from the stricken vessel.

In her deeply touching book *My Moquini* published in 2012, Karen Tocknell writes: *"As our men embarked on their adventure across the ocean, unknowingly their wives and families began a journey of their own. For me, it marked the start of a journey through the depths of darkness and despair into the unfathomable light of God's love; a journey into the deep centre of my soul to discover the eternal treasures of God's mercy and grace."*

****

The call came through on Friday 16th of September 2005 that was to shatter the lives of Karen Tocknell and her family and also the lives of the other crew members. Denise Cochrane had received a missed call from the Maritime Rescue Coordination Centre (MRCC) at 08.30 in the morning.

The MRCC informed her that a single EPIRB (An emergency position-indicating radio beacon, which signals maritime distress) had been received from the yacht Crackerjack.

Realising that the Crackerjack's EPIRB system was aboard the Moquini, Denise was overcome with emotion — she instinctively knew that something was wrong. The single stream of data from the EPIRB was a single 350 millisecond signal that transmitted the identity code of the Moquini, but which was too brief for the MRCC to capture a location. Immediately, Denise phoned the Race Organiser Dave Claxton, who was now faced with the unenviable task of phoning all the families.

Months of extensive searching proved futile and gradually each family had to face the reality of the tragic situation-the six man crew of the Moquini were forever lost at sea.

However, even in this time of sadness there were miracles that showed that God had not abandoned the men of the Moquini or their families in their time of sorrow.

The first week that the men went missing, Karen's friend Cathy Sutherland was praying at the St Agnes Anglican Church in Kloof, asking Jesus to be with the six crew members as they went through their ordeal. Looking up, Cathy noticed that light was streaming through a single stained glass window at the front of the church. The picture depicted in the window was of six men, one of colour like Michael, with Christ in the centre of them. Whenever Karen or Cathy went to pray at the church, even if it was a cloudy day, the same shaft of light fell through that one window.

There were other signs that the Trocknell family had not been abandoned in their grief. One day daughter Jenna, Neil's eldest daughter, stopped in at a Christian bookstore, to choose a Bible that she thought her Dad would like.

Later as Karen unwrapped the Bible, she noted that a scripture had been selected and highlighted in red on the cardboard sleeve that encased the Bible in order to highlight the Bible's font.

The biblical extract chosen spoke of Jesus in a boat with his disciples, with the storm raging around them.

"Jesus responded, 'Why are you afraid? You have so little faith!' Then he got up, rebuked the wind and the waves, and suddenly all was calm.' " (Matthew 8:26 New Living Translation).

This verse brought great comfort to Karen as it indicated to her that Christ was with the men in the Moquini, calming the fear that raged within them.

In the midst of their despair, the wives of the missing crew members showed amazing courage. On the night of the 24th of September, the Prize Giving for the yachts that had completed the race from Mauritius to Durban was held at the International Conference Centre.

Sandy Ostendorf, wife of missing crew member, Kurt, as the secretary of the race, was to present the prizes. She performed this task with grace and dignity, congratulating each sailor who had made it home.

Not only had Sandy lost her husband, but less than two years later she would mourn the loss of her son Warren, who was killed in a motorbike accident.

As is written in Ecclesiastes 3:

For everything there is a season, and a time to every matter under heaven: A time to weep, and a time to laugh

The jubilation of the race winners was tempered by the fact that the popular crew members of the Moquini were not there to join in the celebrations and hope for their survival was virtually nil.

****

Karen had had a premonition that Neil's father would also die and sadly this premonition proved to be correct. Neil and his dad, BCT, had forged a close bond from their years of sailing together. The pain of Neil's death was too much for his father to bear. Collapsing sometime in early October, BCT succumbed to massive internal haemorrhaging.

BCT was taken to hospital in an ambulance and he underwent surgery the following week. A second operation followed the first operation, which was unsuccessful, and on the 24th of October, six weeks after his son went missing, BCT passed away. In her sadness, Karen wondered whether Neil was there to show his father the way home.

Karen was supported through her grief by a network of family and friends. Her parents moved in with her the day the Moquini was reported missing and with their help as well as the assistance of her sister, Sandy Menin, the household kept running, her mother giving her children the love and nurturing that Karen, at that time, was unable to provide; her father being an example to her, as he had always been, of God's unwavering devotion to his children.

Following Michael Goolam's memorable service on the 19th of November, Karen, who was well aware that despite Michael's life of difficulty and hardship, his faith in God had never wavered, asked God for a sign that He was available to all those who seek him.

There was a late afternoon storm that day. At first Karen could see only the dark, forbidding clouds in the sky, but, as she turned to go indoors, she saw a rainbow.

The phone was ringing as Karen entered the kitchen. It was Cathy with a message from her sister Sarah in England. Sarah had been praying for her, asking God to send a sign, a symbol of his faithfulness. As she gazed upon the rainbow in its multitude of colours, Karen knew that even in her darkest hours, God had not abandoned her, just as she was sure that God had been with the men of the Moquini as their final storm raged.

In early December Karen visited a church group who offered to pray for Neil, herself and her children. After some time had passed, the leader of the church group indicated that he had seen a vision of a dove rising above the wreck of the Moquini and the voice of God saying that He had taken Neil to be with him.

This message sent Karen into further despair. Already the trauma had caused physical damage to her body: her hair had started falling out in chunks; her molar teeth were cracked from the effort of her clenching her jaws and she was suffering from severe sleep deprivation.

Her brother Glen, a doctor, decided that she needed to seek medical help. She was admitted to Westville Hospital for sleep therapy. Karen reacted badly to the sleep inducing medication, which pushed her heart rate into the danger zone and she awoke to find herself in Intensive Care.

Karen's prolonged time in hospital gave her time to rest and in her book *My Moquini,* which she was later to write, she says: '*Eventually I found serenity in my belief that God carried Neil and the men of the Moquini through whatever they had faced on the ocean. He was with them. I believe that they rose with Him above the storm; that He lifted them from the pain of the physical into the spiritual realm of His presence where they found courage, comfort and peace.*'

****

A memorial service for Neil was held in the Bethany Chapel on Karen's parents' farm three months after the Moquini was declared missing. Karen was accompanied by her two daughters, Jenna and Sarah, while toddler Ryan was left to sleep in the farmhouse.

Filled with the courage that she has shown since Neil's death, Karen spoke to the many family members, friends and colleagues who had gathered to support the family in their time of sorrow and of loss. She was later to say of the memorial service: "I have never felt so completely loved or so completely alone."

The question "How did Neil die?" was always uppermost in Karen's mind. On Sunday the 5th of February 2006, a capsized yacht was spotted at 33°32S and 38°21E off the coast of East London by a passing tanker, the MT Algarve.

Bill Tyler, the manufacturer of the Moquini, was able to identify the visible hull as that of the lost yacht. On the 8th of February, the MRCC dispatched a towing vessel, the Smit Amandla, to investigate and salvage the wreck. The Moquini was found inverted, with the rudder and engine's sale drive unit in their normal positions but with the keel missing. Absence of the keel would have caused the vessel to roll over completely, while still retaining its mast. It would seem that the ill-fated yacht had hit a container, with the keel taking full impact, pushing into the boat.

With this scenario, the yacht would have immediately inverted 180 degrees within less than a minute. The crew would have had no time to do anything. Crew members who were on desk would have been thrown into the water. Those below would not have had time to evacuate their cabins and would probably have been badly injured as they were flung from their bunks.

Despite exhaustive investigation in the ensuing months, no conclusive information was gathered as to what had occurred to cause the men of the Moquini to lose their lives. The brass propeller of the yacht was mounted on a plaque at the Royal Natal Yacht Club in memory of the Moquini's men who had perished. In an ironic twist of fate, this propeller was stolen from the club one year after it had been mounted.

After nine months of hoping against hope that the crew of the Moquini had miraculously survived, the families finally asked the Durban High Court to declare the men dead. When one of the judges declared that the presumption of death application had been granted, dodging the photographers and journalists who stood outside the courtroom, Karen and her friend Cathy took the children to the beach. Each person took a red rose and threw it into the sea, in remembrance of what they had personally loved most about Neil.

The years that have elapsed since the wreck of the Moquini, have been fraught with difficulties for the four widows and their children. Karen was faced with the challenge of being the sole parent and provider for her growing family as well the need to find her own identity in the midst of her darkness and despair.

It certainly has not been an easy time for her children. Jenna, the eldest, slipped into a state of anxiety and depression, fearful of leaving her mother. For middle child, Sarah, her sadness took on the form of aggression as she lashed out, physically, verbally and emotionally against all those closest to her.

For Ryan, just a year old when the Moquini sank, he has a simple desire — to find a new dad so that he can have a father like his friends do. One day, he whispered to his mother: "I think I know why God is taking such a long time to get me another dad. It is very hard to find one as special as Dad was."

The journey for Karen, while filled with sadness and difficulties, has proved her undoubted mettle as a woman. Not only has she succeeded as a mother and as a business woman, she has become a much sought-after motivational speaker as well as the author of the moving book *My Moquini*.

With her unwavering faith in God, Karen concludes her book with these beautiful words:

"I will remain calm and unconfused when clouds of sorrow and suffering gather again on the horizon; I will reflect on God's faithfulness in those moments when the tumultuous storms of circumstance threaten to overwhelm me, and I will continue to move forward steadfastly even when I cannot see the shore and do not know where I am headed. My eyes will remain fixed on the face of Christ as He walks beside me on the sea.

I will embrace all that lies before me.
I will choose to live and love abundantly.
I will choose to leave behind the life that is lost to me forever and to trust in the creativity of God, to bring life and beauty into the dark chaos of loss."

karen@mangomooncc.co.za

RAINBOW HEART FLOWER

BY LARA EDMONDS

THE HOPE FLOWER

Imagine you found an envelope,
Just lying on the ground.
You picked it up and read the label:
"Plant me!" It said, in scribbled hand.
"Nurture me and I will give you Hope!"
So you planted the single seed of Hope,
And you watched it sprout and grow,
You really nurtured it and waited patiently for its bud to form.
Sure enough before your eyes
A mysterious flower unfurled.
For days you observed its mesmerising colour, shape and grace.
And then, rather sadly,
You watched it fade.
So, you pulled the crumpled, dried out flower off the stem
In an attempt to save the rest of the plant!
But in that moment
You witnessed the true miracle of that flower,
For within your grasp,
Lay the seeds of Hope
And fields and fields of flowers....

Lara Edmonds

We were absolutely devastated when our beautiful eleven month old son, James, was diagnosed with a very rare, chronic leukaemia — it was the darkest hour of our lives. But we were to discover that when you hand your shock, sorrow and fear over to God, that little seed of faith that hides in one's heart starts to germinate and hope, like a bright, colourful flower grows.

This is our story and we hope that it will be of some comfort to parents who grieve for those they have loved and lost.

When our first child, James, was born we won a number of baby hampers and even had the story of his birth published in a magazine — we thought of him as our little 'lucky bean'. We tried to make a cosy nest for our little family, but we found taking care of our new baby extremely taxing. He was a very unsettled baby with a continuous high-pitched whine and, being new parents, we diligently made our way through the tried and tested baby books and baby magazines, we listened to well-meaning advice and we must have tried every colic remedy on the market. All to no avail.

Our family and friends listened to our concerns and consoled us with phrases like, "But he's such a beautiful baby." And James really was a beautiful boy with a kind of classic beauty, complete with dimples he'd inherited from my mother's side of the family, which you used to see in some of the well-known baby advertisements. However, looks can be deceiving and his restlessness troubled me — deep in my heart, I knew that something was wrong.

Besides being unsettled, our trips to the clinic and his 'Road to Health Chart' revealed that his condition was on something of a see-saw. Sometimes he appeared to be thriving; at other times he was poorly.

Trips to our local paediatrician indicated that James probably had a dairy allergy. I was still breast-feeding so I changed my diet and eliminated all milk, cheese and yoghurt from my eating plan. This seemed to help for a time and we settled into a more peaceful routine where we spent many happy hours discovering this beautiful angel that was our very own.

We made a baby gym and we watched James bat the soft toys and rattles around as he discovered how his little arms and legs worked. We applauded when he learnt to roll over and we encouraged him to do it again and again.

I returned to work when James was six months old and, on the doctor's advice, weaned him onto a Soya-based formula. We also found a wonderful nanny to look after James and he was content, so much so, that he even started to sleep through the night.

However, two months later James' struggles started again and so, on our clinic sister's advice, we visited Dawn, a local kinesiologist, who had had great success with allergies. As a pastor's daughter, I was a bit sceptical about this alternative method of treatment, but we quickly warmed to Dawn who was devout Catholic and ran her practice in an old convent.

During the first session, Dawn picked up some really interesting things.

For example, she said that there was lead in his blood stream from car fumes and we concluded that he had probably inhaled this pollution on our many afternoon walks — the route we took included a very busy road in our neighbourhood. She also said that there was something wrong with his spleen and that we should talk to our doctor about this in a month's time.

At the end of the session, Dawn felt that she had cured James of his allergy and she suggested that we change his formula. Again, James seemed to improve and we relaxed and enjoyed playing hide and seek with him as we encouraged him to crawl down the passage; but at the end of autumn he caught a cold, which in spite of the antibiotics, he could not seem to get over. We were battling once more and I was becoming exasperated as all the avenues we had explored now appeared to contradict one another.

At my insistence our paediatrician Greg Wiseman arranged for a comprehensive set of blood tests and he immediately telephoned me at work when he received the results. I remember telling my husband Andrew he says that he needs to see us urgently.

Dr Wiseman was so much more than our paediatrician — he was also a member of our small bible study group — and we could read the deep concern on his face when he greeted us.

He quietly and carefully explained to us that the test results revealed that James had a very high white blood cell count which indicated some kind of cancer and that James would have to have a bone marrow aspirate and lumbar puncture to confirm the diagnosis.

"Take me to my parents," I whispered to Andrew as we left the doctor's rooms. He drove me straight to the Evangelical Seminary where they both worked and I remember collapsing into my bewildered mother's arms and crying inconsolably.

When we got home, we enfolded James in our arms and wept. He, however, was simply delighted to have both his parents home so early. That night, in slow motion, I packed the nappy bag for the trip the next day to St Anne's Hospital.

This numb feeling of shock and disbelief would remain with me for a number of days.

The next day James had a general anaesthetic for the tests and was then discharged from the hospital. Dr Wiseman visited us that same night to tell us that the bone marrow aspirate confirmed his worst fears: Juvenile Mylomonocytic Leukaemia (JMML) — a very rare childhood cancer. Distraught, I telephoned the kinesiologist Dawn as soon as I got the results. She joined us at our home and we had the most amazing session with her. One of the last things she said to me was "Look for the healing power of the white light."

****

Everything happened in a whirlwind after that: James had a central line fitted so that all medication and chemotherapy could be administered intravenously and all arrangements were made for a transfer to a hospital in Johannesburg where one of the top oncologists in South Africa was expecting us.

We left our home in Pietermaritzburg in Kwazulu Natal at midnight to avoid the notorious early morning traffic in Johannesburg, but during the trip James' vomiting increased and half way there, I knew that he was dehydrating rapidly because his fontanels were deeply sunken.

Filled with panic, we called for medical assistance and the paramedics were supposed to meet us on the highway, but they could not find us because we had taken the wrong off-ramp. I wept and prayed as James appeared to be slipping in and out of consciousness, while Andrew tried desperately to get directions from a petrol attendant.

We both cried with relief when an old state ambulance drove into the truck stop where we had halted. We followed it to the local hospital, but our relief turned to acute fear when we realised that there was no doctor or nurse at the small hospital to administer a drip.

We frantically tried to get hold of the paramedic in the private ambulance that had been dispatched and called Dr Wiseman, who told us that the drip could easily be administered through the central line. Thankfully, the man on night duty at the hospital managed to call the doctor on duty. This competent doctor allayed our fears and stabilized James. "If you had passed Harrismith, you would have been in desperate trouble," she told us.

A special high care ambulance arrived early that morning to take us to Johannesburg and the paramedic, Abraham, told me that he had been expecting an eleven-year-old leukaemia patient, not an eleven-month-old baby. He also told us that as a state paramedic he did freelance work on his days off. "I didn't need to take the call but I felt that God wanted me to," he said.

We arrived at the Johannesburg General Hospital in a pretty exhausted and haggard state. James was immediately assessed by the specialist and he then went straight into theatre for another bone marrow aspirate. The specialist sat down with us and told us that because it was a long weekend we would have to wait four days for the final diagnosis, but she explained that they suspected it was JMML. The prognosis was not good because they only saw a case of this nature every five to ten years and that James' only hope would be to have a bone marrow transplant.

"Mr and Mrs Edmonds, we are looking for an exact genetic match and as James does not have a sibling, the chances of finding this are extremely slim," she told us.

During this discussion we were looking for anything positive to latch onto, but there was just nothing. It felt like I had had open-heart surgery and that they had forgotten to sew me back up, such was the agony I experienced as all hope dissolved into dark despair.

In a state of panic, I phoned my parents and told them that we desperately needed them to join us in Johannesburg.

One of the nurses then led us along a labyrinth of passages to a comfortable private room with a television and an en suite bathroom where we were both able to stay with James. I lay awake for most of the night, convinced that I would never be able to sleep again in my life, but the body eventually surrenders and we all slept deeply.

Initially we felt isolated — imprisoned in a little room with a view of an enormous concrete block, but we quickly adapted and learnt to nurse James around the clock. While I was waiting for my parents to arrive, I spent a great deal of time searching for God's face. I read Genesis again:

In the beginning God created the heaven and the earth. And the earth was without form, and void; and darkness was upon the face of the deep. And the Spirit of God moved upon the face of the waters. And God said: Let there be light and there was light. I thought a great deal about this light.

I thought of a spiritual battle as conflict between light and dark; I have always regarded Jesus as the light. I thought about how God had made us in his image, his genetic image if you like. How all that was paradise changed when man sinned and thus created the origin of disease and its genetic heritage. With Noah, God preserved the genetic pool and as a sign/covenant to all generations, he sent his rainbow — a white light in spectrum.

In my heart, I now knew that I was looking for a rainbow and time and time again I found myself looking up at the tiny square of blue sky between the two hospital towers hoping for one.

With this ray of hope, we contacted Tina who told us: "There are only 30 000 potential donors on the registry but it is our goal to grow the registry to at least 100 000 as most patients have a 1:100 000 chance of finding a match." She also told us how to go about initiating a campaign to find a bone marrow match for James.

My parents joined us when the doctors came in to give us the final test results, which confirmed the original diagnosis: classic JMML. We now had to make the decision to treat or not to treat — treatment in itself required such a miracle and so we wondered if we should leave treatment altogether and simply pray for a complete miracle.

The specialist recommended that we attempt to get James into remission and then look for a bone marrow transplant. She told us that this first course of chemotherapy could, however, prove fatal, as patients are very vulnerable to infection when their fighting white blood cells are destroyed.

We wondered how any parent could be expected to make this decision. It's a lot easier to make if you know that you've got a seventy per cent chance, but unlike other children with leukaemia, James did not have this kind of hope.

The doctors could not make the decision for us, so together with my parents, we decided to hand James over to God, as only God could possibly know his destiny. This decision brought both relief and hope.

God reminded me of Abraham's words: 'Go with the flow, don't create obstacles', and so we chose treatment. The course of chemotherapy was started immediately and because it was the winter school holidays, Andrew, a teacher, was able to be with us for the entire treatment.

James refused to sleep in the cot we had been given and so all three of us slept on the narrow hospital bed. For ten days, we watched the chemicals drip into the little Hickman line attached to the artery in his heart and we waited for the terrible side effects of the chemotherapy to kick in. James was well medicated for nausea but the diarrhoea was acute with Andrew changing ten nappies a night.

At one stage, James' temperature shot up to 40°C and the doctors had to experiment with a number of antibiotics to get the infection under control.

We were under acute stress and I remember crying the one day: "I don't want him to die in Johannesburg."

However, God's grace prevailed and we became a very efficient team as Andrew nursed James around the clock, while I wrote articles on the laptop friends had lent us and, together with my friend Claudia, contacted various people who could help us organise a bone marrow drive in Kwazulu Natal.

When the induction phase of chemotherapy was complete and his marrow had practically been destroyed, we held our breath as his white cell count started climbing. The days were ticking by and as the school holidays were drawing to a close, we started making new plans.

One of the biggest challenges I was afraid of facing was being left in Johannesburg alone with James for months on end while Andrew returned to work in Pietermaritzburg. I was terrified I would have to phone him and tell him that we were losing James and he wouldn't be able to do anything about it.

I decided to leave James and Andrew in Johannesburg while I flew down to Durban to meet with the haematologist in Kwazulu Natal who could treat him. That night I agonised over the decision — I didn't want to be the selfish one because I did not have the courage to stay in Johannesburg where James may have had better care. I earnestly asked God for a sign that we were on the right track. I remembered the promise of the rainbow.

Together with my parents we visited the Albert Luthuli Hospital where James could be treated in the paediatric ICU. It was about 3 pm, a cold winter's day in Durban and as we climbed out the car and slammed the doors, my father cried out, "Lord, how could I do this?" as he noticed that he had locked the keys in the car.

"Relax Dad," I said calmly. "Phone the locksmith while mom and I look around the hospital." The locksmith told my father that he'd be there in ten minutes, but he took an hour. Just as we climbed back into the car it started to rain and I remember joking that at least we would not get wet.

It was now 4 pm and as we drove back down into Durban, God presented me with my sign — the most magnificent rainbow arched over the whole of Durban. This was truly a miracle of timing because if my father hadn't locked his keys in the car I would never have seen that rainbow painted in the sky.

****

While I was in Durban I received a call from a journalist who had read our story on a baby website on the Internet. She wanted to publish a story about it. This story was picked up by one of the television stations and I was thus able to make an appeal for donors. More media coverage followed and people flocked to blood banks in their personal attempt to save James. I returned to Johannesburg with renewed hope, ready to face the outcome of our son's final bone marrow aspirate.

When the haematologist walked into the hospital, accompanied by a social worker, we knew that were back to square one and she confirmed this by saying: "James has not achieved remission." It was quite difficult to believe this fact because he sat quite happily on the bed eating a piece of chocolate and listening intently to everything that the doctor had to say.

We sat for some time with her discussing the options — there weren't many. "Further high does chemo is unlikely to be effective and could even prove fatal," the doctor said. So, the decision was taken to go ahead with tissue typing and to look for a match on SA's Bone Marrow Registry.

The doctor advised us to return home where James would be monitored weekly. Regular blood and platelet transfusions would allow James to remain relatively stable while we looked for a bone marrow match.

We were delighted to be home for James' first birthday and I asked my friends to order his cake: a little house with a garden and the hadedas he loved. The cake was encircled by a rainbow because it symbolised our dream to be back home with all our family and friends.

James could only invite adult friends to his party because of his vulnerable immune system, but we had the most wonderful day — it certainly goes down as the best day of my life.

God continued to send us hope in poetic ways. In fact, He seemed to be having fun. For example, a lady in my father's congregation, who had no idea about our 'light signs', told my father: "Keep praying that there's a rainbow at the end of the tunnel." On another occasion I bought a newspaper that I do not usually get because it had a photograph of a rainbow with an aeroplane flying into it. It was taken at Nevada Airport and its caption read Rainbow Nation. It was our quest linked to something in the USA, I wondered?

One day, while were leaving Johannesburg General Hospital, as we entered the lift, we met an old man who asked us our baby's name. When we told him that it was James he said that it was a Hebrew derivative of the name Jacob. We were humouring this old man and answering his questions when I suddenly realised that they were getting quite complicated for a layman.

I asked him if he was a doctor and, in reply, he simply opened his jacket and showed me his stethoscope. We then spoke about a possible second opinion in Cape Town and he told me about a transplant specialist called Professor Jacobs. When my parents picked me up at the airport in Durban, after flying home with James, my father said that he had been given the telephone number of a Professor Jacobs in Cape Town.

This had to be more than mere coincidence … surely God was telling us something. The first Sunday we were back in Pietermaritzburg, we went to visit Andrew's parents on their farm out in the Table Mountain area. I had to tell them our rainbow and Jacob stories.

To our amazement, Andrew's mother then told us that her father called her brother, who was killed in the Second World War 'Rainbow'. James' great grandfather, who had been a lay preacher in the Methodist Church, was very into symbolism and he nicknamed his unborn child after the incredible rainbow he witnessed while walking with his heavily pregnant wife. The child was born the next day.

All his letters to his son during the war were addressed to 'Rainbow', but no-one referred to him as Rainbow after his death so we did not know the story. Apparently during the fighting, Rainbow saw the shadow of his aeroplane in a full circular rainbow as he was looking down on the clouds below his plane.

The Jacob connection also seemed to carry across the generations because Andrew's mother told us that their farm was called Bethel — the place where Jacob had his dream. We now knew that if we had to let James go he would climb the rainbow ladder to heaven to meet his great-grandfather and his uncle Rainbow.

And Jacob went out from Beersheba, and went towards Haran. And he lighted upon a certain place, and tarried there all night, because the sun was set; and he took the stones of that place, and put them for his pillows, and lay down in that place to sleep. And he dreamed, and behold a ladder set up on the earth, and the top of it reached to heaven: and behold the angels of God ascending and descending on it.

The weeks dragged by and each morning I spent an hour in prayer begging God for a suitable match. Then one day we got a call from the haematologist: "There's no match in South Africa, but there's a cord blood match in Spain and some matches in the USA."

My heart soared with hope — God's signpost was definitely pointing to a rainbow in the States and this made even more sense when we discovered that the only South African specialist who was authorised to attain bone marrow from the U.S.A. was Professor Jacobs in Cape Town.

****

Our flight to Cape Town to meet with Professor Jacobs was uneventful until the very end: As the pilot banked the aeroplane to prepare for landing I saw the shadow of the plane on the clouds with a hazy rainbow wrapped around it. Betty Kincaid Smith, the lady sitting in front of me, said: "Did you see the funny little rainbow?" (We stayed in touch and she was later to write these prophetic words: *The rainbow enshrouded the shadow of the plane.*)

We were also amazed when we got to the hospital, Constantiaberg Medi-Clinic, to see the sign Bethel Church hanging next to the hospital sign as they are in the same road. With the rainbow over Cape Town and the sign Bethel, God gave us, so I believe. The exact co-ordinates to the doctor and the hospital where James would have his transplant.

We returned home but we were in constant contact with the team who, under Prof Jacobs, were arranging the transplant. The paediatric haematologists in Cape Town and Durban put James on an experimental treatment, a simple oral medication, which immediately started to bring his high white cell count down in preparation for the transplant. The Registry was proceeding with the necessary tissue typing and the complicated process took months. Eventually one donor in the States was isolated and we were notified that it was a near perfect match.

Initially the transplant was planned for the 21st of January 2004, but then the date was unexpectedly moved forward to the 3rd of November. We arrived in Cape Town completely confident that we were exactly where God wanted us to be. The wonderful nurses in the bone marrow unit made living in isolation quite easy and we quickly became part of the 'Haem Team'. We put up our rainbow banner: *Jesus: our help for today, our hope for tomorrow* and unpacked all James' toys and clothes.

James immediately stole everyone's hearts as he tootled up and down the isolation ward with their mega laundry trolley. Andrew became adept at managing James' drip stand. James had countless tubes and pipes attached to him: a nasal gastric tube kept him well-nourished while saline, chemo, blood or platelets and powerful antibiotics dripped through the little Hickman line fitted to the main vein in his heart. He was not bothered by all of this though — like a little puppet, he continued to play to his captive audience.

We were initially a bit intimidated to meet Prof Jacobs — the walls of the haematology block are lined like a gallery with his achievements over the years. As the weeks passed we got to know him and he allowed us to take a peek at the wonderful 'softie' behind the image of the eminent scientist — he blew soap bubbles with James and it was soon obvious that our little boy had also snuck into his heart.

Dr Lund, our paediatrician, was also incredible — he was just so kind and such a good communicator. When there were no words, he would simply hug us. Right from the beginning he warned us that we could expect a very bad patch after the transplant as James would have no marrow, and therefore no immune system and he would become very vulnerable to infections, hence the isolation.

****

The day of James' transplant finally dawned. I had read in James' file that the donor was a thirty-five year old lady and that stem cells would be harvested in California. The courier arrived with these precious stem cells early in the morning. We were all very emotional and she said that it was a privilege to courier the blood all the way from the United States. As everything is so confidential, she had no idea that the marrow was for a little toddler.

The transplant itself was a very simple transfusion, but a very spiritual experience as along with all our friends, we lit a special transplant candle and said a prayer of thanksgiving and healing. Prof told us that they had done an adult harvest of stem cells and so only half the bag was required — the rest would be specially frozen in case we needed it again.

Then the countdown for engraftment began and each day we crossed off another block on our calendar. We were told that things would only start to happen on day fourteen, but on day eleven Prof surprised us with the news that James had engrafted. We immediately sent out an SMS and asked everyone to 'give thanks'.

The media grabbed hold of the excitement and within hours the good news had spread. Prof and Dr Lund started to talk about discharge but a niggling low-grade temperature would keep us in hospital for a couple more days — or so we thought.

The same week we spotted a very special message on the hospital's notice board. *Then Jacob woke from his sleep and said Surely the Lord is in this place.* Genesis 28. This again came from the passage where Jacob had his dream at Bethel. I thought to myself that if the transplant date had not been moved forward by two months we would not have received this message. I did not know that its true significance would only be revealed to me later.

Unfortunately in the next couple of days, James' temperature suddenly shot up to 39.9°C and his white blood count dropped to a frightening 0.2. Initially this indicated a serious infection and we were rushed to ICU at Red Cross Children's Hospital where a pulminologist would perform a lung biopsy.

Again we found ourselves at crisis point and we prayed for confirmation and guidance. It came as I entered the theatre waiting area where an exquisite mural of Table Mountain with a stunning rainbow over it greeted me. I knew God was with us and this gave us incredible peace in a time of immense stress.

It was such a relief though to return again, by ambulance, to the Bone Marrow Unit at Constantiaberg. We found security in isolation, as we had felt vulnerable in the open ICU ward. We were, however, not completely devastated when Prof told us that the graft had mysteriously vanished because we always knew that this was a possibility and that the extra bag of stem cells could be used for another transplant. James' infection was now also under control and he started looking much better.

In the meantime we heard some very sad news from home. Andrew's mother had had a massive stroke. We were grateful that she did not know that James' second transplant had failed. Being so many miles from home, all we could do was pray for her — we knew that she had only days to live and so we prayed that she would not suffer too long and that her dignity would be spared.

That night I returned to the little garden flat we were renting. (I had to leave Andrew and James at the hospital as we both could not sleep there.) I felt so alone and, overcome by grief, I telephoned my parents. My father answered my distraught call with a special prayer: he asked for a sign that would give us the peace and encouragement we needed to face another transplant.

I was still upset as I drove to the hospital next morning. I said to God: "You can pull a rainbow out of the box — we really need one."

To my amazement a short, hazy rainbow appeared in the sky over the little graveyard in Southfield. I stopped the car and watched it. This was the sign we had prayed for and, again, it held a message that my heart was not yet open to receive: a rainbow ladder leading all the way to heaven. Later that morning, Andrew's sister came to tell us that Mum had died earlier that morning. "It was almost as if she pulled that one out of the box," Shirley said.

James battled with the next phase of chemotherapy to prepare his slight body for the second transplant. He had constant diarrhoea and he became very aggressive. The second transplant was also different because the preservatives in the stem cells made the blood thicker and our wonderful nurse, Pat, had to sit and manually push it down the line.

To the amazement of the doctors James seemed to rally in the next couple of days and he started to eat and play again. My family joined us for Christmas and we celebrated in Prof's private lounge. We took turns looking after James and everyone watched through the window as he shyly opened his presents.

We had been warned that James would take much longer to engraft this second time because of the way the stem cells had been preserved, so we were not too worried when my family left and James still did not have a white blood cell count.

At the end of December when the lease on our little flat was up, we moved in with our friends Buck and Diana, who through their love and support, became like godparents to James. We felt destined to stay with them as their home in St James (Kalk Bay) is three roads down from a long stairway called Jacob's Ladder.

Again, we crossed off the days on the calendar and we held our breath each time they did the 'Buffie Test' to see if James had engrafted — the results were always negative. We were starting to get worried, but the doctors said: "Something good must be happening … look how well he is."

James did seem much better and we enjoyed many happy hours trawling up and down the ward with the big 'transplant truck' we had brought him and the drip stand.

But, one day we noticed that it seemed as if James' batteries were going flat — he just did not have the energy to walk and play as he had been doing mere days before.

I read the scripture in my book of devotions that I had brought together with a rainbow banner at the local bible store in Pietermaritzburg: What a comfort it was to once again receive a message from that special scripture in Genesis 28 — the Bethel story: *"I am with you and will watch over you wherever you go … I will not leave you until I have done what I have promised you."*

By day twenty-six James had developed an abscess on his bottom that had to be lanced under general anaesthetic. While James was in theatre the doctors did another bone marrow aspirate to try and establish what was happening with the graft.

During James' absence we had a meeting with Prof. "The results are out," he said. "The bone is completely empty." We were in absolute shock — this was very unusual as infection, rather than engraftment was normally the problem. Professor Jacobs advised us to go for another transplant. Weeping, we prayed for guidance … we prayed that God would open or close the doors very quickly.

In my car on the way home to St James, I again found myself distraught and saying to God, "I can't believe that after all the signs you have given us — there is nothing now. Where is your rainbow?" He answered me immediately with the most beautiful 'rainbow'song 'The Colour of Love', by the group Boyz to Men on the radio.

When I heard the message that love will colour your soul like a rainbow I wept as God had given me something so much more valuable than a rainbow in the sky. You see, I had desperately wanted to share a rainbow with Andrew and now I could. Buck bought us the CD and this beautiful melody comforted us as we waited to hear if they could use the cord blood from Spain for another transplant.

Three transplants in a row would be unprecedented, but we told Prof to go ahead. While examining James, Dr Lund discovered that he had pneumonia and during the next two nights it became clear to us that James was very, very ill. We would lie awake for hours listening to the unsteady rhythm of his breathing. God's message in the 'rainbow song' was becoming clearer to us, we had to let him go — true love is letting go.

I will never forget our last Sunday morning in the Bone Marrow Unit. We woke up and knew without doubt what we had to do. I told our special nurse our decision — she simply wept and embraced us: "It's the right thing to do!" she said. Together with Buck and Diana and the wonderful head nurse Rowan, we then encircled James praying and then singing 'This little light of mine' and 'Jesus loves me'.

I will always love Prof for the fact that he never gives up on anyone. I remember how we all cried and embraced him when we told him that we had changed our minds about the third transplant. "We've all done our best ... we have to leave the rest to God," we told him. The nurses then carefully removed James' intravenous antibiotics and we sent the following SMS to our special family and friends: "The angels that surround us will take James home in a couple of days."

Our grieving had already started and we struggled to lift the mood so that James would not feel our sadness. The nurses told us to go off for a break and, without thinking, we drove straight to St James where we slowly climbed the incredible flight of stairs called Jacob's Ladder.

At the top, we surrendered James to God and by the time we descended, our dark depression had lifted. For three days, we watched the candle we had placed next to his hospital cot burn and we played his favourite songs, including the lullaby 'Jacob's Dream'. The morphine dose was upped in stages and James was sleepy most of the time.

On the morning of the 20th of January 2004, I asked the nurse if she thought that James would go on that day and she nodded. My heart was in a state of panic that morning because he did not want to be touched — I felt so helpless. My little son was dying and I was a spectator. But a miracle was starting to unfold. James, who was on heavy doses of morphine, lifted his arms and said: "Ma." He was calling for me and a miraculous peace settled in my heart as I embraced him.

I held him for about half an hour while Andrew stood behind me. We spoke sweetly to him: "You have been so brave, our darling, so strong, but it's time to go now. Come on, off you go. Follow the light, sweetheart."

I will never forget how he opened his eyes for a minute — I believe he was looking at the light. In my spirit I had a vision of him, a hesitant figure at a half open door, silhouetted against a bright light, looking back and listening to us … and then laughing, running into the light.

It amazed me how his spirit was gone in an instant. The nurses joined us and we prayed together. Andrew and I gently bathed and dressed him. The nurse had placed a little rainbow in his hands and we took this with us — a final memory.

We left the hospital quickly and sent the SMS: "Our precious baby, James, climbed the rainbow ladder to heaven half an hour ago." We then went for a long drive up the coast.

The gift of peace James gave us when he called out to us will remain. We cry now because we miss him and because our destiny is still so beautiful: Friends continue to catch rainbows for us — there's a sprinkler in our garden and it's making rainbows; there's a beautiful rainbow over Kirstenbosch and so it goes. We still see rainbows everywhere: in soapy bubbles; in the light reflected off a CD; in a smudged oil spill on a wet tarmac; in the rose plant we received from our bible study group called Rainbow's End.

****

Sometimes an incredible gift accompanies great loss – for us the gift is sharing our little son James' beautiful destiny with others. Sharing helps us to heal, but it is also such a privilege to witness how God touches people's lives through our family's story. We are so grateful for God's 'Rainbow Hope Flower' and embrace His grace in our lives every single day.

In loving memory of our son—

Baby James Edmonds

Lara Edmonds © 2013

DAN SEFUDI RAKGOATHE

BLIND POET, ARTIST & MYSTIC

THE DARK NIGHT OF THE SOUL

THE UNFOLDING MAN

Now I know I am crucified
To this wasting shell I call me
Yet — I did not know here to fore
That this mortal matter was never truly me
Now I begin to grow with wisdom
In learning from painful passion
That I am expanding more and more
As every pang arouses rapturous awareness
Of the good that comes out of painful experience
Now I begin to understand in depth
That I am God in God and all that is God
A God — forever unfolding in all consciousness
That I am one with the all big and small
For God — the overall dwells in all
I know ... I know ... I know

Dan Rakgoathe (c. 1991)

The frail woman, Phani Rebecca Rakgoathe, her body crippled by rheumatoid arthritis, lay back on her bed against a pile of soft cushions.

Her hands were bent like the claws of a bird and her body shivered with cold, although the day outside was warm.

Sometimes she called for her sons, Gerson (nicknamed Boy) and Titus (nicknamed Biki) or her daughter Khathazile, but mostly she called for her son, Dan. For Dan, she knew, was the sensitive one, the one most likely to be affected by her death. She longed to embrace him in her stick-like arms. "Oh, my poor little boy," she whispered, before the ambulance came and took her away.

Dan did not cry then. It was only several years later when he was staying with his aunt's family in Phoquane, that he succumbed to his grief. As he sat on the veranda looking at the moon he began, for the first time since his mother's death, to cry. Pleading with the moon, he begged the celestial orb to send his mother back. "Lady on the Moon, is my mother there with you? If she is, please tell her to come back to us."

However, the moon turned a deaf ear to his pleas. For in the fullness of time, Dan, between 1962 and 1967, lost all three of his siblings. His only sister Khathazile died from tuberculosis and high blood pressure; his elder brother, Boy, died from tuberculosis and diabetes; his younger brother Biki's death was due to diabetes. In 1978, his beloved father Ephraim died, leaving Dan alone and bereft.

From 1969 Dan, already deeply upset by the death of his siblings, knew instinctively that he would go blind. He also knew that it would happen in November 1989. In 1967 his linocut self-portrait entitled *Portrait Profile of a Prophet* depicts the artist with one eye closed and one eye opened.

"For me, this symbolised the closure of the physical side and the opening of the psychic side. Indeed, it was only when I went blind that I started experiencing the visions from The Source that I have written down in a series of prophecies that I must share before I die. For I am a God sent messenger. I *need* to be heard."

VOICE OF PROPHECY

The voice of echo called from
the fathomless deep
of sleep:
Awake dreaming sleeper!
To you is given the task
to work and write.
The WORK shall be made
clear by the WORD.
The WORD shall be made
understood by the WORK.
Make haste, we cannot
wait any longer!

The Home for the Civilian Blind in the south of Johannesburg South Africa is not a particularly pretty place. But then it doesn't have to be. However, it serves a useful purpose acting as a home to many unsighted inhabitants who otherwise may well not have a roof over their heads. After all it is not easy for families who have to work all day to look after those who cannot look after themselves.

Dan Rakgoathe has been an inhabitant of this institution since his blindness became total in 1990. It is a difficult place for a man of Dan's undoubted intellect to find himself, for most of the other visually impaired inmates are not able to converse at his level.

No wonder Dan prefers to sit by himself in his room with his radio as company, in particular the talk station Radio 702. In his own way he has much to occupy his time. Since becoming a Rosicrucian in 1964 — the movement, officially titled 'The Ancient and Mystical Order Rosae Crucis' (AMORC) offers a system of instruction and guidance into the Rosicrucian Order of mystical teachings and Dan has become an avid follower of their principles of faith.

For the past eight years a good Samaritan, or as Dan prefers to call her an angel, Beryl Kück, has been coming to visit him once a week for an hour. Beryl reads to him from the teachings of the Rosicrucians, simultaneously recording each lesson so that in her absence Dan is able to revise all that he has heard.

Then with his Third Eye opened, Dan occupies himself with his daily meditation and with chanting. The words he chants in endless repetition, rocking himself back and forth, are RA and MA.

These words have particular significance to Dan for they are connected with his favourite of the many stories that his beloved maternal grandmother used to tell him:

"A long, long time ago there were two people, Ra and Ma. Ra was the father and Ma was the mother. And these two people so loved one another, that they came to live together. And when they were together Ma said to Ra, what shall we create? And Ra said to Ma, my love, we cannot create anything, because we are in darkness. We cannot see — there is no light.

Therefore let us create light. So they came together, and then what came into them was the most powerful force that there ever was — love.

And out of this love they created light, and the whole world of nations sprang from this light. So it is love, my dear, love is what brought the world into being. When they say God is love, it is true according to African Genesis."*

****

The story of Dan Rakgoathe's life is one of struggle. The struggle of being 'different' from his schoolmates; of being an inattentive student who used to daydream in class, so much so that despite his obvious intelligence, he was to fail four times before finally completing his schooling in 1957.

The struggle of continuously being uprooted as his father Ephraim moved from place to place seeking suitable employment; the struggle of losing his mother at an early age; the struggle to become an artist in a society where little provision was made for Blacks who aspired to an artistic career; the struggle against the demon alcohol; and finally the struggle against blindness.

Yet against this harsh backdrop, it is also a story of inspiration and courage. For through tenacity and stubbornness and dogged determination Dan was to graduate from Fort Hare University (he was expelled from Rorke's Drift Art School in Natal from imbibing more than the artistic atmosphere) with a BA in Fine Arts, gaining a double distinction in Painting and Graphic Art. He was already forty by this time and was one of the first of two Black Fine Art students to graduate from the university.

Recommended by Professor Eddie De Jager, Professor of Anthropology at the University of Fort Hare during the time of Dan's studies there, for the prestigious American Full bright scholarship, Dan was to spend two years at the University of California in Los Angeles (UCLA). His studies commenced in August 1981 and two years later, he graduated with a Master's Degree in African Literature and Philosophy.

This was an extraordinary achievement when one considers that he was over forty when he got to the States; with the aid of the Rosicrucians and Alcoholics Anonymous he had won his battle against alcoholism; but he still had to wrestle with diabetes, which was diagnosed during his American stay.

Nevertheless, Dan was to become one of the finest graphic artists and creative philosophers produced in South Africa — with a strong mystical and spiritual thread running through all his work. Unlike many of his contempo-

---
* Reference: The Unfolding Man The Life and Art of Dan Rakgoathe by Donvé Langhan

raries, despite the harshness of growing up impoverished under a regime that regarded Blacks as second-class citizens, the majority of his work has a spirit of optimism and upliftment.

Multi-talented, Dan was also to become an acknowledged poet, gaining membership of the American International Library of Poetry Hall of Fame. Examples of his poetry can be found on the society's Internet web page. This fact delights Dan for he realises that his writing is now accessible to over forty million people.

It is difficult for anybody to go blind; for an artist it must be the most soul-destroying nightmare. Yet Dan has somehow managed, once his initial rage and dismay at his condition had abated, to transcend this difficulty, seeing the all-encompassing darkness as a blessing rather than a curse.

For like all those chosen to be messengers of God — Jesus, Buddha, Mohammed, Dan himself as he believes — there can be no total unity with The Divine Source, without a period of hardship and sacrifice. "We have to undergo many trials on this earth," explained Dan, "for our spiritual growth. I believe that my blindness is my ultimate test. I have come to regard it not as a curse, but as a privilege."

It is this extraordinary faith, this ability to accept dire adversity that I wished to discuss with Dan as I knocked on the door of his room one Monday morning in July. I came armed not only with my notebook and tape recorder, but also with a cooked chicken and a bottle of dry red wine.

"I am by nature a shy man," Dan explained to me over the telephone, "so I need the wine to loosen my tongue."

****

His room is sparsely furnished with a large bed, a wardrobe, a desk and a table. The bathroom is on one side and basic cooking facilities on the other. Despite the authorities constant attempts at disinfecting the inhabitants' rooms, a couple of cockroaches appear to be very much at home.

Dan demanded that the interview begin with the opening of the bottle of wine. I questioned the wisdom of this decision as he had not yet eaten and I was worried that his train of thought would stray. I also knew from what I have read about him of his battles with alcoholism.

A gentle man, Dan has a stubborn streak running through his veins. The bottle of wine must to be opened before we spoke. For me, this simple action brought into focus the difficulties of both living in an institution and the frustration of not being able to see.

Dan was unable to recall where he had put his corkscrew and I was unable to find it. "I will go the kitchen and get a corkscrew," I suggested.

However, the kitchen staff greeted my request with indifferent stares. "We don't have a corkscrew here," one of the cooks said somewhat impatiently, fiddling with the sheet of plastic that served as her apron.

I then went to the small shop and asked the man behind the counter if he had a corkscrew. Running his eyes over the shelves, filled only with basic necessities — soap, washing powder, small packets of sugar, a couple of tinned goods — he shook his head.

"I'm here visiting Dan Rakgoathe," I said.

"Ah, that explains why you need a corkscrew," he replied, nodding his head wisely.

I returned to the room empty handed. In my absence one of the cleaners, obviously used to Dan, had located the missing corkscrew. The bottle of wine was opened and Dan's tongue was able to flow with eloquence and loquacity.

****

"I was a lonely child at school. A dreamer. I instinctively knew that I had lived other lives in other times. I well remember my life previous to this one. I was a young Tswana girl who was born around 1914 and who died around 1927. Yet my elders never spoke of such things and I thought I had better keep these thoughts to myself.

"One day, when I was about eleven, I read an article about reincarnation in a magazine. I wept with joy to find out that my intuitive 'knowing' now had a name."

Conventional Christianity was very much part of Dan's early life. His father was a deacon in the African Methodist Episcopal church and Dan, together with his siblings, was obliged to attend Sunday school.

From the outset, Dan had problems with the teachings of the New Testament. "Why if God was so full of love, did he take my mother away? Also, why does Christianity anthropomorphise God? The priests talk of The Father, The Son and the Holy Ghost? Where is the Mother in this Holy Trinity?"

"Yet, it is the woman who is the most important part of creativity; it is the woman who carries the foetus in her womb for nine months. However, instead of saying 'Mother' we say 'Holy Ghost.' What the hell does this mean? In my opinion, no one has ever been able to explain who or what the Holy Ghost is.

"God should be part man and part woman. The selfish patriarchal nature of Christianity is to blame for not promoting Mother to the Godhead. After all, how could Mary, who is the mother of Jesus, not be held in equal esteem to God, if God is the father of Jesus?"

Shaking his head in wonderment as he sips his wine, Dan then requested me to seek his poem Godhood on the Internet.

Under www.poets.com I find the following poem that well illustrates Dan's lifelong preoccupation with finding who God is and where He resides. For Dan, sceptical from an early age, could not accept God as a distant figure with a long white beard sitting on a cloud and dispensing harsh justice to followers who had to bow down in awe and supplication to this autocratic and imposing ruler.

GODHOOD

A perplexed THOUGHT loomed in a Pondering CONSCIOUSNESS
To ask a desperate question:
*who is GOD so that we may know
What is of GOD so that we may serve
Where is GOD so that we may go to worship
An answer from the deep abiding
WISDOM surged:
GOD, there is no such as of particular*

PERSON

*GOD, there is no such as in need of your WORSHIP
GOD, there is no such as of individualised outside YOU
In all sparks the might O God
In all dwells the essence of GOD
In all moves the creative power of God
That and that comprises GODHOOD
That and that comprises GOD BEING
That and that comprises GOD*

CONSCIOUSNESS

*All is: GOD the PRIME
GOD the PROCESS
GOD the PRODUCT
The overall PRINCIPLE OF THIS
COSMIC TRINITY is LOVE
ATTUNE to it in PRAYER and MEDITATION
Therein lies service to GODHOOD.*

"Dan, what are your views on Jesus Christ?"

"I respect him as a great mystic master, I respect him as one of the greatest teachers that the earth was ever blessed with — a great man. But what grew out of his teachings was to become organised religion, which I reject. I can't understand how people can talk such crap as Adam's rib being turned into a woman, even people like doctors of divinity — it's stupid, it's childish, but people actually believe it literally. We need to put religious beliefs in context with progressive thinking.

"For instance, I don't regard Jesus Christ as God, but as a messenger of God. Humans suffer from inferiority complexes, because they think that there must be a power above them, but in fact I am God, you are God. The power comes from us. I am very critical of the idea of God being a human being."*

On the one hand an artist, a philosopher and a poet with mystical visions, on the other hand an impoverished Black man whose dreams of greatness were constantly being thwarted by the realities of the Apartheid regime that decreed to spend a bare minimum on educating the vast majority of the population, as he grew older Dan's constant companions were poverty, loneliness and alcohol.

For a brief period of his life, Dan was to know the true friendship of a kindred spirit, fellow artist Cyprian Shilakoe. Together the two men shared a belief in ancestors, spirits and dreams. Tools of the medicine men or sangomas rather than of the Christian religious ethos of Rorke's Drift, where they both went to study art.

A strong mystical bond between Dan and Cyprian allowed them to communicate with each other through their thoughts and dreams. By 1972, both men had tasted the fruits of their success — Dan had held successful exhibitions of his art while Cyprian was fast establishing an international reputation as an artist.

As a result of his newfound financial stability, Cyprian was able to buy himself a brand-new Volkswagen combi. On their way to see the Beatle movie *Let It Be* in the township of Soweto, Cyprian, who was an inexperienced driver and who, like Dan, was intoxicated by alcohol, drove too fast, overturning the vehicle and killing himself in the process.

This accident, coupled with his best friend's death, left Dan injured and for a time, emotionally crippled. One of Cyprians' legacies — for he, like Dan, had the gift of prophesy — was a portrait of Dan entitled '*The Philosopher.*' Done in 1969 this etching now forms part of the Durban Art Gallery collection.

The central figure appears to be holding his head in pain. Inside his chest, almost as if in an X-ray, another face appears. The second face seems more peaceful and the eyes are closed as if in meditation.

---

* Reference: The Unfolding Man. The Life and Art of Dan Rakgoathe by Donvé Langhan

Cyprian is here perhaps alluding to the belief that he held in common with Dan — true peace can only be found by going deep within oneself. The closed eyes, maintained Cyprian, were illustrative of the fact that he knew his friend would go blind at some future date.

As for himself, Cyprian, with his psychic abilities, knew that he would die. He had already bid goodbye to his close friends in the preceding weeks. At the time of his death on September 7th 1972, Cyprian, who was nine years younger than Dan, was only twenty-six.

As a man who already wore the cloak of loneliness, Cyprian's death, followed five years later by the death of his beloved father, Ephraim, plunged Dan into an abyss of grief and alcoholism.

His heavy drinking, which had always perturbed his father, suddenly began to worry Dan. It appeared to him that whenever he imbibed too much, he seemed to be the victim of intended violent crime, yet somehow he was always 'saved' from destruction

"I remember," said Dan, "an incident, at the time I was living in Dennilton and was returning home by bus. Unfortunately, the bus broke down and it took time to get it fixed. It was dark when we reached our destination."

"As I walked home, I became aware that three young men were following me. Intuitively, I knew that they meant to harm me. I had no idea what to do as I knew that I could not outrun them.

"An inner voice, I believe guidance from the Rosicrucians, told me, 'Step aside from the road. Stand still'."

"I heeded this advice. I heard one of the young chaps ask his friend in surprise 'Hey, where did that bloke go?' I knew that I had become invisible to them. I was later to read in the Rosicrucians teachings about the phenomenon of invisibility."

"My pursuers started arguing amongst themselves. 'He couldn't have just disappeared into thin air.' Then one of the trio said in a scared voice, 'He must be a ghost.' The others obviously agreed for they started to run as fast as they could," recalled Dan with obvious relish.

Dan took this violence to mean that his heavy drinking displeased his ancestors, particularly his father. He knew that he had to do something about his alcoholism. But what?

He appealed to the Rosicrucians for help, telling the Council of Solace that he felt he was sinking fast. Dan believes that it was the Rosicrucians who guided him to attend his first Alcoholics Anonymous meeting. For when he went in the taxi from the Young Men's Christian Association (YMCA) in Orlando, Soweto to Moletsane Township where the meeting was held, on the journey he could smell a beautiful rose aroma. "I asked myself the question: Was one of the passengers perhaps wearing a rose scent?"

However, on alighting from the taxi, the scent went away. Only to return, when after the AA meeting, Dan went back to his hostel room. "In my room, the scent was very strong. I asked myself where could it come from? Then I remembered that the emblem of the Rosicrucians is the Rose Cross — a crucifix with the symbol of a rose at the intersection of the two arms of the cross.

"Undoubtedly, it was the Rosicrucians who guided me to Alcoholics Anonymous. The AA saved my life. I found such warmth, sympathy and fellowship there. Without the AA, I would undoubtedly have died."

I watched as Dan poured himself another glass of red wine from the bottle. "Is it OK that you're drinking now?"

"Yes," chuckled Dan. "Alexandra, you must not worry. These days, my drinking is under control."

****

In 1989 Dan approached Ferdinand Haenggi of Gallery 21 in Johannesburg about holding a retrospective exhibition of his work. When Haenggi informed him that owing to the gallery's previous commitments, the exhibition could only be held the following year, Dan insisted that the exhibition take place before November.

The exhibition, consisting of ninety of Dan's work, included black and white linocuts, etchings, drawings, photolithographs and mixed media collages, was finally held in October 1989. By the end of November Dan was, as he knew he would be completely blind.

"How did you feel about this?"

"I wanted to kill myself. An artist cannot be blind. I sat and thought to myself of ways to commit suicide. I wanted a painless way out. Then, one day, by chance I heard on the radio a blind artist saying that since he had lost his sight, he had experienced all kind of mystical visions. Suddenly I knew that, just as Beethoven, Van Gogh, Job, even Jesus had been tested, I was being tested. My blindness was my final test. It was what God had ordained for my spiritual growth."

"What have you seen since going blind?"

"So many visions. I do not wish to discuss them all with you.

"But I will tell you of one thing I saw after going blind. I was having an exhibition of my art at the Durban Art Gallery and I asked them to send an invitation to the Rosicrucians in California, which was their headquarters at the time.

"Suddenly I saw that the gallery was filled with people. They looked like Rosicrucian officials. They seemed to be lining up before me, congratulating me for the work I'd done."

Dan went on to talk about religion. "The word religion comes from the Latin 'relegate' which means to reconnect, to rebind. To bring together that which has gone separate. Even they, the greatest of them all, the avatars, were all but human like the rest of us, but they ascended the difficult stairway of trial and tribulation to reach the highest level of Divinity and from there to beckon to the rest of us the path to follow."

Daniel Sefudi Rakgoathe leans back in his chair. He is an elderly man, tired now from all the talking. His clothes are clean, but shabby; and although he cannot see it, the soles of his shoes are coming unstuck.

Yet, if it is true what The Great Masters say that the only true happiness is achieved through unity with the Divine Source, then one must not pity the blind artist.

For while Dan's two eyes see nothing, his Third Eye has opened to show him many mystical visions and he believes, rightly or wrongly, that he is a messenger of the Lord — a sentiment that he has eloquently expressed in this extract from his poem

COMING OF A MESSENGER

His hand shall bear mark of divine skill
his head shall bear the crown of enlightenment
his forehead shall emit a trail of shimmering light
which shall surround him in a vibrant violet aura

> *that will dispel the darkness of ignorance*
> *darkness that covered the yestertime world*
> *he shall cross the threshold of cosmic consciousness*
> *with his physical vision veiled*
> *his kith and kin shall turn against him*
> *they shall dine and wine while whispering scandals*
> *saying he has immersed himself in diabolic folly*
> *but, as sure as sunlight follows night darkness*
> *he too shall rise to shine bright*
> *the alienated shall turn back and say —*
> *we know him of long time ago*
> *he is a spinner of true dreams*
> *he is a weaver of divine visions*
> *he is a true messenger of love ...*

"Most of my waking life is spent in solitude, providing me with the opportunity to meditate," remarked Dan. "When I consider how I live in the dim world of the blind, the more I come to realise that the attainment of cosmic consciousness through this meditation is my sacred sanctuary and source of inspiration.

"I always comfort myself with these words: If the moment of the dark night of the soul is here, then surely the new dawn of the soul's illumination is to follow. No matter how long it takes according to relative time for me to achieve cosmic consciousness, I *know* this will follow this dark night of the soul."

It is time to take my leave of Dan. The last drops of dry red wine have been drunk, but my appetite has been whet. I will visit Mr Rakgoathe again. Not out of pity. But rather to imbibe his wisdom, his spiritualism, his bright eyed optimism.

Following a massive stroke, Dan Sefudi Rakgoathe passed away on the 18th of April 2004. He was sixty-six years old. This book was very close to his heart and I sense that his spirit will continue to light the path of its progress.

MICKI PISTORIUS

SERIAL KILLER PROFILER & WRITER

STRANGLING THE MONSTER WITHIN

> King Richard: Discomfortable cousin! know'st thou not
> That when the searching eye of heaven is hid,
> Behind the globe, that lights the lower world,
> Then thieves and robbers range abroad unseen
> In murders and in outrage boldly here;
> But when from under this terrestrial ball
> He fires the proud tops of the eastern pines
> And darts his light through every guilty hole,
> Then murders, treasons and detested sins,
> The cloak of night being pluck'd from off their backs,
> Stand bare and naked, trembling at themselves?
>
> William Shakespeare

Micki Pistorius, the aunt of blade runner Oscar Pistorius, sits on the sofa in my cottage, a feminine petite woman, with a Barbie Doll perfect figure. One can picture her as a courtesan in some Barbara Cartland novel, carelessly tossing back her flowing auburn curls, flirting shamelessly with some debonair cavalier.

It is less easy to imagine Micki, who has a doctorate in psychology, as the head of the investigative psychology unit with the South African Police Service. Over the six years, she spent with the police as a profiler, she was involved in more than thirty serial killer cases, which meant she had to enter deep into the hearts, minds and psyche of some deeply disturbed criminals, often holding their hands and looking straight into their troubled eyes as she dived into the darkness of their souls.

How did her journey on such a tortured path begin?

"My parents divorced before I was five years old. Later they remarried, only to divorce again. My father remarried, continuing to live in our old house with his wife and her children. My mother also remarried, extending the family to include another brother, a sister and a stepfather."

This loving, although complicated, family structure Micki believes, gave her the ability to become aware of other people's agendas, to become mindful of the many different dynamics within relationships.

As she writes in her best-selling book *Catch me a Killer:*

Although not all profilers need to have gone through the same life experiences that I have, a good profiler, who truly wants to understand the serial killer, must have been prepared by life experiences before he or she can dare to venture into the abyss. A person who has led a protected life will not survive.

By the time she was a young adult, Micki was no stranger to death. While she was in secondary school, one of her school friends died in a car crash. Her maternal grandmother's death was followed by a succession of deaths of ex-boyfriends. Some of her boyfriends died doing border duty in the Angolan War; a fiancé died in a car crash; another died of a drug overdose; yet another hanged himself. Perhaps the most traumatic death for Micki was the death of her stepbrother, who aged twenty-one, committed suicide.

After finishing her schooling, Micki enrolled at university to do a BA in languages. This made sense as she intended to become a writer. After completing her degree in 1981, Micki worked as a journalist. She met and married her husband, a fellow journalist. For a time her life seemed idyllic.

The couple moved to Cape Town and when this move lost its lustre, they decided to return to Pretoria, where Micki decided to continue her studies in psychology. After completing her Honours degree, she went on to do her Masters. She then decided to do her Doctorate on serial killers 'because it was interesting.'

It was when one of her lecturers, Professor Kemp, handed out a list of themes for projects and Micki chose to do her dissertation on the psychopathy of serial killers, that the course of her life was dramatically altered. What started off as a one-off project was to become her life's work.

In 1993 Captain Braam Beetge, a psychologist in the South African Police Force, was looking for university graduates to join the Force and become involved in a project on forensic psychology. Having studied this branch of psychology as an extra subject, Micki was an ideal candidate for the job. She was appointed to the position in 1994, one year after completing her master's degree.

Taking on a career of this nature, Micki felt that after seven years of an idyllic marriage, her career choice cast a shadow on her marriage.

"I didn't want him to be contaminated by the horribleness of my work. I had to choose between my marriage and my career. Fortunately, I never wanted children. You know the Afrikaans word 'broeis'? It means broody. As in Mother Hen. Well, I never felt like that about children, although I like other people's kids.

When we divorced, my husband held my hand in court. We are still good friends. I still don't know if I made the right decision ..."

****

By 1994, The Station Strangler, as he was dubbed, had already killed eleven young boys in Mitchell's Plain on the Cape Flats. Micki joined the investigative team wearing a black miniskirt, stockings and high heels.

However, she was soon to learn that there was little glamour in accompanying the police as they set off to discover bodies in various stages of decomposition, some of whom had been sodomised before being strangled with their own clothing.

Micki had grown up in the Dutch Reformed Church where her grandfather was a *dominee* or minister. While she and her siblings were obliged to go to Sunday School, church was not obligatory and when she married Micki became a Roman Catholic, although she has since moved on from organised religion to a more spiritual and individualistic approach.

Now in her new job where she was obliged to confront gruesome death on a daily basis, and she prayed silently at the crime scene.

"For whom did you pray?"

"I prayed for the detectives working on the job. I prayed for the killer, hoping that his tortured soul would find some escape from his hell on earth. I prayed, too for the victims. Although I could see that their suffering was over. I could see that they were at peace. I also prayed for the families of the victims."

"Are you psychic?"

"For me the word conjures up visions of a gypsy with a crystal ball or a cup of tea leaves. So I would rather say that I am sensitive. I can interpret hidden agendas and I could pick up the killer's vibes."

"How do you mean?"

"I found that I was having the same dreams as the killer I was profiling. So much so that I was able to tell the detective the dreams of the murderer I was profiling. If I left the room and the detective asked the suspect to relate his dreams, they would correlate exactly to what I had already told him. Not only that. I would share the killer's thoughts, his sick sexual fantasies; sometimes my hands would feel the stickiness of fresh blood."

"This must have been extremely disturbing …"

"I started reading the books of the famous psychic writer Edgar Cayce and I began to study quantum physics. I discovered that every molecule has energy that vibrates. Energy never dissipates and forms an energy field, which is also referred to as an aura. I was able to tune into the vibration of energy left at the crime scene. I could tell the detectives exactly what happened there. I also learnt that one's Delta brainwaves are active in interpreting these vibrations. I think all people have this capacity – anyone can pick up the 'vibe' if they walk into friends' homes just after they had a fight. Just as all people can run, athletes are better because they practice. I inadvertently had been practicing this capacity and only later began understanding how it works when I read quantum physics. I am no more psychic than anyone else, but my sense for interpreting vibrations has been practiced."

"Were you able to divorce yourself from your work?"

"No. When I was investigating a crime scene it was as if the killer's mindset took over my own. I forgot to do the normal everyday things like buying groceries and paying accounts. My mood became dark and sombre. Without meaning any offence, I was curt and abrupt with people, even those closest to me."

After six years of entering the minds and psyche of notorious killers like the Station Strangler, the Cape Prostitute Killer and Stewart Wilken, who bit and finally ate the nipples of one of his victims, and Mhlengwa Zikode, who first killed the male partners of his victims, Micki was in an abyss of dark despair.

Suffering from convulsions and throwing up as much as twenty-two times a day, she realised that she urgently needed help. The post-traumatic stress resulting from her work was literally killing her.

In desperation, Micki sought the help of Pretoria-based psychologist, Susan Kriegler. As she walked through the door Susan said: "Well, why are you here?"

Skirting around the issue of her real problems, Micki replied, "Because I want to stop smoking."

Susan laughed and said that she smoked herself and this definitely wasn't the reason that the serial killer profiler had come to see her. Relieved, Micki said "Then do you mind if I go and fetch my cigarettes from the car?"

When the session continued, Susan, who is, according to Micki a deeply spiritual woman, told her patient that she could see two things in her aura. "What are they are?" asked Micki intrigued.

"The first is a nun," replied the psychologist, "and the second is ... I don't know if I should tell you this."

"Look, I catch serial killers for a living. You can tell me anything."

"The other is an assassin."

Micki reflected on this astonishing revelation and it made perfect sense to her. "I always thought that within the Force I was the only one who *really* understood the killers. Not that I condoned what they did. But I could understand why they had committed the crime. You know what they say," she said with a small laugh, "it takes one to catch one."

Susan suggested that Micki should undergo some past life regression therapy with her. Micki was willing to comply.

"I felt that my job had something to do with my karma. It seemed to me that this life was payback time. I had to sacrifice my life and my sanity by doing community service. By assisting the police catch these dangerous men, I was helping to keep the community safe."

Under hypnosis, Susan regressed Micki. "In the beginning I only experienced minor stuff. In one regression I saw myself as a tiger. By the way, the tiger is my spiritual animal. When we first got to the tiger, he was a male, he was hurt and mangled."

Susan said: "What are we going to do to help this tiger?"

"We are going to run," replied Micki. Under Susan's guidance, she began to run, in ever decreasing circles, trying to get closer to the tiger in order to ascertain what had wounded him so. But at this stage, the angry animal was not yet ready to be healed.

Finding the assassin through regression was to prove a fascinating experience for both the patient and her psychologist. "At first," recalled Micki, "All I could see was a giant black iron ball. And what this ball did was to jump through time and space. I was the ball. So I kept saying to Susan, "Now I'm here with the Black Death in England. Wherever there was death and destruction throughout the centuries, this is where the ball landed.

"At one stage I said to Susan that this man, the assassin, doesn't want me to find him, which is why he was throwing the ball as a diversion. However, he had reckoned without my determination ... I made up my mind to find him. The next moment both Susan and I got a vision of a mosque knee-deep in blood.

"This energy started to attack Susan. I realised what was going on and I came out of the trance. Susan was shaking and she had a red rash all over her body. She said that she too had seen the vision of a mosque knee-deep in blood."

Her session with Susan over, Micki drove back to the office, upset and deep in thought. Suddenly, within her mind's eye, she saw the assassin who said to her, "I did it in the name of Christ."

Even the researcher, Micki pondered over this and recalled that her mother's name was Iolanthe Tancred. She also knew that within her mother's personal library, Iolanthe had history books that could help her troubled daughter piece together the puzzle of the blood-bespattered mosque. Paging through a book on the Crusades, Micki came upon a photograph of the blood-splattered mosque and uncovered the following story:

Pope Urban heeded a call from Alexius in Constantinople to rid the east of infidels. Tancrede of Hauteville, an ancestor of Iolanthe, was a Scandinavian Viking who settled with his two wives and many children in Normandy. One of the major sons from the first wife was called Robert Guiscard and his son was Bohemud.

Micki believes that the ancestor whose memories she had tapped into under hypnosis was a son of the second wife, whose name was also Tancrede. (Tancrede 11).

In 1096, Bohemud and Tancrede 11 joined the third Crusade. They captured many cities, including Antioch, which is situated in the present day Syria. Tancrede 11 captured it first, but his feuding stepbrother, Bohemud, who possessed a larger army, forced him to hand it over.

Tancrede was furious, but set his eyes on Jerusalem. Bohemud stayed in Antioch and became regent.

On 15th July 1099, Tancrede 11, was the first crusader over the walls of Jerusalem, opening the gates for the rest of the army. The Moslem defenders retreated to the Mosque of al-Aqsa, where Tancred, flying his banner over the mosque, promised them asylum, assuring them that they would be safe inside. However, in the frenzy of the fighting, the other crusaders killed these Moslems, littering the mosque with corpses and leaving it knee-high in blood.

Micki feels that this betrayal of the crusaders gave Tancrede the karma of guilt he continued to suffer for centuries.

Yet more blood was to be shed. The Egyptians were descending upon Jerusalem and on 12th August 1099, Tancrede and his men attacked the Egyptians while they were sleeping. Tancrede himself managed to kill the standard bearer of the Egyptian leader, al-Afdal, in his tent, but al-Afdal had already fled.

Tancrede became the Regent of Antioch and was known as the Prince of Galilee. He died just before Christmas at the age of 26 in 1112 in Antioch.

Micki decided to travel to France to finally shake off the ghosts from her past. She wrote: *Tancred of Hauteville's sons built The Cathedral in Coutance in 1056. It is magnificent! I went to Coutances and to the Tancred museum in Hautville. There is a statue there of Robert Guiscard, son of Tancrede of Hautville.*

I held my mother's passport up to it. Here, in the lush green countryside I lent my eyes to my ancestor, Tancrede 11, so he could once more see the countryside of his birth, since he had died in the barren desert of Antioch, 889 years before.

"I got a very peaceful feeling. I believe that this was the moment that his karma was finally paid off!

"I don't think I am a reincarnation of my ancestor, but I do think I carried some of his burden, which is now done with."

****

Micki is today in a very happy space. Having left the Police Force, she now concentrates fulltime on her private practice as a psychologist and her writing. Although the subject matter of her books currently focuses on her in-depth knowledge of killers and their crimes, she feels that in future her writing may move in an entirely different direction. She has also completed an Afrikaans historical novel, called *Sorg*, about the Ostrich feather industry in Oudtshoorn.

Certainly, she is very much interested in spirituality and she has studied Reiki and Kahuna healing. She does not particularly like going to church. "I don't enjoy going anywhere where there is a crowd," but she has studied the life of Christ in depth and she now feels comfortable with her perception of man and God.

"I feel that religion as it is taught in church is fine. But for me it is the nursery school phase — one needs to ask one's own questions and go on one's own journey of exploration.

"A friend gave me this interpretation of God and man, which I like. There is a big dam. And this big dam is God. All the little rivers, consisting of man, animals, plants and trees, everything that is on this earth, flows into this big dam. So we are all connected, flowing one into the other. Although we are not God, we are part of God and God is part of us.

"In this stream of energy, if you do something good, clear water is going to flow, but if you do something bad, you muddy the waters for everyone."

With her investigative mind, Micki is forever asking questions.

Pondering on the reason why bad things happen to good people, she came up with the following analogy:

"As souls in heaven, we decide to incarnate as humans on earth, to do God's work. We collaborate with other souls and work out a script. When we are on earth we are actors acting out the script that we decided on up there. As actors we are not conscious of our own true soul's purpose while on stage."

Micki reflected on her words for a few moments. "Of course we fluff our lines, blunder and make mistakes, for there is no rehearsal. Our spirit guides are like the soundmen, light crew etc. whose unseen hands make it easier for us to perform.

"The earth is the stage where everything is acted out — the bad things happen here on earth, as we scripted them up there, but we should all remember that the purpose of the play is to allow goodness, forgiveness, peace, love, charity and mercy to win in the end, which will be to the glory of God.

"Sometimes people get so involved in their designated roles, they completely forget their original higher purpose. We all need to learn to align our earth ego personality with our soul identity, if we want to get it right here on earth."

Micki grew suddenly solemn. "This is the meaning of life. According to Christianity, Christ was the only one who fully succeeded in living his life totally to the glory of God."

"Are you saying that one should condone murder as, at some other level, the whole scenario was planned?"

"I will never condone murder. Taking a life is stealing from God. I have looked into the souls of murderers and assassins and their souls' suffering is beyond our comprehension. Whether you put them behind bars or let them go free, they are imprisoned by their anguish and their anger. I will never agree to a serial killer going on parole either. All that have been released so far, killed again. Why give a serial killer a second chance on life if at the same time you are giving someone else a chance at losing their life?"

Micki believes in angels. "There are legions of angels all around waiting to do your biding. But you must ask for exactly what you want. I have read *The Secret* and I am learning to live my life according to it and I believe that it does work."

Here is this woman who has seen death over three to four hundred bodies — often gruesomely mangled — at close quarters.

For herself she has no fear of death. "I believe it's like waiting to go to a beautiful island. You've got the ticket, but your plane doesn't leave yet. Sometimes, I get very impatient to return to my spiritual form, but I know I have purpose on earth."

Micki Pistorius is at peace. She was even able, through her sessions with her psychologist, to revisit her wounded tiger. "In a field of yellow grass, I saw his ears just pointing out. When I saw him again, his fur was rich and thick and he was completely healed. He was playful, yet powerful. He is often with me. I like to tickle his stomach. Whenever I need courage I call on him."

As Micki stood to leave, I notice that she had been leaning her back against a cushion embroidered with the image of a tiger. The unflinching yellow-green eyes of this tiger stared back at me. I noticed that the tiger's eyes looked pretty much like Micki's.

THE REVEREND OLIVE IZAAKS

SPIRITUAL PSYCHIC

COMFORTING THE LIVING
BY CONNECTING WITH THE DEAD

FOOTPRINTS

*One night I had a dream.
I was walking along the beach with the Lord
and across the sky flashed scenes from my life.
In each scene I noticed
two sets of footprints in the sand:
One made by me and the other made by the Lord.
When the last scene of my life flashed before me
I looked back at the footprints in the sand.
I noticed many times along the patch of life
there was only one set of footprints in the sand.
I also noticed that it happened
At the very lowest and saddest times of my life.
This really bothered me very much,
So I asked the Lord about it.
"Lord, you said once I decided to follow you
you'd walk with me all the way.
But I've noticed that in times of trouble Align
there is only one set of footprints in the sand.
I don't understand why in times
When I needed you most you would leave me."
The Lord answered, "My precious, precious child,
I love you and I would never, never leave you.
During your times of trial and suffering
When you see only one set of footprints in the sand,
It was then that I carried you."*

Mary Stevenson

THE REVEREND OLIVE IZAAKS

The Reverend Olive Izaaks is the head of the Johannesburg Study Group of the Aquarian Foundation, a religion dedicated to God, spiritual miracles, psychical research, individual rights, morality and the family.

In this capacity, Olive serves not only her congregation by leading their regular services, she also conducts spiritual weddings, funerals and baptisms; teaches and counsels people about spirituality; carries out spiritual healing and assists those who she believes have a calling to become spiritual healers and spiritual psychics.

In addition to this demanding schedule, Olive also does one-on-one spiritual readings, the main thrust of which is to bring comfort to those who seek proof that a beloved family member or friend who has passed over is still alive in the spirit world.

"I am not a fortune teller," she declared firmly. "I prefer to think of myself as a spiritual psychic. When I do a reading for someone, I leave it to my beloved guide, Arthur, to determine who gets what. Invariably I also connect with the Ascended Masters who will give guidance and general direction to the person who has come to consult with me."

Obviously, Olive, the Ascended Masters and Arthur form an indefatigable team, for there is a long waiting list for those requiring her insight and wisdom. When I request an interview with her, I, too, have to have to join the lengthy queue. I felt a certain trepidation when I finally rang the doorbell of her apartment in Craighall in Johannesburg. I need not have worried.

A kindly grey-haired grandmother with a ready smile, totally modest and unassuming, opened the door. She declared that she was surprised that I should want to interview her for she is 'so ordinary.'

Mentioning her considerable reputation as a spiritual psychic, I suggested that despite her well-groomed, conventional appearance, she was anything but a run-of-the-mill widow. Olive chuckled and explained her down-to-earth approach to the spiritual world. "When connecting with the spirit world, we need to keep our feet on earth and our head in heaven."

She paused thoughtfully for a few moments. "We need to explode karma* and ask for dharma.** We need to realise that we never do this alone. We are always guided."

****

---

* Karma (Sanskrit) is the consequence of our thoughts, words or deeds of this or previous lives.
** Dharma (Sanskrit) is essentially Buddhist teaching, but in a wider sense, any teaching or truth.

Olive was born on the 16th of January 1942. Her father, William Henry Izaaks, whose family came from Poland, rose to be a second lieutenant in the air force, but his career was short lived. Out on a training mission, he was killed in a plane crash during the war. He was only twenty-two years old at the time and Olive was a baby of just nine months.

At the same time as this tragedy occurred, her maternal grandmother was dying of cancer in the Cape and Olive's mother, Katherine, was forced to go there to care for her ailing parent. Baby Olive was left in the care of her paternal grandparents, Christina and Charles, who later legally adopted her.

Olive was twenty-four years old before she finally met her mother, although this did not bother her. "I knew that I was where I was supposed to be," she said.

Surprisingly, considering that she never really knew him, Olive always felt extraordinarily attached to her father — today his picture has pride of place in her living room and growing up in Kwazulu Natal, every Saturday afternoon, she used to regularly visit his grave in the military section of the picturesque Pietermaritzburg cemetery.

When Olive reached puberty and began dating young men, her astonished boyfriends were taken to her father's graveside to be introduced to her late dad.

In 1957, when she was fifteen, Olive's grandfather died. "I vividly recall the night of his death. I was standing in my room trying on a dress when I unexpectedly heard my grandmother shouting. Grandpa had already left us when suddenly we saw a spirit hand, a man's hand, coming down from the ceiling. My cousin who was with us also saw it.

"I'm sure that my grandfather was just trying to tell us that we mustn't worry, that he was alright, but I was terrified. So frightened, in fact, that I wouldn't sleep in the house. My bedroom was in the front of the house and, in those days, the toilet was outside, at the back of the house. I was too scared to go there alone. From that moment, I blocked out my spirituality."

Olive married Gerald van Rooyen at the tender age of seventeen and had two sons, Michael and Henry. Today she is the proud mother of two adult grandsons on whom she positively dotes.

Thoroughly modern in many respects, Olive is quick to show me their picture on her cell phone. Alas, her married bliss was not to last. By the time she was twenty-four, Olive was widowed and she reconciled herself to the fact that she was destined to go through this life on her own.

With a mischievous twinkle in her eye, she confided in me, "It's not that I don't like men. I think they're adorable. I like to give them a kiss on the lips and pinch their cheeks. Then I like to send them home. I'm a Capricorn and I love the privacy of having my own space."

Light years away from any sort of spiritual path and busy with bringing up her boys and working in the field of Human Resources — Olive is very much a people's person — her interest in the esoteric was reawakened by a colleague at her work who introduced her to the works of Lobsang Rampa. She soon developed an interest in Transcendental Meditation and became a voracious reader of spiritual books.

When a friend from Johannesburg came to visit her in Pietermaritzburg, Olive was distressed to see his physical deterioration. Suffering with severe back problems, he told Olive that he was destined to end up in a wheelchair.

A few months later, the same friend came back on another visit. This time, he appeared vibrant and healthy. Far from being wheelchair bound, he was playing golf once more. Olive could not believe the extraordinary transformation in him. She questioned what had happened to change him and he told her that he had been receiving spiritual healing.

Intrigued, Olive wondered if there was a spiritual church in Pietermaritzburg. Her friend then took her to the small spiritual church and she was amazed — she didn't know how many times she had walked passed it without even noticing it. She resolved to attend a service there, but somehow she didn't get around to it. Her friend kept phoning her from Johannesburg.

"Olive, have you been to a service yet?" he queried. Each time he phoned, Olive was obliged to say that she still had not found the time to attend a service. Finally, running out of excuses, Olive stepped inside the spiritual church in Pietermaritzburg.

She listened to the service, finding it not all that dissimilar from conventional church services, but towards the end of the service there was something different — the church leader tuned into his spiritual guide(s) and began delivering messages to various members of the congregation. Olive was fascinated and intrigued.

Olive knew that, despite blocking out her spirituality for so long, there was a spiritual world — she instinctively felt that her deceased father was safe and that he was looking after her and she knew, too, that other departed family members were with her in spirit. It was in that moment that Olive knew that she had found her spiritual path.

****

When she relocated to Johannesburg, Olive continued her exploration of the spiritual world. She visited the spiritual church in Troyeville; she went to the Three-in-One Church, services for which were held in the Scout Hall in Parktown, but still she felt her quest for a deeper spiritual knowledge was not being satisfied.

It was only when she walked into the Aquarian Foundation, where the services were held in a little house in Webb Street in Yeoville, which at that time could only claim a membership of around fifteen members that Olive knew that she had truly found her spiritual home.

****

Once she was in this spiritual milieu, Olive found that her intuition was developing at a rapid rate. More than ever, she was aware of Spirit. A friend asked her for healing for her sick cousin who lived some distance from Olive. As Olive was completing writing the letter, she became aware that her hand was not her hand, but that it was being controlled by someone else. With her delightful sense of humour, Olive recalled with a laugh:

"I thought I was being psychically attacked. I screamed at the entity, "Go to the Light. Go to the Light." It was only after some time that I realized that my writing was being assisted by my guide, Andrew. I was so privileged. Such lovely information was coming through."

Now, blessed with the gift of automatic writing, Olive used to write down a question and her guide would provide her with the answer. "We wrote reams and reams of stuff together," she recalled.

"Explain automatic writing to me," I said.

"I believe it is the spirits' way of communicating with the living. Sometimes one is not even aware of what is being written and often the handwriting on the page is markedly different to one's own handwriting."

"What happened to all these writings?" I asked.

"I threw them all out when I moved to this flat."

She sees me looking at her in dismay. "I shouldn't have done that, should I? Who knows what gems of wisdom I have destroyed?"

I suggested that her lost writing could perhaps be likened to a Buddhist monk's mandalas. In Tibetan Buddhism a mandala is an imaginary palace that is contemplated during meditation. Each object in the palace has significance, representing some aspect of wisdom or reminding the mediator of some guiding principle.

When a mandala is done as a sand painting, the sand is dyed and then carefully placed on a large, flat table. The construction process takes several days and the mandala is destroyed shortly after its completion. It is testimony to the Buddhist ideal of non-attachment.

As Olive's automatic writing skills developed, she realized that as she was writing, she instinctively knew what the next word would be. From here, her psychic skills developed apace. Olive became clairaudient, able to hear the next word that her Spirit Guide was giving her.

Soon, as she communicated with the spirit world, she found that she was using the same words as her client's departed relative or friend used to use; that she could adopt their mannerisms; laugh as they used to laugh. All of which makes a reading with Olive an extraordinarily moving experience.

Curious to know more about Olive's ability to communicate with the dead, I asked her, "Is there any information the departed do not wish to give you?"

"Their names. Very seldom am I given a name. But the reader always knows who is present. They'll say something like 'Oh that's my mom. She always used to use that expression. Or that's my dad. You laughed exactly like he always laughed.' "

****

While Olive feels a particular closeness and affinity to her main psychic guide, Arthur, a Knight Templar whose been in the spirit world since 1146, "He's such a beautiful soul ... he guides me through reading and interaction with The Masters," she believes that her main master teacher is Djwal Khul, a master teacher, who also connected to Alice Bailey.*

"DK as he is sometimes known as, has a vast knowledge of the mysteries and he trains souls to embrace the Christ Consciousness in order for them to serve humanity. He works on the indigo ray and his colour is blue — deep royal blue. Even before I connected with him I knew that my soul colour was blue."

Olive is also privileged to receive information, via Arthur, from various other Ascended Masters, in particular Babaji, Koot Humi, Master Buddha, Master Emil, Master Jesus, Master Zoser, Ascended Master Lord Sananda, Rameses II, Imhotep, Lady Master Leandra, Master Elmorya and also beings that have never been to this planet, such as Clarion and Metatron.

With regard to the Space Masters, Olive said simply that she connected very closely to space beings. She also said that during a recent reading with a client, a new Ascended Master, someone who has never connected with her before, came into the reading. "Master Lady Claire came in and introduced herself. After all the years of doing readings, this was the first time I met her."

Often working as a spiritual healer, Olive needs the services of a healing guide and Many Colours, a North American Indian, came in to fill this important role. "Many Colours may seem a strange name to some people, but colours mean so much to me and I work on all the colours of the healing rays."

"Do you wish to tell me about any of your other guides?" I asked.

Olive burst out laughing. "Well, I have a financial guide. He's Jewish and his name is Joshua. He's got his hands full trying to keep my spending under control."

In October 2005 twenty-eight members of the South African Aquarian Foundation went to America as a pilgrimage to celebrate the fifty year anniversary of the church which was founded by the Reverend Keith Milton Reinhardt.

---

* Author and channel Alice Bailey produced a total of twenty-four books of esoteric teachings, including her autobiography. Nineteen of these books were supposed to have been written by her Tibetan Master Djwal Khul.

Amongst the many planned events which were to be held to mark the celebrations was a masked ball. Needing beaded shoes to go with her gown, Olive went out and bought not one, but three pairs of beaded shoes as they all looked right with her outfit.

"No wonder I have to have a guide to look after my financial affairs. After this shopping spree, Joshua simply looked at me and shook his head," she chortled.

Despite her seeming levity, Olive takes her work extremely seriously, and as she works, she continually thanks her Guides for the information which she feels blessed and privileged to receive.

Yet this side of Olive, the spiritual psychic, healer and spiritual leader, which may seem strange to some, can be kept under wraps if needs be. During the many years she worked for The Southern Suns Hotel Group in the Human Resources Department, Olive's true vocation only came to light shortly before her retirement and proved a great source of surprise to her fellow staff members.

****

Curious to learn more about The Aquarian Foundation I went to a meeting at the headquarters of the Johannesburg Study Group in Randburg in Johannesburg. On the first floor of an office block, there is little to indicate the presence of this spiritual meeting.

Olive explained this thus: "We do not advertise. Rather we believe that those who need to be here will be led here." The session that I am attending is a Saturday afternoon meditation. When I arrive, I am warmly greeted by an assembly of approximately twenty-five people, all with name tags. Their ages vary, anything from eighteen to eighty years old, and I notice that there is a liberal sprinkling of masculine energy, which is unusual in most spiritual circles.

When Olive appeared, she greeted everybody warmly. It would appear that she knows all the congregants' names as well as their personal details.

"Lovely to see you again, Annie. Is your mom better?"

"Thank you for coming, Clive. How's that sore knee of yours?"

On the tables running along the walls are large scrapbooks filled with cuttings of various newspaper articles pertaining to The Foundation, including many accounts of the late Reverend Keith Milton Reinhardt's extraordinary psychic powers, which were put to the test time and time again and which were never found to be lacking.

Indeed, so charismatic was the Reverend Reinhardt's personality, that today The Aquarian Foundation's Church of The New Age in Seattle Washington is the largest psychic and occult centre in the United States.

I am drawn to ask Olive about the core Aquarian belief system.

"Aquarians are spiritualists to the extent they believe in and practice communication with the so-called dead, some of whom serve as 'guides' or 'guardian angels' through human instruments called 'mediums.'

"This would seem to presuppose a belief in the continuity of life beyond the grave and in other planes of life than this physical plane. Aquarians are not content, however, with presupposing this claim, but tend to investigate thoroughly the field of psychic phenomena and mediumship until absolute proof is found to the satisfaction of each of them."

Later, we go into the inner sanctum, which is simply furnished with a pulpit and rows of chairs. Photographs of the Ascended Masters gaze down from the walls and sacred objects, mainly large and unusually shaped crystals, are much in evidence.

Olive began the simple service by welcoming everyone and some prayers were read. Today, she was leading the congregation whose meetings are open 'to all sincere people' (apart from the master classes, which are only open to members who wish to enhance their spiritual and psychic development) in meditation. The women were all given either simple blue and yellow or white irises from a vase and the men were given single sheets of blank paper.

We were then asked to concentrate on these objects and to meditate looking at the flowers or else at the sheet of paper and to ask questions. "Who planted the flower as a seed? Who prepared the ground? Go back to the time when that paper was a tree. Who cut the tree down? Try and see the bigger picture."

Following the meditation, Olive went around the room asking each person what they experienced during this meditation. The answers that came back were intelligent and thought provoking. One woman read aloud a poem which she said had been channelled to her:

> *This small flower*
> *is but an infinitesimal*
> *part of the Universe.*
> *It is part of God's perfect creation.*
> *But we are all part of God's perfect creation.*
> *So next time you feel*
> *lonely or afraid*
> *Remember that you are*
> *as perfect as this flower*
> *Without blemish or flaw*
> *And that you are deeply loved*
> *by God.*

Then Olive, assisted by two of her Master Class students went around the room giving messages that they had received from Spirit to each member of the congregation.

The following week, I attended another session, this time of spiritual healing at the Foundation. I notice that there was a disclaimer on the leaflets of their monthly schedules which suggested that spiritual healing should be given not in isolation, but rather as a complementary adjunct to competent medical advice.

At the end of the service, Olive began administering spiritual healing to some members of the congregation. Deep in prayer she appeared to pass her hands over the person as they sat quietly on a small stool. The whole process was over in a matter of minutes.

Again, two of her Master Class students were also chosen to administer spiritual healing. After the service, while everyone was standing around chatting, I asked Brigid, a congregant, if she believed in spiritual healing. Her reply was one of the most charming testimonials that I've ever received.

"My husband, Raymond, and I breed rabbits. A mom deserted her litter of six baby rabbits of two or three days old. The vet gave us instructions as to how feed these little orphans and five of them survived. We found homes for four of them and kept one for ourselves, which we named Emil, after Master Emil.

"One day this rabbit became ill. To the surprise of the congregation, we brought her to the church for spiritual healing. We thought that even if she survived, she would be crippled or would end up with a curved spine.

"She came to two sessions. Everybody said prayers for our little rabbit.

"She survived, thank God, and we found her a mate, Rasha. Three weeks after their introduction, she gave birth to a litter of healthy snow-white babies. Isn't she beautiful?" asked Brigid, proudly producing a photo of a plump rabbit for my inspection. I had to agree that her white rabbit certainly seemed to be in the pink.

****

It has been a long journey for Olive from her first visit to the spiritual church in Pietermaritzburg to head of the Johannesburg branch of the Aquarian Foundation, a position which she was given in 2000.

Olive began as a spiritual helper within the church. From there she was given the responsibility of administering to the spiritual welfare of one of the groups and became a spiritual teacher in training.

When her predecessor elected to retire to the Cape, Olive's succession had to be approved not only within the local community, but by the Board in America, whose spiritual leader is Jann Werner, an ex-South African. Over and above all this, the Ascended Masters had to approve her appointment.

After spending time with Olive, I'm sure that The Masters did this with much alacrity and joy. For, whether she is leading her small, but very special church, or giving personal readings at her home, Olive is a remarkable woman, filled with humour, warmth, compassion and a profound wisdom that must have taken many lifetimes to acquire.

JASON LIGHT WING

SOUND ENGINEER, CONSERVATIONIST, PSYCHIC, RECOVERED DRUG ADDICT, HEALER

FLYING HIGH AFTER HITTING ROCK BOTTOM

THE WINDHOVER

To Christ Our Lord

I caught this morning morning's minion, kingdom of daylight's dauphin,
dapple-dawn-drawn Falcon, in his riding
Of the rolling level underneath him steady air, and striding
High there, how he rung upon the rein of a wimpling wing
In his ecstasy! Then off, off forth on swing,
As a skate's heel sweeps smooth on a bow-bend: the hurt and gliding
Rebuffed the big wind. My heart in hiding
Stirred for a bird, — the achieve of, the mastery of the thing!
Brute beauty and valour and act, oh air, pride, plume here
Buckle! AND the fire that breaks from thee then, a billion
Times told lovelier, more dangerous, O my chevalier!
No wonder of it: sheer plod makes plough down sillion
Shine, and blue-beak embers, ah my dear,
Fall, gall themselves, and gash gold-vermillion.

Gerald Manley Hopkins

Vanessa Wallis was only nineteen when her son Jason was born. Her husband, James, was both aggressive and abusive when he had been drinking. Consequently Jason grew up before his time, feeling that he had to be strong for his mother and his small sister Sherri-Lynn. James committed suicide when he was thirty-six, blaming Vanessa and fourteen year old Jason for his unhappiness.

Consumed by guilt, Jason's downward spiral began as he started experimenting with alcohol and drugs, until by the time he was in his early twenties he had graduated from marijuana to the harder stuff — crack, heroin and cocaine.

His drug problem was compounded by the fact that after leaving school he studied sound engineering in the USA. While he was in the States, Jason spent time with the Hopi Indians, who awakened his spirituality while teaching him to experiment with hallucinogenic cacti.

On his return to South Africa, Jason's sound engineering career meant that he was working unnaturally long hours, handling the sound at pop concerts for thousands upon thousands of people. The only way Jason found that he could cope with the pressure and the sleep deprivation was by snorting coke.

"I thought I was on top of the pressure. I was filled with ego when I did the large concerts, being responsible for rocking the stadiums with the sounds of heavy metal. There used to be a joke in the industry — the difference between a sound engineer on coke and God is that God doesn't think he's a sound engineer on coke." Jason packed up with laughter as he said this.

At work one day, Jason was startled to receive a call that his bedroom in his student digs in the suburb of Melville was burning down. Rushing to the scene, Jason found that a short in his electric blanket cord was responsible for the fire, which had now blazed out of control, destroying both his bedroom and all his possessions, including his freshly ironed clothes which the char had left for him on the bed.

Only three things could be rescued from the fire — his much prized Samurai sword and his two bass guitars —"I sometimes used to sing in a band and play bass."

There was little time to dwell on his loss, as he was doing the sound engineering for a large fifteen piece band at Bassline, the in-club at the time.

That evening, there was a promotion and Jason was given a couple of sample cans of deodorant.

"Do you know the deodorant was called Phoenix?" Jason remarked, chuckling at this irony. "I knew that the Universe was giving me a subtle wake-up call. I wondered if I would be able to rise from the ashes."

"Following the fire, I didn't take any drugs for about two weeks.

Then, as they say, the proverbial shit hit the fan. My second car was stolen. My good friend died of a drug overdose and my ex-fiancée announced that she was marrying my best friend.

"I decided that the Universe had it in for me. In victim mode, feeling very sorry for myself, I left my girlfriend and moved in with an Ecstasy dealer. I started taking drugs again. Illegally, I began to race nitrous oxide vehicles — this will be news to my mom, which could go about 70% faster than normal cars. However, you could only drive them about twice before they burnt out. At this stage of my life, it didn't seem that I could sink much lower."

Aged twenty-three years old and weighing a mere fifty-eight kilo he's still lean today at seventy-five kilo, Jason realised that he had to tackle his drug addiction before it destroyed him.

Finally, he felt obliged to confess to his mother the extent of his problem. Although she was shocked, as a strong woman, 'my mother is my inspiration' and so Vanessa decided to tackle her son's addiction head on.

"Do you want to go into rehabilitation?" she asked Jason.

Vehemently Jason shook his head. "According to the Chinese horoscope, I'm a snake and according to the Western horoscope, I'm a Leo. Either way, I was too proud. I knew that if they put me in a clinic I'd find a way to get out and to go to Hillbrow, to the nearest drug dealer.

Vanessa decided to take Jason and Sherri-Lynn on holiday to Umhlanga, a popular seaside resort in Natal. Once they were ensconced in the hotel room, Jason knew that he had to confront his demons.

"Seven days of hell followed as I tried to clean up my act and wean myself off my cocktail of drugs. I went cold turkey and I suffered from uncontrollable vomiting and nose bleeds. My skin crawled and I had a burning sensation in my sinuses and chest.

"I had terrifying hallucinations. Big spiders seemed to be pinning me down. I got to see what I thought was the devil. A dark entity about seven feet tall was omnipresent and he kept putting his hands around my heart until it seemed as if the life force would be drained out of me.

"I have always believed in a force greater than myself and I told this force that I was not ready to die, that I still had too much work to do on this planet.

When I said this I felt my body flooded with light, with a feeling of complete peace and harmony.

"The primeval monster got very angry at the fact that I was still alive and, indeed, it is a miracle that I pulled through. Only 3% of heroin addicts make it, the rest die. When my seven days of hell were finally over, I went to see a doctor to see whether I was clean. The doctor was astounded that I had survived — I still had enough drugs in my system to put down a small elephant."

When he was feeling stronger within himself, Vanessa asked her son if he wanted to see any of Natal's tourist attractions. Immediately Jason produced a pamphlet advertising the Umgeni River Park Bird Show.

"I didn't know why, but I knew that I had to see that show," recalled Jason. "Actually, when I was still on drugs I went to The Crystal Cave in Rustlers Valley near the Lesotho Border. I began meditating in the cave and I immediately became aware of a Higher Force and of birds of prey bonding with me and settling on my shoulders and on my arms and on my glove."

Jason watched the Umgeni Bird Show with quiet fascination while he listened as the handler told the audience about the habits and habitat of each bird. He watched as the birds flew around the open air auditorium before returning to their perches. Jason observed how the handlers controlled the birds — for he was aware that unless properly disciplined some of these birds of prey could inflict grievous harm on humans. By the time the show was over, Jason knew that he had found his perfect career path — he wanted to work with birds of prey and to save those facing extinction for future generations.

Meeting with Paulette, the show's organiser, whom he would later refer to as 'an angel in my recovery', Jason did not beat about the bush.

"I'm a recovering drug addict," he said, "and I need to clean up my life. I'd like to work with wild birds of prey."

Despite the CV of a sound engineer seemingly being little suited to a career in ornithology, Jason managed to secure a job at Umgeni River Park. On reflection, however, he decided to take another position closer to home offered to him by Dr. Steven Van Der Spuy, who was in charge of the bird show run by the resort complex, Monte Casino, and who Jason affectionately describes as his mentor.

"I immediately felt a great affinity with these birds of prey. Although I had no previous experience with birds apart from working in a pet shop when I was about eighteen, I managed, under Dr. Van Der Spuy's guidance, to produce a unique show that was attended by visitors from all over the world.

"I worked with many kinds of birds including Wattled Cranes, Cape Vultures, Goliath Herons, Macaw Parrots, but the birds that I grew closest to were undoubtedly the falcons."

"Why were the falcons your favourites?"

"I believe that I have had many incarnations on this earth and I feel a strong connection to ancient Egypt. Horus, the revered Egyptian god of humanity had a falcon head and falconry is the oldest sport known to mankind, originating over 3500 years ago. It is no accident that I have come to work with these birds in this lifetime.

"Falconry, like the martial arts, involves a special code of honour. What falconers do is that they trap birds in their first year of passage. 75% of birds of prey will die within their first year due to starvation, not knowing how to hunt, poisoning, being run over by cars, that sort of thing.

"After we trap the birds, we train them, and teach them how to hunt and make them strong once more. When they moult from their juvenile feathers, we'll hunt them three or four times before releasing them into the wild and starting the process all over again, thereby bringing up the number of birds of prey all over the world."

"Tell me about the falcon named Fugly."

"Falcons are very special birds of prey. Being precognitive, they see movement of their prey before it happens. The Saker Falcon that I had at Monte Casino and I had a very special relationship. He was a full human imprint, which means that he was hand raised by human beings. As a result, he thought that he was human. His stage name was Gaia, but I used to call him Fugly, because he was very ugly.

"He became so comfortable in my space that I could actually take him and hold him up against my chest, put his beak against my nose and he wouldn't bite me. There was a certain element of trust that he had with me that he didn't have with anybody else. We got so close that I could tell if there was something wrong with him. I watched his health deteriorating as he got incredibly sick and he ultimately died of bird pneumonia.

"On my day off I made him a hood, which I wanted to get it to him before he died. I put the final bead on the top of the hood and I was just about to take it to him when I got a call from Monte Casino, telling me that Fugly had passed on."

"What was the purpose of the hood?"

"We use hoods on the birds during training to cover their eyes. It has a calming effect on them when we transport them. Birds are like kids. They think if they can't see you, you can't see them. When we take the hoods off, the birds know that they are ready to hunt."

Jason paused for a moment, obviously still finding the death of his animal friend painful. "A while ago, I did a Brandon Bays *Journey* process during which time I discovered that Fugly has become one of my animal guides. During this Journey he actually took me on a flight and it was absolutely incredible."

"Are you still doing bird shows?"

"No, I have moved onto the conservation and preservation of these birds. I realised that a connection can be made between bird and man in business … when the Black Eagle goes hunting, it knows exactly what it wants."

****

Once weaned off the drugs that threatened to destroy his life, Jason became a keen follower of the disciplined Japanese martial art of Ninjitsu. He also now follows a deeply spiritual path, light years away from his drug popping days as a sound engineer.

"Do you follow any particular teachings?"

"I try and learn all that I can about all religions, all teachings, especially Eastern philosophies. I don't want to ever be put in a box. By learning all these different things, my soul keeps finding new levels of understanding. My thoughts create my reality, manifested into physical things which are tangible."

"Such as?"

"I have a Samurai sword that was bent from mock fighting. I wanted to get it fixed. When I mentioned this to a friend she said that she knew a guy who had the largest collection of Samurai swords in Southern Africa. I asked her if he repaired swords. When she replied in the affirmative I told her that I would really like to meet him. Then she said, 'Well, there he is — he's coming out of the supermarket across the road right now.'

"I believe when you put out your intention to the Universe, provided that it is honourable and you stay 100% focused, the Universe will support you."

"Is this is what is known as synchronicity?"

"For me, that is human understanding of the word. In my opinion, everything happens for a reason. Things happen not by time ordained by a watch or by a calendar. I believe that there is only one time. And that is God's time. It is one's ego that tries to push things forward into my time. And through my ego wanting it, I find that my soul pushes it further and further away."

"Are you clairaudient? Do you receive messages from the spirit world?"

"Yes. I used to be clairaudient, but that gift was taken away from me because of my drug use. However, my psychic powers have been restored to me.

"During the last four months that I used drugs, I saw the dark energies who work only on the lower realms of vibration. A black figure used to lie in bed with me and attack me."

"What did you see before you started taking drugs?"

"My father's alcoholic abuse made my childhood extremely difficult. When he was at his most violent, I used to be comforted by a lady with a dog. I remember sitting outside on the veranda steps and being consoled by her. I must have been about four or five at the time. Now I understand that this must have been a spirit guide. Her presence gave me a small insight into what Divine Love is.

"However, I now realise that my father's addictive personality was my addictive personality and that I would never have learnt life's lessons without his example."

"Let's talk about you being psychic. Do you know who your guides are?"

"I have a good idea. In a psychic reading I was told that my main guide is not of this earth, but comes from another realm and has been given to me to look after me. This entity is neither male nor female, but both and has no name — it just is.

"Apparently I have seventeen guides in all. A whole entourage, in fact. I have been in many situations where I should have died — when I get to heaven I'm going to give each one of them a big bunch of flowers and I'm going to apologise for keeping them all so busy.

"I know that I have four Bushido warriors that look after me. Bushido was the understanding that was taken from Buddhism and from Daoism. "Every in breath is a new life. Every out breath is a new life."

"Do you have any other animal guides besides the falcon that you trained?"

"It is my understanding that I also have some horse guides. Trusty steeds that help me carry my load through this life."

"Do you have any cognisance of your previous lives?"

"I know that I have lived as a Tibetan monk. I also think that I was an army general in the Ming Dynasty, which probably accounts for my interest in martial arts in this lifetime. It is part of my karma. I do not think that there is good or bad karma. No good or bad luck. Your karma just is."

"Do you fear death?"

"No. The soul is eternal. There is no death. The cycle of life and death is continuous. Although I believe that this is my last lifetime on this earth, which is probably why it is so eventful," Jason concluded laughing heartily.

"Then how will you reincarnate?"

"I will return as a spirit guide. Having been in so much trouble myself in such a comparatively brief space of time, I will be there to look after my friends.

"But before I die, I hope I can achieve my greatest ambition. To race in the falcon race in the Gobi desert in Kazakhstan in China, territory where Attila the Hun fought.

"The race there is like the Eagle World Cup. Riding on horseback and hunting with eagles, the winner is the one who brings back the most foxes. However, unlike the other contestants, I will not hunt with the Golden Eagle.

"Oh no! I will hunt with the Black Eagle. It's smaller than the Golden Eagle, but with its incredible grace and power, strength and cunning, it proves one thing …"

"And what is that?"

"Africa is not for sissies."

****

Sometime has elapsed since I first saw Jason and meeting him again, I find that although his incredible energy has not abated in any shape or form, his life has moved on. Leaving sound engineering in 2010, he has now opened a healing centre in Roosevelt Park called The Centre of Well Balance. From where he does energy healing, psychic channelling, tarot and palm reading, aura and space cleansing.

"Let us talk first about your healing. How did you come to be a healer?"

"I believe that all the best healers have been seriously injured themselves at some stage. Well, I broke my spine when I was fourteen. It was an L1 compression fracture."

"How did you manage to do that?"

"I fell down an abandoned mineshaft at Pilgrim's Rest. I was trying to catch a snake, a rock python. The snake disappeared into some bushes and I followed it. There was no ground on the other side of the bushes and I fell about fifteen metres. I had to lie in a brace for what seemed like an eternity."

"What other injuries have you had?"

"I was working as a sound engineer at Emperor's Palace when I fell off a rig. I threw up from the pain. I told the attending paramedics that I had broken my spine.

"They said that that was impossible because I was still able to walk … I do have a very high pain threshold. I asked the guys if they could get me an ambulance. When they were too slow for my liking, I drove myself to the Rosebank Clinic, which is quite some way away. The orthopaedic surgeon who attended to me told me that I had broken three vertebrae — L1 again, as well as T12 and T5. He told me that I was destined to stay in hospital for quite some months."

"Were you prepared for this?"

"Not at all. I walked out the hospital in agony and made my way to an acupuncturist. He did some X-rays and then his eyes went very wide for a Chinese guy. He said: 'Do you want the good news or the bad?'

"The good news was that he would be able to heal me. The bad news was that I would have to come to him for acupuncture every day for three weeks. In addition to needles, he would be shocking me with electrodes into my spine and also he would hang me from the roof.

"I had been a vegetarian for twelve years and the Chinese doctor said that I had to eat protein and more protein. This involved eating fish three times a day …for breakfast, lunch and supper.

"After three weeks, I was able to quit these sessions. I have never felt stronger or healthier in my life."

"What kind of healing do you do at your Centre?"

"I work with Orgonite. This is the energy which comes off lightening and which transforms negative energy into positive. In addition to reiki, I do electromagnetic audio healing with a soundtrack that I have worked out myself. It takes thirty-three minutes and thirty-three seconds exactly. It is brainwave therapy. I transport people from the Delta to Alpha to Theta to the Shamanic dream state."

"Tell me about your psychic readings."

"My guides said that it would take me about six months to fully realise my psychic ability. After which they said I would be a psychic equal to no other."

"Isn't that somewhat conceited?"

"Not at all. They didn't say higher or better … they said EQUAL to," replied Jason, seemingly surprised that his guides' words should be questioned.

In conclusion, owing to his hectic schedule, trying to get hold of the ubiquitous Jason to update this interview proved so difficult, that I can only conclude that in the eyes of his guides as well as in the eyes of his clients he must be doing something right.

BRANDON BAYS

INTERNATIONAL SPIRITUAL TEACHER & COUNSELLOR

JOURNEYING ALONG THE PATH OF HOPE

THE ROAD NOT TAKEN

Two roads diverged in a yellow wood,
And sorry I could not travel both
And be one traveller, long I stood
And looked down one as far as I could
To where it bent in the undergrowth;
Then took the other, as just as fair,
And having perhaps the better claim,
Because it was grassy and wanted wear;
Though as for that, the passing there
Had worn them really about the same,
And both that morning equally lay
In leaves no steps had trodden black.
Oh, I kept the first for another day!
Yet knowing how way leads on to way,
I doubted if I should ever come back.
I shall be telling this with a sigh
Somewhere ages and ages hence;
Two roads diverged in a wood, and I —
I took the one less travelled by,
And that has made all the difference.

Robert Frost

For Brandon Bays, spiritual teacher and counsellor, adversity is not adversity at all. She sees it rather as a 'wake-up' call. Writing in her acclaimed book, *The Journey*, she sees us starting out our life as a pristine, pure, flawless diamond, that as we progress along life's difficult path, our innate brilliance becomes hidden by a load of rubbish, so we forget who we really are.

Adversity, in Brandon's opinion, is the wake-up call or catalyst that forces us to deal with our demons, to peel back the layers, to remove the blockages that prevent us from being our shinning beautiful true selves.

As I watched Brandon at her Intensive *The Journey* workshop, which was being held in Durban, South Africa, I observed that this small American-born woman, simply dressed in a bright silk top and black trousers, her beautiful face wet with perspiration from the unaccustomed heat — she and her second husband Kevin live in a cottage in a rural part of Wales — I saw not only a highly polished performer, I saw a woman truly committed to helping others conquer their pain and anguish.

Oprah-like, Brandon listened intently to the sad stories which poured forth from the audience as they opened their hearts to her. Her blue eyes filled frequently with tears. When she heard the heart-breaking story told by an Indian woman who was advised not to hold her premature stillborn daughter before the doctors took the small corpse away, she wept openly.

Eager hands were there to supply her with tissues, for Brandon has a legion of paid workers and devoted volunteers, mainly in the UK, Australia and now in South Africa, who willingly assist her whenever she needs help with her seminars and workshops. *The Emotional Journey* is a process developed and perfected by Brandon, who herself has gone through profound suffering and difficulty to reach the place of contentment and serenity at which she finds herself today.

Brandon's creed is as follows: *Know whatever comes to you unexpected, to be a gift from God, which will surely serve you if you use it to the fullest. It is only that which you strive for out of your own imagination that gives you trouble.**

****

Brandon has the ability to talk to and to counsel the grief-stricken and bereaved from the depth of her vast experience of a life filled with considerable adversity, which in the fullness of time she has come to regard as a great blessing from Source.

Born into a dysfunctional family where abuse was common and rage and violence so frequent, that the authorities often had to step in order to prevent

---

* The Journey by Brandon Bays

the parents from physically harming their offspring, Brandon experienced life's difficulties from an early age.

By the summer of 1992 Brandon seemed, however, to be in a pretty good space. A health conscious vegetarian, deeply fulfilled in her marriage, a committed mother, a motivational speaker who travelled the world as a member of the Anthony Robbins — America's leading personal growth teacher's team — she seemed to be in complete control of her life.

Nevertheless, she was about to receive a wake-up call of mammoth proportions. Brandon was diagnosed with a tumour the size of a basketball, that had grown all the way up from her pubic area to the ribcage, until it was pressing against her diaphragm, making it difficult for her to breathe. This pelvic mass was causing Brandon to bleed profusely — what she had thought to be an early period was in fact internal bleeding of an extremely serious nature.

She was advised by her doctor to undergo immediate surgery, but being in the field of mind healing, Brandon felt this to be against all she taught. She pleaded for time. The doctor told her that she had just a couple of days to stop the bleeding and a month to get rid of the pelvic mass, before having to undergo surgery. "There is not one case history in all these books of a woman who has healed naturally from a pelvic mass the size of yours," she warned ominously.

With a childlike innocence and a trust that she would discover what this tumour had to teach her, Brandon embarked on her own personal journey.

It was while she was being massaged by Surja, a deeply spiritual massage therapist, the masseuse suggested that Brandon go deep inside her tumour to see what it looked like. She did so and from deep within she came across an area that looked particularly dark and foreboding.

"Why don't you go down there?" suggested Surja. "Your body wisdom is probably coming up with that memory for a good reason. Even if your thinking mind is doubting this, what have you got to lose?"

Tears began to stream down Brandon's face. She was finally experiencing all the natural emotions that she had not allowed herself to experience at the time of the trauma, for as a small child she had been taught not to show her true feelings.

Surja suggested that Brandon imagine herself at a little camp fire and pull all the people in her memory at this camp fire with her. So, in her mind's eye,

Brandon visualised a crackling camp fire, with both her much younger parents there and herself as a four year old.

Brandon turned to her parents and asked them why they behaved as they did. Finally she was able to understand the source of the pain. Her young sister had drowned at the age of four and unfortunately their inexpressible anguish would sometimes get directed at her.

"Now that you understand are you able to forgive your parents?" demanded Surja. "Not just forgive, but truly forgive from the bottom of your heart?"

Brandon nodded, knowing instinctively that once her issues were completely healed and forgiven, her tumour would be able to leave was pretty much on track.

"It is my firm belief that emotional memories are stored in the cells of the body and get passed on from one cell generation to the next, and that real healing begins only when you can let go of these cellular memories," she explained. "Successful survivors get access to this cell memory and are able to clear out all the debris."

It is the practical approach to this healing journey that forms the basis of all Brandon's Journey workshops, which, it must be said, have helped thousands of sufferers overcome their illnesses, anger, fear, depression, grief, hurt and anxiety, allowing them to free themselves in order to live their lives at their highest potential.

In her eventful life, Brandon would not only have to rid herself of a tumour through non-surgical means, she would also have to deal with painful loss. In the autumn of 1993 there was a big fire storm in the hills of Malibu where Brandon was living at the time. Flying back from New York to Malibu, Brandon was to find her home burnt to a cinder.

The television crewmen, ever anxious for a good story, approached her. "Okay, so how does it feel to be a survivor of this disaster?"

Brandon looked at the reporter and quietly said, "Well, actually I don't feel myself to be a survivor, either."

"Okay, so how do you feel?"

"Well, truthfully, what I'm feeling most right now is gratitude," replied Brandon.

"Gratitude? How could you feel gratitude at a time like this?" the cynical reporter asked Brandon.

Quietly Brandon replied, "I feel gratitude because I am truly aware today of how most people would gladly burn down ten houses to experience the kind of love that I have in my life — to have the deeply fulfilling relationship I have with my husband, and to feel how blessed I am to be so close with my daughter."

Talking some years later about the enormous loss she and her family had suffered in this fire, Brandon was only to comment that it was sad not to have the family photograph albums, the precious baby pictures.

Financial devastation was to follow the fire. "A year went by. We had to receive Grace in whatever form it came. I am not proud of this, but we took the money that we had been saving to pay our taxes and used it to get our lives back together again."

Following a much needed holiday in Australia, which included a stopover in India, where Brandon drank in some much needed spiritual nourishment, the family returned to their simple two bedroomed flat.

Awaiting the returning family were some official letters from the US Government. "Because you've not paid your taxes, we are docking 100% of your wages," read the first letter. Worse was to follow. "Because you have failed to respond to our previous correspondence, we have frozen your bank accounts."

However, the letter that really broke Brandon's heart came from her cherished daughter Kelly. "While you were gone, I got a divorce. I don't know if I want to see either of you again." The letter pierced like a knife through Brandon's breaking heart.

"Nothing else can go wrong in my life," thought Brandon, ignoring her husband's increased hostility towards her. As he was putting his clothes in the cupboard he turned to her and said "Brandon, I've fallen in love with another woman."

Brandon was astonished that she'd missed all the signs. She'd always regarded her marriage as perfect. Trembling, crying, shaking with abject terror she walked towards the refrigerator and digested the words pinned onto the fridge door, words which have become her mantra:

Know whatever comes unexpected, to be a gift from God that will surely serve you if you use it to your fullest.

Some weeks went by. Her husband was wrestling with his feelings. He still loved his wife but was also passionately in love with another woman. Brandon asked nothing of him but that he was completely honest with her. Finally her husband made his decision. Over the phone, he told Brandon that he was leaving her.

Rage welled up within her. Absolute rage. "This is not right," Brandon told herself, adding, "You're not going to create another tumour." Brandon decided to open her heart to her rage, to her anguish that she had lost the great love of her life.

After the rage came an overwhelming grief. "In six days I lost eleven pounds," she recalled. Then she remembered being told that there was no grief so great that it could not clear itself in seven days if the person was prepared to open out.

Working with her friend, Vicky, Brandon made use of her own *Journey* therapy.

"This growing knot in your stomach, what might it say if the pain could talk?"

"Betrayal," wept Brandon. "That I had been betrayed."

"Let us get to the Source. Come to the campfire and tell me what happened when you were about seven years old."

"I made a vow that I would marry my true love and live happily ever after," sobbed Brandon, realising that in order to heal she had to forgive herself for not sticking to her own promise.

Brandon busied herself with *Journey* seminars and she was in England one year later when her former husband told her that he and his new love wanted to get married.

"Then, I will throw you an engagement party," Brandon heard herself say. She invited all the trainee therapists on her *Journey* course to the celebration. She was busy preparing food when someone called out "They've arrived."

"I froze in abject terror," recalled Brandon. "Then I remembered to take the strongest emotion that I had and went straight into the heart of it. There, I knew

I would find peace. So digging deep into my feeling of terror I took my ex-husband's fiancée into my arms and I hugged her. She looked at me in astonishment and a single tear fell down her cheek. 'So much love,' she whispered. "I knew then that my camp fire was finally healed."

More joy was to follow. Three months later in London Brandon received a call from her daughter Kelly. "I have to see you," she said.

Brandon met her daughter at Heathrow. As they embraced Kelly gave Brandon the joyous news that she was pregnant.

"My grand-daughter is a beautiful child. When I look into her angelic face I see the light shining from her eyes and I rejoice in the living proof that each of us does indeed come into this life as a pristine, pure, flawless diamond."

****

Brandon's two-day *Journey* Intensive Seminar is hard work, both for Brandon, who spends long hours on stage leading the assembled participants in meditation, talking about how she came to The *Journey* process, telling stories of people who have been cured by Journey therapy, listening to participants tell their moving accounts of pain and anguish (and hopefully release of their deeply embedded hurtful memories) and also for the audience who are expected, after careful instruction and with comprehensive notes, watched by vigilant trainers, to lead a randomly chosen partner through the undeniably painful *Journey* method before undergoing the process themselves. The final outcome of which should be healing and transformation at the deepest level.

At the Durban seminar a middle-aged man called Faizel, a victim of Apartheid South Africa, and now a *Journey* therapist in Australia, courageously agreed to undergo the *Journey* therapy on stage in order to demonstrate how it worked.

Cushioned by the love of all those present, Faizel, tears streaming down his face, went deep within himself to dredge up old memories of a hateful White boss, who abused the young and powerless Coloured boy.

Going through the Journey process Brandon reached the point where she was able to ask the younger Faizel, "Even though his/her previous behaviour may not have been acceptable by any standards — even if you in no way condone his/her behaviour, are you willing to completely and utterly forgive him/her from the bottom of your heart?"

After a few moments hesitation, Faizel slowly nodded his head.

Gently Brandon repeated, "When the present you is ready, even though his/her previous behaviour may not have been acceptable by any standards — even if you in no way condone his/her behaviour, are you willing to completely and utterly forgive him/her from the bottom of your heart?"

Once again, Faizel with tears falling freely from his tightly shut eyes, nodded his head. Then Brandon led him and the imagined mentor who accompanied him on this journey from the camp fire, which is the Source of all that is, of unconditional love and peace, back to the filled auditorium.

"How do you feel now?"

"I feel beautiful ... wonderful," murmured Faizel.

"Then go in peace, knowing that your damaged self will continue to heal automatically of its own accord and that the part of you responsible for making your heart beat and your eyes shine and your cells replicate will continue the healing process perfectly without you even thinking about it," smiled Brandon.

Although the call for forgiveness is nothing new — *Father forgive them; for they know what they do* pleaded St Luke, Brandon's call, honed by her obvious sincerity and years spent watching Anthony Robbins at his craft — is pretty highly polished.

****

Overcoming all her adversity-even seeing her divorce from Don ultimately as a great blessing ... "What I didn't realise was that he set me free to do what I am here to do, for since his leaving taking, I have finally been able to give my whole life to Serving Truth," Brandon is today a truly international spiritual leader.

Following the tragic September 11th events in America, Brandon was to send out an e-mail that was circulated round the world. This is an extract from this letter:

As you know, it is the first time in six years that I've returned to the U.S. to offer Journey Work. The summer holidays over, I thought I would be writing to you of an amazing book launch tour and the exciting news that I've been invited to speak before Congress.

I had so wanted to share with you the heart rending stories of our time in Soweto South Africa and our extraordinarily beautiful Therapist Accreditation Programme in Australia, but what is burning to be shared is what is currently in my heart right now.

It was not long ago that a great wall divided Russia from the rest of the western world. To hear their heartfelt support moved me beyond words.

To see Germany standing alongside Israel; to hear the words of alignment from Japan and China; to hear how personally England took the news to heart and immediately offered to stand 'shoulder to shoulder' alongside us — you would have to be made of stone not to be touched.

I have always been more globally orientated that nationally. As a child of the sixties when flag burning was popular, I learned to be untouched by either our flag or our national anthem. Yet when I heard that they played 'The Star Spangled Banner' at the changing of the guards in England, my heart exploded and for the first time in my adult life I actually felt proud to be American.

These words indicate to me that while Brandon may be deeply spiritual, she is still very much part of the modern world — a steel core runs through her slight, blonde, blue-eyed frame and she is not afraid to speak her mind with unflinching conviction.

Indeed on her CD *The War-Zone of the Mind,* Brandon courageously does not edit out a woman who questions her teachings. "When I retreat into my mind, my critical mind, I get very angry and rebellious with you. I don't know whether you are telling the truth or inventing little truths to comfort us.

"At times, I feel the examples you give us are too neat, too easy. Rather than encourage me, they offend me. I don't want to come out of here as a floating can of feathers," remarked this doubting soul.

In reply, after explaining her own truth and reality, Brandon concludes her answer with a tough, no-nonsense, hard-nosed, New Yorker reply: "Those that know Brandon personally would say that she is a fierce raiser of Truth with a crisp, clear cutting mind that can cut through the bullshit of the mind and cut through to the truth that is behind the bullshit."

****

Sometime had elapsed since Brandon's *Journey Intensive* workshop, which I attended. I was standing in a department store and watching the interplay between a confident, self-assured mother and her awkward, teenage daughter whose body language clearly stated, "I feel that I am not good enough. That I am unattractive. That I am unworthy."

I looked at this ungainly girl, at her raw complexion, covered in unsightly acne spots and I am reminded of a story told to me by Jayshree Mannie, former head of *The Journey* in South Africa.

"As a grown woman, I suddenly came out in the most hideous acne. I went from doctor to doctor, but nothing they prescribed helped my blemished skin. I was ashamed. I wanted to hide my scarred and swollen appearance. I went out with my face covered in scarves."

"Finally, I stumbled across Brandon Bays' *The Journey*. I decided to try the process. So I peeled off my armour and shed layer upon layer of old emotional issues and blockages. As I did so and as I experienced the love, beauty and truth that is at Source, my skin began to clear.

"I have no way of expressing gratitude to Brandon, except by devoting all my time and effort to making *The Journey* known in this part of the world. I don't feel that only adults need this cellular healing. I want *The Journey* work to go into the schools, so that no child, no matter how difficult the circumstances, will feel himself/herself to be unworthy or unloved," Jayshree told me.

Now, as I looked at this awkward teenager as she reluctantly looked through the clothing rails, I had a brief vision of Brandon herself taking this unfortunate youngster through *The Journey* process. I imagined the young girl being told that she was beautiful and special and that the Divine was within her.

In my mind's eye I saw her layers of hurt and pain, her hostility towards her mother being peeled away as she forgave the older woman for all the anguish that she was unwittingly causing her.

For the first time I noticed how beautiful the young girl's blue eyes were as she threw back her hunched shoulders and walked confidently out of the store, her head held high.

www.thejourney.com

VICTOR VERMEULEN

FORMER CHAMPION CRICKETER, MOTIVATIONAL SPEAKER & QUADRIPLEGIC

A MAN OF IMMOVABLE FAITH

"I will live each day in courage and gratitude, showing a deep sense of appreciation to people like my Mom, who has encouraged my progress and development and supported my efforts to be the very best that I can be.
I will operate by the values of integrity and continuously strive to fulfil the commitments I have made to the people around me and to myself. I will never take life for granted and I will endeavour to live each day to the full, remaining aware that my strength of character and optimism can make an essential difference in the lives of others. My sense of self-worth is constantly reinforced by my own personal triumphs and victories. I will not allow myself to become bogged down in self-pity or anger, because I realise that life is too precious to waste. Regardless of the fact that my physical body is confined to a wheel chair, I will encourage my spirit to soar, so that I can help those in need through my ability to motivate and inspire."

Victor Vermeulen

Victor Ben Ned Vermeulen was born on July 16th 1973 and looked, said his mother Isabella, "like a marshmallow. His skin was white, his cheeks were pink, his eyes were blue and his hair was red when I took him home from the hospital ..."

"Hey," interrupted Victor, "You said you took me from a tree. You cut down my tail and I jumped into your arms."

There is a lot of laughter and playful bantering in the Vermeulen home, despite the fact that a diving accident when he was nineteen left Victor with a broken neck and mobility only in his head, neck and shoulders. Nothing it seems can break his indomitable spirit.

"You can't sit there moaning about your lot in life, you've got to get on with it. Deal with the hand that God has dealt you. Be the best you can under the circumstances in which you find yourself. And you need to laugh — you can't get through this life without a sense of humour," smiled Victor.

A sense of humour is something that he has in abundance. My interview with him is interrupted by a call from one of the airline personnel, who wants to know what his requirements on board the aircraft will be when he undertakes yet another of his inspirational motivational talks, which he does, not just in South Africa, but all over the world. This is a man who might not be able to walk but who is nevertheless flying high.

Understandably, Isabella is annoyed. "We are Frequent Flyers on the Voyager Programme, yet they keep losing his details," she complained.

Speaking into a small microphone as he lies on his specially adapted hospital bed at his home, Victor tells the girl at the other end of the line that, "No, he isn't a cripple, he's a quadriplegic and that he is paralysed and that he will therefore need a forklift to hoist him into the plane."

He relates this to her in a matter-of-fact tone without a hint of self-pity in his voice.

"I'm so sorry," said the girl.

"There's no need to be," replied Victor, consoling her. "I'm not sorry for myself."

Her long list of questions continues for the difficulties of transporting a 6' 3" quadriplegic are numerous. "Will you need oxygen on the flight?"

"No, I can breathe on my own." This statement bears testimony to Victor's fighting spirit and courage. For the doctors told Victor after the accident that he would never breathe by himself again. Bit by bit, however, Victor, refusing to take his doctors prognostications as gospel, taught himself to breathe without the respirator to which he was attached to after the accident.

Finally, the conversation with the lady from the airline ends. "Are you sure there's nothing else you would like to know?" demanded Victor good humouredly. "My shoe size, perhaps?"

****

Victor was an active, if accident-prone child. On weekends, he would rush into his parents' room and jump onto Isabella and Tokkie's bed. One day he landed on the bed with such force that he broke the base clean in half.

When he was eight months old, Victor developed abscesses in both ears, which had to be removed by emergency surgery, for if they had burst, Victor would have been deaf.

After her grandmother's death, Isabella opened a hairdressing salon. Victor used to accompany her there. Unable to sit still for a moment, one day he banged his head against the wall and broke his nose.

A month later, when Isabella was feeling unwell, accompanied by her young son, she went to see the doctor in hospital. Following her examination, the doctor offered to give Victor a check-up.

"His appendix is abnormally long. It will have to be removed immediately," said the doctor.

That night Isabella slept on the floor of the hospital next to Victor's cot. It was perhaps a foretaste of what was to come. For following her son's accident, Isabella has not spent one night in her bedroom. She prefers to sleep on the couch next to her son's bed.

"What if he gets cold during the night and needs the blanket pulled up? He might be thirsty and need a drink of water," she told me without a trace of self-pity.

When Victor was three years old, Isabella, gazing out of the window, saw the toddler playing with his older cousins. Victor was jumping from the top of the gate.

She would have stopped the game then and there had she been aware that the purpose of the game was to see who could jump from the highest point. Highly competitive and always anxious to win, little Victor ended up jumping off the roof.

Seemingly, and somewhat surprisingly, Victor had not injured himself. However, the following morning, when the child tried to get up, his legs crumbled beneath him. An X-ray revealed that Victor had pulled his leg right out of its socket. He would have to be in bed for four months.

"I remember lying in bed, all my friends and cousins playing outside. My Mom gave me puzzles and read to me and we listened to records, but it wasn't the same. It was very frustrating." Victor pauses and gives a quick grin. "I think now, maybe the big guy upstairs was preparing me. Maybe he wanted to see if I could handle the situation."

Always on the move, with remarkable co-ordination and with boundless energy, four year old Victor went with Isabella to see *Saturday Night Fever*.

Fascinated by the dancing, when they got home Victor put his half-brother, Teddy's, copy of the record on the gramophone and began gyrating in a remarkably good imitation of John Travolta's *Staying Alive* routine, wiggling his little bum and pointing his fingers to the heavens.*

When the Vermeulen family went to a record bar, Isabella noticed that young Victor was missing. Then she saw a crowd was gathering and she knew that Victor must somehow be involved. To the delight of the crowd, the youngster was performing his John Travolta routine, boogying and bopping like a professional.

Clearly, Victor was born to perform. "The shop manager even offered to pay Victor to dance at the shop on weekends," laughed Isabella.

****

These days, Victor is still performing. One August evening in October 2003, I was privileged to hear this accomplished speaker in action, addressing the pupils of St Andrews School for Girls on their annual speech day.

Looking handsome in a suit and tie, he was wheeled onto the stage by Isabella, who, always conscious of his needs, stood unobtrusively behind her son. A slight inclination of his head and she was immediately there to give him water.

Ever the joker, Victor told the school's headmistress, Pauline Jackson, who, by some coincidence, once taught the younger Victor, that he was glad to see that she still had a great pair of legs.

Just as Isabella once had to watch her hyper active son's every action, so Mrs Jackson paid careful attention to Victor's words in case he said something

---

* The Victor Within by Victor Vermeulen and Jonathan Acer

too risqué. "Despite my accident," smiled Victor, "I can still play the piano. No wonder they call me Clever Dick."

His speech is sprinkled with jokes like this. "I would have loved to be a stand-up comedian ... only I can't stand."

Despite the humour, the story Victor tells on stage is deeply moving and with its slick slide presentation it is highly professional.

The audience learned of Victor's illustrious sports career. Given a much coveted Duncan Fearley Magnum cricket bat as a young boy, by the time he was about ten years old, Victor was to score his first century with this bat.

At his primary school there was a tradition that any boy who scored a century, would be given a cricket bat. Until Victor came to the school, no boy had ever scored a century — a pretty difficult feat because the pupils only played 25 overs per side. Nevertheless, Victor was to score a century once in Standard 3, four times in Standard 4 and four times in Standard 5.

After receiving his prized bat, the headmaster, Mr Labuschagne, told him that he didn't need any more bats — he was bankrupting the school. Recognising Victor's talent, Mr Labuschagne used to take Victor into the school hall and threw tennis balls at him so that he could practice his cricket strokes. "He was a great coach," recalled Victor with obvious affection.

By the time Victor was twelve, he was captain of the Northern Transvaal team, earning the nickname Turbo because he was so quick running between the wickets. Not only was Victor an accomplished cricketer, he was also an excellent rugby player, being twice selected in his final years of schooling to play for the Craven Week finals.

Ever the joker, when he scored a try against rival school, King David Linksfield High School, much to the delight of the spectators, Vic celebrated by doing the Michael Jackson moonwalk under the rugby poles.

With his boundless natural sporting talent, Victor also excelled at South African Schools Soccer. So much so that when he was fifteen he was invited by Jomo Sono, the South African soccer legend, to play professionally for Jomo's Premier League team, Cosmos. After giving this invitation serious consideration, Victor declined the offer. Cricket was his first love.

Thousands of schoolboy cricketers attempt to make the team that plays at Nuffield Week and only thirteen boys are chosen to represent the South African

Schools' side. When Victor represented Transvaal at Nuffield Week, he put in a masterful performance. In just over three hours, he hit twenty-two fours and a huge six to score an unbeaten 175 runs. A record which remains unbeaten to this day.

Not that cricket was Victor's whole life. A party animal, Vic could be up all night having a good time. Much to the envy of his team mates who would have to go to sleep early before a match, the next day, showing no ill effects after his night on the town, Victor would still produce the highest score of the game.

After leaving school, Victor was snapped up to play for the Transvaal A under twenty-four team. In a match against Natal, the game was petering out to a draw. Victor's bat handle broke and he selected to play with a new bat — one on which the guys had pasted a naked woman centrefold.

The first ball Victor blocked, hit the girl on her breasts. Turning to the umpire, Victor called out "Tit shot, hey?" Still brandishing the 'Porno Bat', Victor was able to hit the ball outside the grounds for a tremendous six. Loud enough for the people close by to hear Victor remarked, "Right in the sweet spot."

Just four months after he left school, Victor made his debut against an international side, when his team, the legendary Transvaal A played against English county team, Worcestershire. This should have been the proudest moment of his life, instead of which it was marred by tragedy. Vic's beloved father, Henry, who was affectionately known as Tokkie, the young cricketer's most ardent and loyal fan, was murdered.

Tokkie, a sales representative for a grocery supply company, was working in the townships, where he sold mainly to small family shops. On the morning of March 16th 1992, three men were hanging around outside the shop where Tokkie had been to collect some money owing from a difficult client.

As he was climbing back into the seat of his small truck, these three men started firing shots at Tokkie. One bullet landed in his back, but somehow he managed to continue driving, as the men continued firing, smashing the vehicle windows with their bullets.

Tokkie drove the truck to Garankua Bakery, where the owner of the shop had been a client of his for the past twenty years. Tokkie gave him the money he had just collected for safe keeping and, leaning heavily against the shop counter, asked for help to the nearest hospital as he had just been shot.

In the operating theatre of Garankua Hospital, Tokkie suffered a heart attack, although the doctor managed to stabilise him. He then had another heart attack and died, leaving his widow Isabella and son Victor heartbroken and devastated.

"I don't think our relationship with Tokkie has ended," said Victor thoughtfully. "We still love him and talk about him. The lessons he taught us will never die and our fond memories of him will always remain. There is definitely an afterlife. This life is just a dream. This life is like going to school. We are here to learn lessons. Only when you've passed one test, can you progress to the next level. When I think about it, I'm sure that we'll see Dad again."

Victor was about to achieve his life's ambition, to play at Lord's Cricket Grounds, without his father there to watch him.

The hard lessons that Victor has learned, have given him wisdom and insight that he is now able to impart to others. "Don't take what you've got for granted," he tells the hushed audience of scholars and parents who fill the auditorium. "Go and give your dad a big hug. Say how much you love each other. You never know when it will be taken away."

Just as Victor the sportsman reached new heights, so Victor the quadriplegic turned motivational speaker, holds his audience spellbound with the brilliance of his delivery.

In one moment you're wiping away the tears as you hear Victor talk of his father's tragic death; the next you're crying with laughter.

"I realised my dream. There I was playing cricket in England. My team, Transvaal, wasn't doing well. We were 52 for 5 when I went out to bat.

"The bowler, a 6' 6" guy, called Joel Garner, sent the ball screaming down the pitch. I suddenly realised that I had forgotten my 'box'— essential equipment for a guy who doesn't want to get hit where it hurts. I had a choice. Either to bat my best or else to protect my goolies. I decided to do what any wise man would have done; I protected my goolies."

The delighted schoolgirl audience applauds this story as Victor, a consummate master of timing continues, "When I returned from England in 1992, I had high hopes of making the South African team. I played a few friendly matches and then I was invited to the Wanderers Club cricket braai. That evening, I dived into the pool and I broke my neck."

Victor paused for a moment. "Sometimes in life things aren't going to go your way. Sure, I could have played cricket for South Africa. But then would I have been able to influence as many people as I do now through my talking? I might be a quadriplegic, but there's nothing wrong with my mind and my soul ... two things which are often neglected in this materialistic world.

"It's no use concentrating on what you don't have. There is a plan. God's plan. I urge you to make the most of the talent that God has given you. Don't live in the past. Don't live in the future. Live for the present. That's why they call life a gift."

****

A lesser woman than Isabella Vermeulen might never have risen from the ashes of her destroyed life. In a short seven months span, she was widowed and her son was rendered a helpless quadriplegic.

Isabella and Victor are with each other twenty-four hours a day. She is responsible for bathing her son, washing his hair, cleaning his ears, blowing his nose, bathing him, exercising his fingers, arms and legs, removing his stools and catheterising him. If it wasn't for his mother's indomitable will to do all that she can for her son, Victor would find himself in the care of a round-the-clock team of nurses.

Life for Isabella has never been easy. Her mother died when she was only two weeks old and she and her three siblings were raised by her grandmother and by her grandmother's son who was a bachelor.

"Where was your father?"

"My father was a very religious man. He gave everything to the church, but after my mother's death, scared of being hurt again, he began to neglect his own children. He rode a Harley Davidson and he was always away going here, there and everywhere."

"Did you love your granny?"

"She was very strict, but she was like a mother to me. When my sisters went to high school my dad got a little flat in town for them and my brother went to stay with my dad in the Bushveld. I stayed behind with my gran and my uncle. It was a very happy time for me.

"My granny always suffered from bronchitis. When I was in my mid-twenties, she became gravely ill. One night, while I was sleeping next to her, in case she needed me, she began to choke and she died.

"After her death, my uncle sort of lost it. He never married and he became depressed. I decided to move to town and I opened a hairdressing salon. What was it called again, Victor?"

"My mother," Victor told me, "has had a slight stroke. Sometimes she can't remember things. She's also had cancer."

"Yes, but we won't discuss that," interrupts Isabella. "You need to take what has happened and move one. It's no good living in the 'what if' syndrome."

"Then you married Dad."

"Yes. During the ceremony, the priest produced a rosebud from his pocket, which he had picked that day. He said to us, 'Henry and Isabella, look at this rose. See the tiny thorns on the stem. You will have thorny days in your marriage: when you do, look at this rosebud to remind yourself of how beautiful it is, and remember what you promised each other here today.' When my husband died, I put the rosebud in the coffin with him."*

"You've certainly had some difficult times ..."

"You can get through anything if you believe in God. God is first and foremost. You need to put your faith in this Higher Being. There must be something like that. You haven't got anything if you haven't got something to believe in."

"Aren't you angry with God after all the adversity that's happened to you?"

I'm not bitter. I'm just so proud of Victor. Of the wonderful, caring and compassionate man that he has become. He is an inspiration to so many people."

"And you, Victor? Are you angry about what has happened to you?"

"No, I miss having my independence and my privacy. But would I change diving into the swimming pool? No, I wouldn't. Since the accident, I've learnt so much about compassion. For most people of my age their biggest problem is that they've lost their girlfriend or their boyfriend. They haven't had to go through what I've been through.

---

* The Victor Within by Victor Vermeulen and Jonathan Acer

"But what I know is that what is right for us, isn't necessarily right for God. Through my accident and the talks that I give, I've been able to reach so many people. So what if I'd been the best cricketer? What is a celebrity anyway? It's so superficial."

"Victor, do you remember that flight we were on and I had to change your catheter?"

"I use a condom catheter and it came off. Mom asked the stewardess to hold up a blanket so that we could have a bit of privacy. Well, the stewardess obviously never heard mom's request. So I took the blanket and put it between my teeth," Victor said laughing together with Isabella.

"You've kept your sense of humour."

"Sure. Lots of religious people can't laugh. But you've got to laugh. If you don't laugh, you'll cry. Mom and I make a good team. We make each other laugh."

It's lucky that Vic and Isabella can see the funny side of life, for the endless work of looking after a quadriplegic is certainly no laughing matter.

The Vermeulen household routine works as follows: "At 10 pm Isabella turns me in order to prevent bedsores. This can take up to twenty minutes. Then I'm strapped to the bed in case I have spasms during the night. At 3 am, the alarm clock rings. Then Mom turns me for the second time during the night. While I'm turned, we catheterise. My stomach works three times a week, so if it's 'bollie' night, after the catheterising, my mom inserts a suppository. At 4.30 am my stomach works. But if it doesn't, Mom has to remove the stools manually. At 4.45 am we are finally able to settle down and get some sleep."

"When do you start your morning care of Vic?"

"The alarm rings at 7.30 am. Then the morning routine starts. I give him breakfast, off go his pyjamas; then I shave him, clean his teeth, sponge bath him, catheterise him, wash his hair…"

"Yeah. Mom does the Shit, Shave and Shampoo thing every day. If we don't work together, we won't win together."

"Yet neither of you seems to be the slightest bit bitter …"

"Accidents happen. It's no use asking Why me? Rather ask Why not me? And remember there's always someone worse off. At the Hope Home, I met this guy who was paralysed and blind. Character doesn't grow in a comfort zone. Don't give up on life. Winners make it happen."

MAUREEN WIGODER

MOTHER & GRANDMOTHER

FINDING LIFE AFTER LOSS

THE CREDO OF THE COMPASSIONATE FRIENDS

*We need not walk alone
We are The Compassionate Friends.
We reach out to each other with love,
with understanding and with hope.
Our children have died at all ages
and from many different causes,
but out love for our children unites us.
Your pain becomes my pain,
just as your hope becomes my hope.
We come together from all walks of life,
from many different circumstances.
We are a unique family because
we represent many races and creeds.
We are young and we are old.
Some of us are far along in our grief,
but others still feel a grief so fresh
and so intensely painful
that we feel helpless and see no hope.
Some of us have found our faith
to be a source of strength.
Some of us are struggling to find answers.
Some of us are angry,
filled with guilt or deep depression;
others radiate an inner peace.
But whatever pain we bring
to this gathering of The Compassionate Friends,
it is pain we will share,
just as we share with each other*

our love for our children.
We are all seeking and struggling
to build a future for ourselves,
but we are committed to
building that future together,
as we reach out to each other in love
and share the pain, as well as the joy,
share the anger, as well as the peace,
share the faith, as well as the doubts
and help each other to grieve,
as well as to grow.
We need not walk alone.

We are sitting on the veranda of Maureen's charming suburban home. Although the garden is compact, the lush greenery of the foliage gives one the feeling that is in a verdant forest. As we sip our coffee, the sun is shining and a gentle breeze is agitating the wind chimes, causing their own gentle harmony. The house harbours a wonderful feeling of warmth and tranquillity.

The great tragedy that plunged the Wigoder family into grief, the death of their nineteen year old son Alan in 1985, while still painful, has been put to rest.

"Alan," said Maureen, "is my eternal teenager. I know that, albeit he is in another realm, he is still with us, watching over me and my husband, Aubrey. I want him to be proud of me. He would not want me to live my remaining years in a cloud of grief.

"I owe it to him and to my two other children, Larry and Debbie, who are now adults, not to live in the dark mire of despondency and despair that enveloped me after his death. When I go I would like my children to rejoice in my living — and not to be blighted by my going."

Maureen, daughter of Sonia, a Lithuanian Communist and an atheist, and South African born Julius Taylor, grew up in Bloemfontein, in a household rich in the Yiddish culture, but devoid of much conventional religion. "My father Julius attended synagogue only on the high holy days and he was also a follower of the late Kavi Yogiraj Mani Finger. I remember my dad standing on his head in our lounge and saying that the only thing that made sense was reincarnation," reminisced Maureen, with a smile.

"My mother, Sonia wrote many detailed stories with amazing recall about her life in Lithuania, which she bequeathed to her grandchildren. "One of the stories was about my grandmother, who appeared to have psychic abilities. This is what my mother wrote:

The family who lived next door to us included two grown-up daughters who had lost their mother. The father soon remarried a much younger woman, by whom he had a baby boy.

In the early hours of the morning, whilst I was still very young, I was woken up by my mother's voice, which sounded very agitated and upset. I heard my mother telling my father that she had had a terrible dream in which she saw the dead first wife going through the wall of the next door house into the boy's room. Later that morning the baby died after choking himself on a little bottle top that he was playing with.

"My grandmother had witnessed the return of the first wife from the spirit world in order to take the dead baby 'home.'"

I became terribly upset, my mother wrote, *and very frightened. When I began to dress, standing up on my bed, I suddenly saw through my window, which faced the next door window, the baby being lifted by a woman, while another woman poured water on the stiff, wax-like corpse. I screamed at the sight of death.*

"The scene took me years to forget. I kept remembering my mother's dream," said Maureen.

After completing her schooling in Johannesburg, Maureen went to Teacher's Training College, studying to become a nursery school teacher.

In 1960 she married Aubrey Wigoder, whom she fondly describes as 'the one stable influence in my life.' Within seven years this union produced three children — two boys and one girl.

"I celebrated the birth of our oldest son, Larry. When my youngest child, my daughter Debbie was born, I cried with joy," commented Maureen. "Yet when my middle child, Alan, was born, despite the fact that he was a planned and much wanted baby, I had a strange reaction — I was overcome with a deep sense of sadness. I think I knew, at soul level, that this child would not be with me for long."

Larry, the eldest son's birth, was extremely difficult for his mother. "I never had the instinct to push," recalled Maureen. "As a result the baby was tearing me inside. I lost a lot of blood and I had to have a heavy blood transfusion. I was in the most unbelievable pain.

"And when he was born, with the release from pain, I experienced a sense of great euphoria and ecstasy. I can't explain it, except to say that I had an out of body experience and within my trance-like state, I actually saw and understood it to be an explanation of the creation. I saw wheels, within wheels, within wheels. They were all rotating and in the middle there was an open round space and within this space there was a tremendously powerful magnetic Life Force, The Creator, who was holding all these rotating circles together.

"At first, I wanted to know where I was in this scheme of things. But then, the thought came to me that it actually didn't matter where I was for I was part of the universe and the universe was part of me. I knew with certainty that every little thing that was within these circles had to be there in order to maintain the whole harmony and balance. Every insect, every leaf, every blade of grass.

"When I told this story to a rabbi he looked at me in amazement saying that I had achieved what the Jewish mystics aspire to see — the creation as it happened."

Some years later, Maureen was to undergo another mystical experience in that she had a near-death experience. Having delayed undergoing a necessary hysterectomy, she was rushed by ambulance to hospital, suffering from massive internal haemorrhaging. Her doctors feared for her life. In her semi-conscious state, Maureen heard two women praying for her: "Liewe Here, in the naam van Jesus, bespaar hierdie arme vrou."*

This prayer brought little comfort to the patient. As one of only two Jewish scholars in primary school in Bloemfontein during the Second World War, Maureen had been the victim of anti-Semitism. Her classmates called her a Christ killer and told her that the Jews were to blame for all that was evil in the world. She therefore had the conviction that it was the existence of Jesus that caused her suffering. Thus in her state of near death, the mention of Jesus brought her little comfort.

"Then a voice said to me, 'Jesus didn't do this to you. People did this to you.' I experienced such a feeling of such sadness, fearing that I was about to leave this life, still filled with old prejudices. I knew then that if you don't sort out all

---

* Dear God, in the name of Jesus, spare this unfortunate woman.

your prejudices in this life, you have a great deal of reconciliatory work to do on The Other Side.

"It was also revealed to me, that, warts and all, I was about to depart this life exactly the way I was. You are not about to become a better person because you are entering a spiritual dimension.

"As I lay in the emergency ward I felt myself go through a tunnel. It was the most wonderful release. We don't realise how shackled the soul is in this physical body.

"There was such an amazing peace and harmony and waiting for me there, enveloped in a brilliant light, with the most welcoming smile, was this friend who had died recently. I thought, hell, we don't die alone. There is always someone there to meet us.

"It took a great deal of will power to turn back. What I felt was so indescribably beautiful. I said please don't call me now. My children are too young. They still need their mother. I don't know if it was my imagination but I thought I saw a lost a look of disappointment on my friend's face as she disappeared.

"I wondered if she knew that I was taking on too much karma if I came back. That I would still have to survive the enormous tragedy of my son's death? But if I was taking on too much karma, it's typical of me, because I overdo everything," said Maureen with a wry laugh.

Her near death experience was verified by her gynaecologist who gently chided Maureen: "Do you realise what a scare you gave us? Do you know that you were clinically dead? For two minutes, you had no blood pressure, no pulse."

Maureen reflected for a moment before saying," Death is something to look forward to. We are actually imprisoned in our bodies. It's just so beautiful on The Other Side. I now have no fear of death whatsoever. I wish people could go through this experience and then come back again. They'll never be the same again. They'll see for themselves that death is not a dark cloud hanging over one, but rather it is a joyous release."

****

The week before Alan's death, Maureen had a premonition that something terrible was going to happen. "My whole world is going to fall apart," she told her husband and a close friend. "I don't know exactly what it is that is going to happen. I only know that although I will be shaken to the core, I will somehow come through it."

Alan had always been a secretive child. He liked to keep his bedroom door locked while he worked in his room. He didn't want to be disturbed while he listened to classical music or played computerised chess. Aged nineteen, almost twenty, he was in his second year of study for his Bachelor of Science degree.

Science was not the only thing that fascinated him. Alan also liked to discover the inner working of things. So he could often be found studying instruments like microscopes and telescopes and cameras.

For some reason that she cannot explain, a week before her son died, Maureen took the spare key of the French doors that led from Alan's bedroom to the garden and placed it on her dressing table in the bedroom. Because the doors were made from glass, as a security measure, Alan himself always took his own key out of the lock in the evening.

"Why have I got this key?" Maureen wondered as the week went by. "Why don't I put it back in Alan's room?" But some inner voice prevented her from removing the key from her dressing table.

"It was very strange. Very strange indeed."

Her behaviour that week was also out of keeping. For she felt compelled to take out the drawings that Alan had done at nursery school, all his old school reports and go through them with him.

"With Larry and Debbie I might have kept the odd report or picture, but with Alan I had each and every report that he'd ever received; and many of the pictures that he'd drawn or painted.

"That day, about two days before he died, as mother and son looked through these records of his young life, they talked, for the first time, not as mother and son, but as equals."

The breadth of Alan's knowledge astounded Maureen. He not only had a deep grasp of spiritual things, unbeknown to his mother, he had been studying art, literature, classical music, philosophy. He spoke of the spirituality in Rembrandt's Night Watch with a maturity that amazed her.

"Alan, I didn't know you were interested in all these things. In addition to working for a science degree, you seem to be working towards your Bachelor of Arts degree," joked his proud mother.

"My brain will not stop. I have so much to learn," Alan replied. "It's as if I have to pass some exam. I just can't put the brakes on."

Maureen poured herself another cup of coffee as she reflected, "I reckon his soul knew that he had to go. So he was required to squeeze in a certain amount of knowledge in a limited time."

To earn extra pocket money Alan had been working as a parking attendant at a motor show in his spare time. The pay was good. He told his parents that he was going to buy himself a gun. Maureen was horrified. "He was a gentle boy. He always used to say that the only way that he would go into the army was as a chef."

"Why do you want a gun?"

"I'm going to practise target shooting," Alan told his parents.

Once he had the gun in his possession, Alan wore it strapped to his ankle. He asked his mother if she could let out the bottom seam of his jeans as he didn't want the bulge of the gun to show.

When Aubrey returned home from work on that fateful Friday evening, Maureen told him, "I know what my terrible feeling is about. It's to do with Alan. If he goes out tonight, then everything will be all right. But if he stays home, something awful will happen. On reflection, that was a strange and contradictory statement to have made."

A popular boy, Alan had many friends. He was going to see a Beatles movie at the local suburban cinema with one of them that Friday night. The boys were to have gone to the eight o' clock show, but at the last minute his friend phoned to ask if they couldn't rather go to the ten o' clock movie as he still had to work on his university project.

That night Alan gulped down, rather than sipped, the traditional Jewish Sabbath wine. Maureen advised him that wine must be sipped slowly, asking him why he appeared to be in such a hurry. "Aw Ma! Don't tell me how to drink."

Trying to ignore the anxious feeling she was experiencing, Maureen had a cup of tea and a slice of chocolate cake. She offered some of the cake to Alan who declined it and went to his room. A while later, thoroughly ill at ease, looking for an excuse to enter Alan's room, Maureen went and knocked at Alan's door.

"Are you sure you don't want some cake?"

"I told you I didn't want any," replied Alan with some irritation.

Thinking back on that evening, Maureen said, "I also remember looking into Alan's eyes that day and I had a strange realisation. "The light of my father is in his eyes I thought with wonder."

Reluctantly, Maureen returned to the sitting room, feeling increasingly apprehensive. Another friend arrived to visit Alan. "Go and see him. He's in his room," said Maureen.

The friend returned a few moments later. "I've been knocking at the door, but there is no reply," he stated.

Alarmed, Aubrey and Maureen knocked on Alan's door once more.

Still no reply. Aubrey immediately took a tall ladder so that he could peer into Alan's room through the fanlight. "He's lying on the floor and making funny noises," he cried.

"I knew then that he was dead," said Maureen softly.

"How can we get into his room?" demanded Aubrey.

"I have the key of the French door," replied his wife.

On entering though the garden doors, his shocked parents found Alan lying on the floor, his gun between his legs in the position he used to hold it in order to clean it, except that he was lying down instead of being in his usual sitting position.

"The bullet had entered his skull and he was brain dead on his arrival at hospital, although mercifully he died a few hours later," recalled Maureen. "In fairness to Alan I would like to state that the coroner recorded a verdict not of suicide, but of accidental death.

"My husband said that he would have preferred it if Alan had committed suicide, for then it would have at least been his choice to die. I have come to realise that there are no accidents — you go when you are meant to go."

There was another strange occurrence on the night of the accident. In Maureen's words: "Aubrey and I needed a lift home from the hospital and a most empathetic woman, warm, loving and very comforting took us in hand. She was dressed in the uniform of the operating theatre and I remember looking down at her feet as she drove — she was wearing theatre slippers.

"In my state of shock, I could not remember the woman's name and when I phoned the hospital at a later date in order to thank her for her kindness, despite supplying them with many relevant details, no-one had any record of her. I was very disappointed as I felt that we had established a special bond with her.

"I sometimes wonder if she was an angel sent to help us in our time of anguish."

****

Several days after Alan's sudden death, Maureen who was totally exhausted and in a state of extreme shock, went to bed early. Almost the moment her head touched the pillow, she started to shake uncontrollably. She felt that the bed was also beginning to shake violently. Deeply concerned, Aubrey said that he was going to call the doctor. "Please don't. Just let me be," replied his wife with astonishing calmness.

"The shaking became even more violent, until the whole room seemed to be moving. I felt that I was being catapulted outside of my body. I actually looked down and I could see myself lying on the bed. I felt as is my arms were outstretched and I could feel the vibrations coming out of every finger. Just like a radio transmitter.

"Then suddenly I had a complete mood swing and a sense of perfect calm and peace came over me. I could not understand this, but several years later, with my increasing awareness and understanding, I realised that what I experienced was that I had tuned into the peace that Alan felt when his soul was leaving his body.

"Aubrey said that I was talking and talking, but I didn't know this. I think I must have been in such a deep trance. Then it became lighter and all I know is that I made direct contact with my late grandfather, who had died when I was two years old. I had no memory of him, yet I was able to recognise his vibrations. (Many years before a psychic had told me that my grandfather was my guardian angel.)

"I made contact with my father, again on a vibrational level. I also made contact with Alan, although his vibration was weaker."

Maureen grew quiet for a few moments. "I started to speak with my grandfather and my father. I was extremely angry. "Why didn't you call me?" I asked. "Why did Alan have to die? He was only nineteen.

"The answer came, very clearly. They said 'Alan's life and the lessons he had to learn were completed. You still have lessons to do. Your mission on earth has not been finished.'

"There could be no argument. I understood exactly that this was the absolute truth and I became quite submissive. Then I said, But Alan was still a teenager. They laughed at me. Not derisively, but as if I was a child who had made a cute naive remark.

"They replied 'Your time is man-made. We live in the time of eternity. Nineteen or ninety, where we live is like the blink of an eyelid.'

"Then Aubrey said to me, 'Ask if they are all together?' Suddenly, a form of stick-like drawings came into my head. And I said to Aubrey, 'Yes, they are together, in a way that we do not understand. Actually, I did understand it when I was in the trance, but the minute I 'woke up', I could no longer comprehend exactly how they were together.

"Then I said to Alan — something I would not have done today with my greater understanding of life and death — "Help me. I am missing you so much.

"Alan responded: 'Why would you want me to return to life on earth which is so filled with difficulties? Where I am there is no pain. The memory of pain is already beginning to fade. I cannot help you. Only you can help yourself.'

"I also asked why he was so careless with the gun? To which he replied 'Why do you ask me that when you knew that I was going to leave?' "

This vision of eternal life, while bringing a measure of comfort to Maureen, still did not lessen her anguish. She felt utterly alone and unable to speak to any of her friends and relatives about her despair at losing her beloved child.

No-one in her immediate circle had ever lost a child. "I felt that I should be pickled in formaldehyde and placed in a jar with a label 'Typical specimen of a bereaved mother,' " she reflected wryly.

Her pain was unbearable. "I remember a night which I call the dark night of the soul where I was in so much pain that I felt that I was not made of flesh and bone, but it seemed to me that I was reduced to a pulsating blob of protoplasm, lying on the bed throbbing with the most excruciating pain. I felt that I had lost my humanity."

It was a time of suffering for the whole family. Shortly after Alan died, his sister Debbie dreamt that she was sitting with friends in her bedroom, which was next door to Alan's room, when strange, animal-like noises came from his room with increasing intensity. Debbie was becoming more and more embarrassed and uncomfortable as her friends began to comment on these sounds.

Then Debbie saw Alan in his familiar brown towelling gown, sliding snake-like to the bathroom, making these inhuman noises. Turning to his sister Alan said, 'Would you have liked me to be like that? That's how I would have been had I survived.'

"I realised then that it was better that he had died rather than be faced with a living death," remarked Maureen quietly.

****

It was at this dark time in her life that Maureen was able to turn to the recently formed South African branch of Compassionate Friends.

Linda Abelheim, grieving for the death of her young son, Joel, and feeling, like Maureen, totally isolated in her grief, decided in 1983 to start Compassionate Friends, a League of Bereaved Parents.

It was Linda's belief that not even trained counsellors can give the understanding and comfort that bereaved parents need to work through their sadness and loss.

Linda maintained that mothers need special help and that only a similarly bereaved person can understand the feelings of guilt and strange mixed reactions of a mother and help her move back into a circle of family and friends without her sorrow affecting everyone.

She understood that fathers needed help because they have to store up their grief and often they behave in strange aggressive ways towards wives and surviving children. She knew too that siblings required help with regard to the loss of their brother or sister and they also needed to understand their mother's grief.

"If I can establish an organisation that will help other bereaved parents and families, then my son will not have died in vain," she declared.

For Maureen, the counselling, love, support and friendship she and her husband received from The Compassionate Friends was to prove invaluable along her long and difficult road to recovery.

In the fullness of time, she felt herself sufficiently healed to become a counsellor for the organisation and today, while she no longer counsels, Maureen is still associated with Compassionate Friends, working as a librarian — one who is possessed of a deep and special understanding of the spiritual books that these particular readers need in order to find some explanation of the profound tragedy that has forever altered their lives.

Where does Maureen find herself today, now that some years have elapsed since Alan's tragic death?

"Well, in the intervening years I've had a lot of dreams where we are together. I know, beyond any shadow of a doubt, that when I die we will be reunited. The thing that has pulled me through is that I want him to be proud of me. I don't want to give him the burden that because of his passing my life is over, because I think that's a terrible burden."

In his famous book *Man's Search for Meaning* the late Holocaust survivor and psychiatrist Victor Frankl wrote that even in the most tragic circumstances there are still choices — positive or negative, to be made.

Maureen has taken this message to heart. "I could choose to be bitter or twisted and become a professional mourner or I could choose to turn my suffering into something positive to be used to help others. I strive to achieve the latter."

www.compassionatefriends.org

CARI-ANN

CHANNEL, SPIRITUAL COUNSELLOR, EPIDERMOLYSIS BULLOSA SUFFERER

LAUGHTER IS THE BEST MEDICINE

From **TO A CHILD**

By what astrology of fear or hope
Dare I to cast thy horoscope!
Like the new moon thy life appears;
A little strip of silver light,
And widening outward into night
The shadowy disk of future years;
And yet upon its outer rim,
A luminous circle, faint and dim,
And scarcely visible to us here,
Rounds and completes the perfect sphere;
A prophecy and intimation,
A pale and feeble adumbration,
Of the great world of light, that lies
Behind all human destinies.

Henry Wadsworth Longfellow

The pain started on the day Cari-Ann was born. Her mother, Ruth, sporty and popular, initially rejected her new baby with the sprinkling of characteristic Epidermolysis Bullosa blisters on her fingertips. "I was the sort of person who couldn't even look at people in wheelchairs," she remarked with a rueful laugh, "so when Cari-Ann was whisked off to an incubator for three days, I initially found bonding with her difficult."

Epidermolysis Bullosa (EB) is a rare genetic disease characterised by the presence of a free floating epidermis, with the layers of skins not being well constructed and therefore failing to move together, causing blistering and shearing of the skin from even the mildest friction. While not contagious, the disease is unsightly, extremely painful and, currently, incurable.

"I remember the day I was born," reflected Cari-Ann. I recall watching over myself. I felt abandoned without the contact with my mom. I was wondering what I was doing here and I was angry that I had had to return, but I knew that my purpose was to go on my spiritual journey."

"I could only look at my baby for a few minutes before they whisked her away and I was in pain because it had been a difficult birth. But when I looked at this tiny creature and I saw the wisdom in her eyes, I said to myself that she'd been on this earth before," smiled Ruth.

Once Cari-Ann left hospital, the difficulties continued. She refused to breast-feed and she was unable to suck a bottle. The tubes that the doctors had put down her throat had damaged it so badly that she almost died at ten days old. It was only when her grandmother found the baby sucking a teat with a huge hole, and the baby was able to feed, that the bonding with her mother Ruth began.

A bonding which has resulted in an extraordinary closeness as both mother and daughter have fought tirelessly to make Cari-Ann's life as normal as possible, under extremely trying circumstances. "I believe that my mom and I are twin souls who have come together to assist each other in this lifetime, although we have been together in different roles in many lifetimes," remarked Cari-Ann. "We are two halves of the same being."

Trying to find a nursery school that would accept Cari-Ann was one of the first hurdles to be faced. With about eighty per cent of her small body covered in blisters and sores, the authorities were afraid that Cari-Ann's condition was contagious and that the other children would be affected.

One pre-school after another rejected her application, until finally when she reached official school going age, the principal of Winston Park Primary School in the Kloof area of Natal, agreed to enrol the eager little girl.

"The younger kids were amazing," recalled Cari-Ann. "My feet were so badly blistered that often I couldn't walk. Then I was pushed in a pram and the children used to fight over who would push me. The teachers were great too. They supported me as much as they could as often the pain was so excruciating, that I was frequently absent from school."

It was when Cari-Ann was about eleven that the unpleasant reality of her condition struck home. "I suddenly became more aware that I looked different from everybody else. The boyfriend/girlfriend thing was starting amongst my classmates and I knew that I wasn't going to find myself a boyfriend. That realisation hurt even more than my skin condition.

"When I was about fourteen, my coping mechanisms shut down. I felt depressed and I never wanted to leave the house. My friends, who had been so devoted, were now more interested in boys and going on dates. Throughout all this, my mom was always there, counselling me, giving me words of encouragement and love."

"I didn't realise it at the time, but I always knew exactly what to say to comfort my daughter to let her know that she was loved, totally loved. I know now that Spirit was guiding me," said Ruth. "Putting words of solace into my mouth, filling me with healing energy."

Carrie-Ann's condition was deteriorating. Her feet were so covered in blisters that they had to be popped before she could walk. Her socks clung to her blistered soles, sometimes taking as long as two hours to remove when she bathed. The blisters on her knees meant that her mobility was almost nil.

"Get Cari-Ann a wheelchair," advised friends.

Ruth and Cari-Ann had other plans, however. Determined not to be thought of as handicapped, Cari-Ann mastered using her younger brother, Justin's skateboard.

"We kept things light, made everything less serious than it was in reality. It was our coping mechanism," explained Ruth.

Medically, the family tried everything to make things easier for Cari-Ann. "When I was eight, the Lions Community Fund raised money for me to go to Israel to be treated by a doctor there. He gave me very strong alcohol-based medication. It stung like hell when I put it on. However, there wasn't sufficient improvement in my condition to say that it was working."

Cari-Ann was taken from doctor to doctor, but no-one could help her.

She was continuously taking antibiotics, but these failed to produce any positive results. In the humid heat of Natal, her skin seemed as if it as burning up.

Disenchanted with the failure of conventional medicine to deal with her rare skin condition — "I only know of forty-two fellow sufferers in the whole of South Africa" — Ruth and Cari-Ann turned to homeopathy.

Cari-Ann was introduced to naturopath, the late Irma Schütte. "She was an astonishing woman. She became my guru. She immediately stopped all the antibiotics and neutralised the cortisone. Irma was more than just a healer. She tried to understand my internal world. She introduced me to homeopaths and herbalists who all helped me tremendously. For the first time, I had some relief."

Back at school, Cari-Ann was experiencing problems. Due to the severity of her condition, she often missed as much as a third of the school year. With her quick mind, she always managed to catch up the work, but now she was in high school, she was finding it increasingly difficult to cope.

"Perhaps your daughter needs a special school," suggested the headmaster. The Open Air School was a learning institution for children with genetic problems, a place where they would receive extra tuition and counselling. Carrie-Ann was sent there as a boarder.

"I lasted at the school for five weeks. I missed home so much and I hated having my physical disabilities pushed in my face. I had always tried to appear as normal as possible, now it was abundantly clear that there was something wrong with me. It was a huge lesson ... learning to accept myself as 'different.'

"I was able to wrap the school psychologist around my little finger, so he supported my desire to leave school. Nevertheless, my departure brought on another spate of severe depression."

Carrie-Ann returned to Hillcrest School, only to fail the year. It was suggested that she move to The Brown School, a school for children with cerebral palsy and learning disabilities. The curriculum was easier, but the move involved a change of subjects. "I had to repeat the year that I had failed. At this stage my brother Justin, who had learning difficulties, was at this school and he was my protector, my bodyguard.

"But my heart wasn't in it and the pain from my feet was excruciating. I decided to give up school. I was emotionally and physically drained. I stayed at home for six years, away from the pressures of society, away from peer pressure."

"What did you do during this time?"

"Very little. I made chocolates, I did a bit of screen printing, and I tried to rebuild my shattered energies."

Faced with financial difficulties, the family decided to relocate to Pinetown. "Being closer to Durban, It was even hotter there, which aggravated my skin condition. I had the air conditioner on all the time, but nothing helped. I experienced some really dark times. It was my closest to want to be out of here, to wanting to end it all. This period was truly 'My dark night of the soul.'"

The family's financial predicament worsened and they decided to move to Johannesburg. As unhappy as she was in Natal, Cari-Ann was fiercely resistant to change.

Once again, Irma, the naturopath, came to her rescue. Irma began treating the troubled girl with Bach Flower Remedies. With a shift in her energies, Cari-Ann realised that the move was the start of new opportunities, of significant changes in her life.

"I think that this was my true beginning on the spiritual path. I had always been aware of guides and angels. I had always spoken to Spirit on an unconscious level. I had always asked God and the angels to help me through. Now, my connection was really starting to open up."

At this time, there was an article written about Cari-Ann in a well-known, popular magazine describing her tremendous suffering due to Epidermolysis Bullosa. As luck would have it, the article was read by an old family friend, Frank Polley, who decided to do a cycle run for DEBRA, the charity which raises money to help people suffering with this condition. "During her lifetime, Princess Diana was patron saint of DEBRA," remarked Ruth.

The money Frank raised was enough to send Cari-Ann, who was now in her early twenties, to Parktown College in Johannesburg. At first, she considered doing a business course, but Ruth told her daughter that it was a shame that she had neglect her art, for as an artist, Cari-Ann had a remarkable God-given talent.

For Cari-Ann doing art was a tremendous challenge. For one thing, the art department was about half a kilometre away from the main building and after staying at home for such a lengthy period, she had great difficulty in walking that distance.

"With the cooler winters in Johannesburg my condition was not nearly as severe and the blisters on my feet were far less pronounced. Nevertheless, it took about three months for my feet to adjust."

It was during her time in college that the physical evidence of her condition seemed less significant and Cari-Ann felt less self-conscious and more socially acceptable.

Cari-Ann started making friends and socialising out like a normal young person. "We had some wild times. I matured a lot, Mom," she laughed looking at Ruth, who was present during the interview, "if you knew some of the places that I went to, your hair would stand on end."

Determined to be one of the gang, and not to be thought of as different, Cari-Ann experienced difficulties that are hard for the majority of us to perceive. After going to the toilet, she struggled to do up the button of the jeans with her sore, blistered fingers.

"But I made a plan. If Mom or a friend wasn't around to help me, I always wore a belt with the jeans. Then I'd simply do up the belt," Cari-Ann laughed. (On listening to the recording I did with Cari-Ann, it was surprising just how much laughter from both Cari-Ann and Ruth, permeated the interview.)

"Then I devised a new plan for closing my jeans. I pushed a piece of string through the buttonhole, which I used to loop around the button in order to close it. There were other things I couldn't do, like pull open the metal ring of a cold drink can. I'd have to use a knife or a spoon for that."

Cari-Ann enjoyed college, calling the two and half years she spent there "the happiest time of my life." Not only did she complete her schooling, she stayed on another six months to get an additional qualification in art.

Initially, Cari-Ann had thought that she would become a graphic designer, but then she realised that she didn't want to spend all day sitting in front of a computer screen. Indeed, it appeared as if the Universe had other plans for her as much wider canvas was opening up for the blossoming artist.

****

At college, Cari-Ann found much needed love and acceptance amongst her peers and, because of her improved self-esteem, this is where her counselling of others started.

"I met a friend who was psychic. She introduced me to crystals.

"I was like a sponge. I just wanted to know everything she could teach me, and it was from that time that I became consciously aware of Spirit. I knew that I knew things, but I didn't know that these were messages from Spirit.

"Now, with my growing awareness I started reading every esoteric book I could lay my hands on and people just came into my life who could guide me on spiritual matters. I joined a meditation group and this helped me to open up my awareness even more."

It was around this time that Cari-Ann, looking for a career, began doing portraits of people's guides.

"What exactly happens during one of these readings?"

"I channel people's guides who will bring through information that is pertinent to that person's growth, in particular their spiritual growth. If there are issues that they haven't been looking at, their guides will draw their attention to these. My readings are on the deepest spiritual level, rather than merely predictive. They focus on the meaning of Spirit in our lives and how we are not separate from the spiritual world."

With her extraordinary artistic ability, Cari-Ann also began to draw people's guides and with this came the knowledge of how to activate a person's chakras.

"This information was channelled from beginning to end, enables me to activate the Christ consciousness, which every individual possesses. I do a meditation for each chakra to enable people to find a blueprint of their own Christ energy, which is contained within the core of each of the chakra energy centres. You could say that I am able to help awaken the God that is within us all."

Cari-Ann herself is in close contact with her own spiritual guides.

"There is Ze-arch, who refers to himself as a Master Angel. He is my universal angel who brings to me information about shifts that are occurring on the planet. He was involved with the re-aligning of the earth's grids.

"Although he works very closely with me, he is not exclusively for me. He also works with other channels, for example my mom, when he can't get through to me." This remark was accompanied by much laughter.

"Ze-arch has helped me tremendously by giving me an understanding of my situation and what my process is. Through his inspiration, he makes me aware of how to help other people. I have no idea how I do what I do but the energy that I hold (and this is not being arrogant), moves people, enabling them to see their own uniqueness and the brilliance that exists within each and everyone of us.

"My form of channelling consists of counselling. I feel that I am able to counsel a person's soul and that, I believe, is what I am here for, what my purpose on this earth is."

"Do you have other guides?"

"I have two other guides that work with me. Herion, who is a winged messenger. He has come to me to teach me to fly again. To spread my wings. To take control of my life and to expand my awareness and to go out into the world without fear and to rise to the heights to which I can rise, in spite of whatever physical difficulty I may have."

"It is inspiring that you think of flying when you have difficulty even walking!"

"I used to think that I could only change my life if my physical condition was healed, but my guides dispute this saying that this is irrelevant. I can still help heal as many people as possible and I can live a life that brings me joy. This need not centre around my being healed. I can still rise to my full potential regardless, and this knowledge is part of my healing process."

"Who is your third guide?"

"Merlin, the magician."

"You're kidding."

"No. Merlin and I have a very interesting relationship, whereby he doesn't let me get away with anything. In the sense that if I'm starting to feel sorry for myself in any way, he'll say 'Oh no, I don't think so.' He knows exactly what I'm going through, what is causing this slump in emotions or whatever. He tries to keep me strong and refuses to let me enter into any sort of depression. He'll say, 'Pull yourself together, now.'

"We play a lot. I appreciate his sense of humour. It's playful. Never disrespectful. He helps to keep the energy light with laughter. My nickname for him is 'Sparky.' He is obviously a Light Being and he is also a spark of light who is always coming up with bright ideas. He has brought me a deeper understanding of myself and myself in relation to Spirit. Despite my disability, laughter has always been a constant in my life and I guess that I have Merlin to thank for this.

"However, as time has gone by, I believe that although all these guides played an important part in my life, they have now merged into one and I now receive guidance from the highest source of all — my own soul."

Cari-Ann works not only with her guides but also with the Ascended Masters, in particular Sinanda, or the Jesus energy, the Buddha, who, working on the green ray, offers her tremendous help with healing, and Kuan Yin.

In times of trouble Cari-Ann also calls on the Archangels, especially Gabriel, Michael, Raphael and Uriel. With her ever-present capacity for humour, she calls these helpers her A-team.

"I never specify who I wish to speak to, but in order to bring divine clarity to those who wish to consult with me, my intention is to connect only with the highest vibrational beings."

"You seem to have made peace with your condition. Do you have any idea why you have been obliged to go through so much suffering in this lifetime?"

"Yes. This is a very interesting story. I had been doing a couple of past life regressions, but nothing major. One of these is of particular relevance to my present condition. I was taken back to Lemurian days where, I 'saw' myself standing over what appeared to be an operating table and I was performing an operation of some kind. No tools were being used, I was working only with energy.

"In a subsequent regression more of the vision came back and I saw this dark tunnel with row upon row of what looked like incubators. I opened one of these incubators-you had to actually lift the lid — and what I saw was this human being who was so deformed that it was barely recognisable as being human. I understand that what I was doing in that time was performing genetic experimentation and that I was responsible for creating this monster.

"I created these monsters at a time when I was an 'ice princess', without feelings or emotions. I literally couldn't see the end of the rows of incubators for I had maimed and disfigured such countless numbers of people.

"The realisation of this was distressing, particularly as in this regression I changed to a child, the same being, but just at a younger age. This was my understanding of it. I went to touch this creature that was so disfigured that the slightest touch would cause it pain.

"What is extraordinary here is that people who suffer from E.B. are called 'The Untouchables' because in its worst form, mothers can't even touch their Epidermolysis Bullosa babies without the infants blistering.

"In order to touch this unfortunate being, I changed my hands into etheric shafts of pink light. Being able to hold the creature in this way appeared to soothe the pain."

Cari-Ann paused for a moment, then she said softly: "Now that I had this knowledge that I caused so much suffering to so many, I didn't know what to do about it. I was totally overcome with shame and guilt. It finally made perfect sense to me why I was experiencing a genetic problem in this lifetime.

"I ended up asking for forgiveness for all of this. I was told that it would be appropriate for me to appear in front of the Karmic Board because, despite the horrific things I had done, I was asking for healing."

Guided by Spirit, Cari-Ann carried out this entire regression by herself, with no help from a hypnotherapist or any other kind of alternative healer.

"In front of the Karmic Board I was asked whether I thought that I had suffered enough for all the untold misery that I had caused. I replied that I had no idea when someone's suffering was sufficient."

"Who comprised this Karmic Board?"

"I know that Kuan Yin was there as well as some Light Beings that I took to be Ascended Masters. The only being who spoke to me directly was Lady Portia. And she is a tough cookie, let me tell you."

"Who exactly is Lady Portia?"

"She is one of the Ascended Masters. Her role is to facilitate the dark times in one's life that we all have to go through."

"What did you ask the Karmic Board?"

"My guides prompted me to ask for a pardon, so that I could receive physical healing in this lifetime. From a very young age I knew instinctively that I had come here in this lifetime to heal myself.

"Lady Portia asked me if I knew one good reason why I should be granted this pardon. I replied that if my physical condition was improved I would be better equipped to help heal as many people as possible. I told her that I would also like to travel and to take my story to as many people as I could, working with love as my most important tool."

"What was her reaction to your request?"

"I got the distinct impression that I failed to win her sympathy. I was surprised that I was able to hold all this energy through my tears and through my hysterical crying.

"Then I turned around and I saw this beautiful, beautiful golden being of light. I knew it was a masculine energy. And behind him, like a ship's wake that simply gets wider and wider, was a whole host of other golden light beings. I felt instinctively that this was the deformed being that I had connected with in the regression. That this being had come in its true spiritual form, to let me know that my victims had forgiven me completely and that they wanted this healing for me."

With this extraordinary revelation into her condition, Cari-Ann has come to realise that, on a spiritual level, she has healed her condition and that she will no longer have to incarnate with her present disability.

She feels that she has already incarnated seven times with her genetic disorder, but because the energy of those times did not supported a healing, she was made to suffer time and again. In this lifetime, she believes her spiritual healing is complete, but on a physical level her pain still continues to sometimes overwhelm her.

"What I am now working with is that if a spiritual healing has occurred there is no reason why a physical healing may not occur as well. I am actually working with reprogramming my DNA structure and it is a process which takes time."

"On another level, I am afraid of being healed physically, I have become accustomed to my condition. I have become used to being known as Cari-Ann with the terrible skin problem."

"I need to stay detached from the outcome. I need to understand that Divine Timing is not necessarily our time. I need to know that I am whole and complete at every moment. I have faith in my ability to choose my destiny and to create my future."

When one gets to know Cari-Ann, when one is given the immense privilege of looking beyond her blemished face into her heart, one sees such overwhelming beauty of soul, that it is not surprising that she is greatly loved — A prophecy and intimation of the great world of light that lies behind all human destinies.

STEPHEN LOEB

HUSBAND, FATHER, ALS SUFFERER

MIND OVER MATTER

Amyotrophic lateral sclerosis (ALS) commonly called Lou Gehrig's disease, is a progressive neuromuscular condition characterised by weakness, muscle wasting, fasciculations and increased reflexes. The disease is most commonly diagnosed in middle age and affects more men than women.

It usually presents with problem in dexterity or gait resulting from muscle weakness. Difficulty in speaking or swallowing is the initial symptom in the bulbar (affecting the medulla oblongata) form of the disease.

Over a period of months or years, patients with ALS develop severe, progressive muscular weakness and other symptoms caused by loss of function in both upper and lower motor neurons. Sphincter control, sensory function, intellectual abilities and skin integrity are preserved. Patients become completely disabled, often requiring ventilatory support and gastrostomy.

Death usually occurs within five years of diagnosis and is attributed to respiratory failure or cachexia.

I am privileged to have received Stephen's permission to publish this profoundly moving letter that he wrote to his family and friends in 2004.

I AM THAT I AM.

I was thirty-seven years old, young and healthy, or so I thought when I was diagnosed with ALS. I was very active and loved the outdoors. I loved sport from a young age and played as much as I could —you name it and I played it. I became obsessed with the martial arts and practised many different styles of this ancient sporting discipline from about the age of eleven.

At twenty-eight I got married; at thirty I had my first child; a boy, and two years later, along came my daughter. Life was good and I could not have asked for more, and, like all of us, I thought that nothing could possibly go wrong. I thought that I would continue riding the crest of my life's wave well into my eighties and then move onto greener pastures, as we all eventually do. I would get to see my beautiful children, Gabriel and Jessica, grow up and finish school. I would be at their weddings and maybe even have grandchildren. I imagined my beautiful wife Darice, and I would enjoy our retirement years, strolling hand in hand along the beach, enjoying each other until the end of time. How true the saying: 'Man plans and God laughs.'

Having Motor Neuron Disease has taught me to understand the meaning of 'Be in the moment' and 'Live in the now as tomorrow may never come.' We have all heard these words at some stage of our lives, but not too many people are able to live in this truth. The present moment is all there is, there is no other reality, the past and the future do not exist ... so don't waste your energy delving into them; there is only NOW.

All of you with MND probably felt the same as me when diagnosed — that your world had come to an end. At that moment, I thought my life was over, but a year later I am still here. I have learnt to live in the moment, my moment. I cannot talk as well or walk as well or do anything as well as I used to and physically I am not the same as anyone else. But so what? We are all on our own journey; we are all very special and we need to carry on in our special way and be the best we can be in our own unique way. We are all winners. Life is all about perception and how we perceive it, so it is. We create our own reality. TRUST THE PROCESS. THINGS ARE EXACTLY AS THEY SHOULD BE. Don't fight it, just BE.

We are all on a train ride and this train has no brakes. Nothing you or I do will stop the train and it may be a very long ride or may be a short ride. We don't know. Only God knows. Trust him. He knows exactly what is happening to us and we are all a piece of Him. He won't let you fall harder that He thinks you can handle. Trust and faith are the best brakes you could have on this ride and with them you hold the power to stop that train right now.

We have chosen to have MND because we are all special. Enjoy this ride of your life and turn that obstacle into an opportunity. At times I feel so grateful to be where I am in my life. My journey has brought me so much love, so much wisdom and so much spiritual growth, that I know I would never have attained if I were healthy and able bodied.

After all, what is the meaning of life, what is our purpose down here? Surely it is to achieve a state of beingness, of Godliness and this can only be achieved through working on our spirituality and not on our physicality; so maybe our illness is a blessing that we have received. We have been forced to work on ourselves to attain greater heights. Our physicality has been taken away, leaving us only with our spirituality.

We may not understand the process, but that does not mean it's wrong. Maybe we need to change our perception and truly trust our Creator. He does not make mistakes. Let your faith carry you. Remember everything in life is based on either love or fear and there is NOTHING to fear except fear itself. Love yourself and love life. Just be, and try to discover the beauty of the inner you, the bigger you, the real you, the person within, which is perfect and has no flaws. You do not need any part of your physicality to be truly happy. Your beauty and happiness are within yourself. You don't need anybody to make you feel special. You are all special. You are all a spark of The Divine. Use this time to ignite this spark and discover the light within you and you will find out that life is beautiful. Let your life burn brighter now than ever before and I pray that we may all experience God's Grace. If you don't go within your inner self, you go without.

Strength to you all.
Until we meet
Shalom
Stephen Loeb

www.alsa.org

Stephen passed away on Easter Sunday 2008. Memorial services were held for him in various centres throughout South Africa. The many, many mourners agreed that he was one of the bravest and wisest of men. They all felt privileged to have known such a beautiful soul.

JOHAN CALITZ

HUSBAND, FATHER, BIG GAME HUNTER

HUNTING FOR GOD

Extract from COMING OF A MESSENGER

Far, far south in Mother Africa
where the Springbok prances and sprints
where the leopard sprawls upon a tree branch
to camouflage its presence in the polka dotted shade
where the hippopotamus thumps the ground with muzzle
where the tottering tortoise make tortuous, soundless footsteps
to mark a countdown to eternity.
where the zebra kicks the air with vigour
where the hyper-active monkey plays hide-and-seek
where the proud silverback prances and shouts
to alert his ape community of approaching danger
where the crocodile with its sinister grin
ominously way-lays the unsuspecting prey.
the land of the elephant
shall be where cosmic wisdom,
love and creativity will be channelled.

Dan Rakgoathe (Composed during the early 1990's)

Born in Pretoria South Africa in 1956, Johan Calitz, whose father was a hunter, grew up with a love of hunting. Today Johan operates one of the most successful hunting operations in Africa, managing approximately 2.1 million acres of hunting concessions on behalf of the Botswana Government and communities in northern Botswana. For the past decade, in addition to his camps in Botswana, Johan has been involved in pioneering the incredible Niassa National Reserve in Mozambique.

Johan, although extremely modest and unassuming, is an African hunter who is known and respected across the globe. His clients include royalty, government officials, highly reputable members of the medical fraternity, as well as the rich and famous. He has gained this reputation by always ascertaining that if he is the leader of the hunt and is totally in command and that no-one is to question his authority and leadership.

Today Johan lives in Maun, Botswana and getting to interview him in Johannesburg about his run-in, some years ago, with enraged and injured buffalo, was no easy feat ... ever since his boyhood he has been most comfortable in the wild. However, I pursued Johan with dogged determination ... I knew that his near death experience — which was well-documented in hunting magazines — needed to be told here from a different point of view ... for its strong spiritual element.

Finally Johan and his first wife Berna were sitting on the veranda of my suburban home and I was able to capture the following incredible story:

"Johan, where did you spend your childhood?"

"I grew up, together with my two younger sisters, Lucia and Karen, in a traditional Afrikaans-speaking Protestant family in Wepener in the South Eastern Free State.

"We three children attended Sunday school regularly where we dutifully learned all the doctrines prescribed by the Dutch Reformed Church. There was nothing in these teachings, however, that could have prepared me for the miracle that I was to witness deep in the Tanzanian bush on the fateful day of 30th September 2001," recalled Johan.

Miracles were not part of what the Calitz children were taught by their Sunday school teachers, although the siblings saw their mother, who passed away when Johan was only fourteen, as a deeply spiritual woman, one who had a very close connection to God.

"How do you remember your mother?"

"Everyone who knew her, described her as an angel. The day she died, everybody in the town, even people drinking in the bars, started crying," said Johan, who despite his tough macho image, has a deep spiritual side to his nature. With a reflective smile he remembered the following anecdote:

"There was a strange spiritual occurrence linked to the family for which there seemed to be no logical explanation. My grandfather's mother predicted the day of her death. She knew that she was going to die on a certain day. When that day came, a white dove flew into the house and started circling around. My great granny went outside the house to whiten it.

"The sky was clear that day, there wasn't a cloud to be seen. Out of the blue, lightening suddenly struck, killing her instantly. As soon as she died, the white dove flew out from the house, heading towards the heavens."

It was this knowledge of occurrences like these that set the young Johan pondering on the fact that there was perhaps something different out there, something bigger and divorced from the normal everyday life he and his sisters knew.

"When did you first become aware that you were being protected by God?"

"In 1976, while I was doing my military service when, after having finishing school, the South African military were busy laying landmines in Nova Radondo in Angola to eliminate tanks and heavy vehicles of the enemy.

"Our unit was given the instruction to withdraw. Driving towards the last line of people to call them back, I was forced to steer the vehicle into enemy territory, where numerous landmines had already been laid.

"As I drove through this high risk area without hitting a single mine, it began to occur to me that for a reason that I could not fathom, I was being protected by a higher power. I couldn't understand why, but I knew that God had sent one of his angels to look after us and guide us through. By the grace of God, we were given the gift of living to see another day."

He grew silent for a moment before remarking: "Our unit wasn't the only lucky one. A South African author wrote a lovely book about how God miraculously saved various members of the military when death stared them in the face.

"The name of this book has slipped my mind, but I do remember that I began to think a lot about why God seems to help certain people escape from harm. Often, there doesn't seem to be a logical explanation as to whom he chooses and what the reason for his choice is.

"But this sort of thing is well documented. Remember The Battle of Blood River, when the Voortrekkers were fighting the Zulus? Although it appeared that the mighty Zulu warriors had the upper hand, the deeply religious Boers suddenly saw white light surrounding their lager of wagons.

"This gave them the strength to win the battle believing that their hard fought victory came not from their technically superior armaments, but rather from this sign from God."

After his stint in the army, Johan returned to South Africa and what he terms 'normal life.' He married his first wife Berna and prayed that their firstborn would be a son. After Cobus was born, Johan prayed for a little sister for Cobus and in the fullness of time Stefani was born. The Calitz family considered themselves to be very blessed.

Johan was going to work for South African Secret Service Bureau of State Security in the Transkei. However, his grandfather got very ill and Johan and his family went to look after the old man's farm in Zastron in the Southern Free State.

Even as a small boy, Johan had been a hunter. By the time he was fourteen he was already shooting dangerous game like elephant and buffalo.

"So many times I painted myself into a corner, starring death in the face. Yet somehow, I always managed to extricate myself from these violent situations. When it came to hunting, I began to consider myself as pretty damn good — almost invincible, one might say."

Despite this seemingly impregnable image, in his quieter moments Johan would often think about spirituality and about God and how he seemed to be protected.

In his heart, he was very grateful.

****

One Sunday afternoon in 1999, following a prayer meeting at their house, Berna and Johan were relaxing and watching TV, although, as is his wont, Johan was continuously in radio contact with his game camps in Botswana.

Earlier that week, a plane had taken off from Lanseria Airport and halfway to Botswana, the one engine of this twin-engine plane had failed. With only one engine, the pilot flew over miles and miles of emptiness.

Eventually he was forced to crash land the plane and following this accident. Immediately search parties were set up for to look for the missing pilot and passengers. The initial likelihood appeared to be that the plane had gone down in the vicinity of Maun in the Delta, but the pilot's Global Positioning System proved this assumption to be erroneous.

Following the accident, Johan went to Botswana to check on his camps there. The usual quietness of the bush was disturbed by the continuous roar of planes as they searched for survivors. For three or four days nobody could find any sign of life. The Botswana Defence Force and members of the private sector all joined in the search, which so far proved fruitless.

Back home that Sunday with Berna and his family, Johan was surprised to get a call from his camp manageress at around five that evening.

"What was the reason for the call?"

"The pilot told the manageress that they had been walking north for three days. They were in the wild, far from any living soul and they had walked for approximately 200 kilometres without being attacked by either man or beast. This coupled with the fact that the manageress had put on the pump's engine just at the time the two weary survivors were nearing the camp, can all be construed as pretty miraculous."

The camp manageress let the pilot of the plane talk to Johan.

"We have no idea where we are," said the pilot. "All we know is that we have walked north. We have no idea where the other passengers are."

"Who were the other passengers?" I asked Johan.

"There were two men and a lady and the lady was very badly burnt."

Johan asked the pilot what he had seen before the plane went down.

"A fence," replied the pilot.

"Do you think it was the buffalo fence?" asked Johan, referring to the buffalo fence that runs from east to west through the country.

"Where did the plane go down?"

"In a forest of green trees."

Johan realised that they had gone down in a green teak forest, which was very lush during the March/April rainy system when the accident had occurred. Using his home GPS System, Johan was able to locate the approximate vicinity of the crash.

"It was too late for the Botswana Defence Force to search for the wreckage or the remaining passengers that night, but they set off in a chopper at dawn the next morning. Following my directions they soon located the burnt out plane, which was so badly damaged it seemed impossible for there to be any survivors.

"I was astounded when the pilot and the passenger walked into my camp. The three other passengers were found near the wreckage and although they were extremely weak and dehydrated, they were still alive — one severely burnt woman, in particular, was in a critical condition. Fortunately, the Botswana Medical Rescue Emergency team were on hand to render medical assistance."

"How did they manage to survive?"

"It was totally miraculous. Not only were they in the wild — leopard, lion, buffalo, snakes and many other dangerous species inhabit the territory — but they had no water, except for the few drops they managed to gather from the hollow of the trees. They applied elephant dung to their burns to try and soothe their inflamed skins."

Johan shook his head as he recalled the crash. "If they had been found one day later it would have been too late."

The story of the crash and the miraculous survival of the passengers was later filmed as a documentary which was shown all over the world. Not surprisingly, the documentary was entitled *In the Hand of God*.

****

The extraordinary events that occurred on 30th September 2001 went against Johan's usual iron grip on the safety and security of a hunting party under his leadership.

"Why weren't you in control of the hunt on that particular occasion?"

"For one thing, I was not the leader of the expedition that set out that day. A regular high profile client of mine had asked me to join him on a hunt in Tanzania."

(As a master of diplomacy, Johan declined to give any further details of the client's identity.) "Because he was hunting with another company, he asked me merely to go along 'for the ride,' so to speak," recalled Johan.

The assembled hunting party resembled a veritable Tower of Babel. Johan spoke English but no French, the other professional hunter spoke French but no English. Consequently they were accompanied by an interpreter whose job it was to bridge the communication gap between them. Four trackers who spoke Swahili, a language unknown to the remaining hunters, accompanied the men.

"On the Sunday before the accident there were a lot of things in my life that went wrong. I am not proud of this, but the fact was that I was arguing with my God, who is the Christian God, what was the point of man's existence on this earth?"

"Hunting is a dangerous profession. Do you often call on God when you are in the wild?"

"Yes. That day, in particular, I was wrestling with a thousand questions. Asking God Why? Why? Why? What particularly bothered me was the question of whether our attendance at church every Sunday is merely a game we play to please those around us or is it a true sign of our spirituality? Other people, the San Bushmen, for example, exercise their spirituality in a different way. Whose spirituality is correct?

"That Sunday morning as I woke up in the Tanzanian bush, I knew that something bad was going to happen, but I went out hunting anyway."

"What was the first thing that gave you an indication that things were not as they should be?"

"We were baiting a leopard, which the client missed when he shot him. The whole day I was not in harmony with the professional hunters who were with me. My emphasis now was to get the client to regain his confidence in his ability and then to get him into a situation where he had to take an animal's life.

"The other hunter also persuaded the client to shoot another animal before returning to the enclosure to await the leopard's return. As the day progressed, we went further and further away from the enclosure where we were supposed to be at four o' clock and also further and further away from the camp where we were to spend the night.

"Just after lunch that afternoon, I saw two buffalo standing on the side of the riverbank. I said to myself that I shouldn't mention this to the others, as I felt that if these guys attempted to shoot these buffalo it would be a disaster."

"What happened next?"

"My reason for being on this shooting expedition was to ensure that this high profile person in the party didn't get hurt. I suppose I was there in the capacity of a glorified bodyguard. So I was upset when the one tracker pointed out the buffalo as I know how dangerous these animals can be.

"The trackers got out of the car and they handed him his rifle, which was a 470 Nitro Express — a very powerful calibre hunting gun.

"The other professional hunter had put the client in a position to shoot and he was looking back at the hunter while he did so. Consequently he did not notice that the buffalo, aware that there were people in the riverbed, had changed direction.

"The client then asked him which way the buffalo was looking. Standing at the vehicle I whispered loudly, "He's looking to the left, shoot him on the shoulder. The hunter took aim and I could see from the reaction of the buffalo, who ran picking up his tail, that the shot had wounded him," Johan related.

Following the tracks of the injured animal, Johan discovered a leaf with a piece of stomach contents on it, mixed with blood. "The professional hunter was having problems with his firearm and asked the client if he could borrow his Nitro Express. Taking two cartridges from his gun belt, the other hunter then walked off in the direction that the buffalo had run off in order to see what had happened to the wounded beast.

"I did not want to accompany them. In my soul I knew that it was a disaster waiting to happen."

Against his will, Johan then followed the other hunter and the four trackers. He tried to communicate with them — he thought that their method of following the buffalo was incorrect.

"However, because of the different languages that the men spoke, nobody could quite understand what I was saying … I am seldom frightened while hunting in the bush, but this time I was distinctly ill at ease."

Shortly after that, the men noticed the buffalo running away from them.

Johan then attempted to shoot the buffalo, but his shot, under these difficult circumstances, also did not hit it properly.

"I went to the spot where the buffalo stood to see if the shot had hit. The other hunter rushed passed me. I heard the buffalo bellow that familiar sound of a charge. I saw the hunter pick up his rifle and I ran towards him to help him. We both shot at the buffalo who charged, focusing his attention on me.

"The tracker, scared and not thinking clearly, ran away with the gun belt. The other hunter ran after him in order to get more bullets."

While this chaotic situation played itself out, the wounded buffalo was almost on top of Johan. Taking aim, he pulled the trigger of his gun once, twice. By the time he fired the second shot, the enraged buffalo was on top of him. In the first three seconds of what Johan refers to as 'the battle royal' the buffalo shattered his ankle, threw him up in the air, then charged at him again. As he tried to shield his face by covering it with his arm, the buffalo stuck his horns into Johan's arm, before tossing him into the air once again.

As he landed on the ground, the buffalo started goring Johan with his horns, boring huge holes into his left upper leg. He then tore open Johan's stomach on the right hand side and pulled open his chest on the left hand side. Johan knew then that he was going to die.

"Dear God, why me? Why here in Tanzania? Why now?" he asked.

"I couldn't fight the buffalo because of a nearly amputated right arm and my shattered, crushed ankle on the left side meant that I had no chance of running away. I thought that the only thing that I could do was to lie there as if I was dead.

"As I lay motionless on the ground, the buffalo tried to crush me with his bosses — his helmet of hard horn on his forehead. He attempted to drive me into any object that could resist my weight," recalled Johan.

By this time the buffalo had been hit five times, but no shot had yet been fired that had harmed his vital organs. The enraged beast had lost very little of his enormous power and in his fury, every time that Johan made eye contact with him as he hit the ground, the animal attacked the dying man once more.

Still conscious, Johan heard one shot being fired and then another.

The buffalo crumpled to the ground and as he fell, he landed right on top of Johan, who was lying on his back. The buffalo was finally dead and Johan was, at this stage, barely clinging to life, hardly able to breathe with this 1800 pound (850 kg) carcass lying on top of him.

The hunter and the trackers immediately tried to roll the dead beast off the seriously weakened Johan. It was probably rolling the animal over his broken leg and gaping stomach wounds in this fashion that served to injure his crushed ankle even more severely.

The other hunter ran towards Johan and putting his arms around his head, started talking to him in French.

"Go to the car," Johan said to him in almost inaudible English, "and try and get a doctor here as soon as possible."

"With such severe injuries you must have felt that you had absolutely no chance of surviving the attack," I said to Johan.

"As I watched the hunter's retreating figure I said to myself I know that I am dead. Even if he walks quickly, the car is at least one hour away."

The frightened trackers did what they could to assist the injured hunter. Cutting two branches, they tore their T-shirts and made up a rough splint. Still Johan knew that if he didn't find some way to help himself, he was definitely going to die.

"The only thing that I can do is pray," he thought. Gasping for breath, he managed to whisper, "Lord, please let me see my family and my friends again. Dear God, I don't want to die."

Opening his eyes, Johan looked down at his wounds. "There was a broken body lying on the ground, with ribs showing, stomach showing. As an experienced hunter, I knew that there was no way I could survive such severe injuries. The horn had gone through my left upper leg and if it had hit an artery, I knew that I would bleed to death. I looked at my arm and I could clearly see the veins and the arteries. I realised that if my lungs were punctured, I would suffocate long before the other hunter returned."

Johan grew silent for a few moments. Then, closing his eyes and grimacing from pain, he cried out again: "Please God help me get through this."

After a few moments had elapsed, Johan opened his eyes once more. He did not see the vivid green of the foliage or the clear blue of the sky. Instead he saw a soft white triangular light coming down from heaven and as he basked in its gentle glow he knew that God had heard his prayers and had answered them.

"I looked down at my wounds ... sure there were holes everywhere, but the bleeding had miraculously stopped. I knew that for whatever reason God wanted me to live and my heart over flowed with gratitude."

****

With this certain knowledge that, no matter how grave his injuries appeared, he was going to make it, Johan lay there as calmly as a person who had not been injured at all. His pants were torn, his shirt was torn off, his belt was broken.

Addressing the trackers, who spoke only Swahili, in English, Johan asked them to give him their T-shirts. Despite the communication difficulties, the trackers somehow understood his request and Johan tried to use the torn shirts they handed him as pressure bandages. One tracker kept Johan's mouth moist by drenching a small cloth from his water bottle and letting him suck on it.

"I will never forget that kindly gesture. It meant a lot to me."

Johan looked down at his crushed ankle. There was no blood coming from this major injury. He looked down at his arm. He saw this huge piece of muscle hanging right down to the bone, an enormous gaping wound, yet there was no blood spurting from this severely damaged limb.

He stared down at his torn chest. Through the ripped flesh he could see his ribs. Yet there was no blood. Johan could see the white lining of his stomach. This injury too was bloodless. "It was unbelievable. It was as if my eyes were playing tricks. God and his angels were definitely looking after me."

An hour went by before help finally arrived. Carrying him in a canvas, the men put Johan, who, now that the initial shock of the attack had worn off, was in the most unbelievable pain, on the back of an open Land Cruiser. There was no mattress of any kind to cushion his agony.

"Nobody wanted to look me in the eye," recalled Johan. Not the client, not the other hunter, not anybody. Nobody wanted to give me water or help with my wounds. Everybody was convinced that I was going to die."

It took three and a half to four hours of driving over uneven ground with no roads or even roughly hewed tracks to reach the camp. Johan's already broken body was subjected to further battering and bruising. Of all those present, it was only Johan who, having witnessed the awesome beauty of the white light, knew that he was not going to die.

The doctor who was in camp — by virtue of his position, the client always travelled with his own physician — used an alcohol-based disinfectant to cleanse the wounds, thereby decreasing the risk of further infection, but adding greatly to Johan's already considerable discomfort.

Throughout his ordeal, Johan was well aware that he dare not lose consciousness — "God and the angels had done their bit, now I had to put up my own fight for survival. When the chips were down, I trusted no-one but God to come to my assistance," he said with a wry grimace.

Fortunately, the doctor was able to put him on a drip and give him morphine before flying Johan to Dar es Salaam. Owing to the severity of his condition, nothing could be done for him there and so finally Johan was flown to Nairobi where he was eventually operated on in the early hours of the following morning.

All this time, despite the morphine and the pain, Johan had struggled valiantly against losing consciousness. Now just before he dosed off in the operating theatre, he heard the doctors discussing the amputation of his injured arm, which had lain open and in the dirt for over twelve and a half hours.

"No," replied the French doctor in broken English, "you must not amputate his arm for you cannot give him blood." (The danger of getting AIDS from contaminated blood is extremely real in African hospitals.)

"What happened when you regained consciousness?"

"When I woke up in the small room, I found two people standing over me. My cell phone was ringing. I was grateful that despite all the drama someone had had the presence of mind to make sure that my cell phone accompanied me to the hospital. I was even more surprised that, after not being charged for so long, my cell phone was still operational.

"The caller was Niekie Nel, my good friend and house doctor from Kroonstad. 'You've got to get me out of here,' I pleaded. 'Whatever you do, get me on a charter flight to Johannesburg.'"

The doctors in Nairobi had closed off all Johan's wounds, thereby sealing in the infection, thereby worsening his already critical condition. There was bleeding in the lungs and Johan was having difficulty in breathing. He was drifting in and out of consciousness.

A charter flight with two doctors on board flew Johan to The Garden City Clinic in Johannesburg. He was taken to surgery where all the wounds were re-opened and the blood drained from his lungs. It was a full month after the accident before they closed the last wound. The doctor said that there was some strange bacteria, probably from the buffalo, that needed treatment.

A great friend of Johan's walked into the hospital ward where he was recuperating. "You were so badly hurt that God didn't send an angel to help you, he sent his son," remarked the man.

For Johan his faith and belief in God is total. "When I prayed to my God, he answered my prayers. He stopped my body bleeding. No major artery was severed, despite the severity of my injuries."

Johan reflected for a moment before saying: "You don't have to be someone special. You don't have to have lived a flawless life to be connected to God. When you ask him to do something and he decides that he will help you, he will not let you down. It is so comforting to know that miracles still exist in the 21st century and that there is a living God."

www.johancalitzsafaris.co.za

JOANNE, ANDREW & FRANKIE BROWN

TSUNAMI SURVIVORS

MIRACLE IN THE MIDST OF MAYHEM

EXTRACT FROM **THE DRY SALVAGES**

The river is within us, the sea is all about us;
The sea is the land's edge also, the granite
Into which it reaches, the beaches where it tosses
Its hints of earlier and other creation:
The starfish, the horseshoe crab, the whale's backbone;
The pools where it offers to our curiosity
The more delicate algae and the sea anemone.
It tosses up our losses, the torn seine,
The shattered lobsterpot, the broken oar
And the gear of foreign dead men. The sea has many voices,
Many gods and many voices.

T.S. Eliot

The Chabad movement, a Hebrew acronym for wisdom, understanding and knowledge, originated in Belarus in Eastern Europe. Until the death of the 7th Chabad leader, Rabbi Menachem Mendel Schneerson in 1994, the followers were governed by a succession of leaders, each descended from the founder of the movement. The death of the Rebbe (rabbi or leader) in 1994 came as a great shock to members of the movement for many believed that he was the Mosiach — the Jewish Messiah and that he would be revealed to the world as such.

An extraordinarily learned and enlightened scholar, in 1943 the Rebbe published Hayom Yom, a pocket-sized booklet with a Chassidic saying for each day of the year. Misleadingly humble in format, it soon became a veritable guide to the life of the soul of the Chassid.

A prolific author, the Rebbe then produced more than 200 volumes of essays, letters and talks over the next half century, pertaining to and illuminating virtually every area of The Torah — the vast body of wisdom and law derived from over three thousand years of Jewish study and application of the Divine word revealed at Sinai. Many Chassidic Jews believe that the Rabbi is even more powerful in death than in life and thus they continue to seek his wisdom and guidance.

Consequently, when Andrew Brown was on a trip to New York, he went to visit the Rebbe's grave. In his hand he held a letter that he had written, a letter that came straight from his heart, asking, amongst other things, that Hashem bring him a life partner. Having read this letter to the late rabbi, as is the custom, Andrew then tore it up.

Joanne Segal had been going out with someone for the past eight years, but she felt unfulfilled in the relationship. She was going to move into a new townhouse in February, but come September she had nowhere to stay until the townhouse was completed and so, when her ex-boyfriend invited her to continue staying in their home until hers was ready, she accepted this arrangement.

In December she met Andrew at a party. "Are you single?" he asked her. She nodded her head.

"Where do you stay?" queried Andrew.

"Well, actually I stay with my ex-boyfriend."

While Joanne's reply might have baffled Andrew, the couple were delighted to discover that when Joanne finally moved into her townhouse — No. 10 Oakwood Manor, her neighbour in No. 9 was Andrew.

Romance blossomed and when the couple married, Andrew felt that the late Rebbe had answered all his prayers.

****

As a young and affluent couple, blessed with good looks and an abundance of friends, it seemed that the Browns had it all; but there was soon trouble in paradise. Both Andrew and Joanne longed for children, but when Joanne failed to fall pregnant, tests followed and the results were not encouraging.

She was diagnosed with polycystic ovary syndrome (POS), a hormonal disorder that is characterised by the follicles failing to ovulate and remaining as multiple cysts which distend the ovary.

Her gynaecologist told her that the chances of her conceiving naturally were remote and he suggested that she undergo fertility treatment. As the couple had only been married a short time, they decided to postpone the treatment until they were quite sure that Joanne was unable to fall pregnant naturally. So imagine the couple's joy when, after a year, Joanne conceived without any medical intervention.

The pregnancy was progressing smoothly and Andrew and Joanne heaved a collective sigh of relief. However, when she was in her sixth month, Joanne fell down a flight of stairs. Anxious in case the fall had harmed their unborn baby, Andrew rushed his wife to the Milpark Hospital. There were fears that Joanne might have broken her back and that the baby might have stopped breathing.

Following X-rays, the radiographer was able to allay their worst fears. Not only had Joanne not been seriously injured, but the baby was also unharmed. "By the way, your baby is a boy," remarked the radiographer as the couple were walking out of the hospital.

Joanne turned to Andrew and took his hand. "No, our baby will be a little girl who will look just like her daddy. Let's do her nursery in pink and red."

Being a spiritual person, Joanne did not want her baby to be born in a conventional hospital. She wanted to go to a birthing clinic and have a water birth, with only a midwife in attendance. Andrew and her gynaecologist tried to dissuade her.

"What if something goes wrong? What if you need a Caesarean? The Linkwood has no neo-natal facilities."

Stubbornly, Joanne insisted on the Linkwood Clinic. "Initially, the birth process was very pleasant. Only Andrew and I and the midwife were present. We listened to the sounds of dolphins and we burnt rose coloured candles. However, after I had been in labour for thirteen hours, things started going wrong. It was thought that the baby had swallowed the placenta and suddenly I found myself giving birth between the bathroom and my bed.

"When the little girl emerged, she didn't cry. Her Apgar score — (a method of rapidly assessing the general state of a baby immediately after birth) — was very low. The attending doctors had to get the baby breathing manually as the birthing clinic was without the necessary equipment. There were fears that the infant would die. But I knew that no matter what the doctors said, my child was going to live," smiled Joanne.

The baby was immediately rushed by ambulance to the nearby Park Lane Clinic where she was placed in the Intensive Care Unit. The doctors were worried that the lack of oxygen from not breathing naturally might have resulted in brain damage and they felt the chances of the baby being a Down's Syndrome child were high.

While friends and family members were tense during the following days, while they anxiously waited for the results of the barrage of tests that the baby had undergone, Joanne was surprisingly calm.

"I guess it was my spirituality that carried me through. I told everybody that if she was a Down's Syndrome baby, we would manage. I said that God only gives these special children to parents who are able to love them unconditionally. And yet I knew that she was going to be fine, absolutely fine."

Joanne's motherly instincts again proved correct. Little Frankie Brown was indeed fine — she soon developed into the most beautiful baby, perfect in every way.

When Andrew and Joanne took their new daughter to be named by the rabbi at the synagogue, he gave her the Hebrew name of Chaya Mushka. Andrew, in particular, as a devout member of the Chabad movement, felt honoured.

His little girl was being given the same name as the late rebbetzin. The Rebbe's beloved wife of fifty-nine years, Chaya Mushka, who died in 1988, had been a wise and erudite woman, much loved by her husband's congregation. When she died she was given a farewell fit for a queen — a procession of fifteen thousand strong, led by an official police motorcade accompanied her to the Chabad cemetery in Queens New York where she was interred near her father, the previous Rebbe, Rabbi Yosef Yitzchak Schneerson.

"You've quite a name to live up to," smiled Andrew as he proudly carried his daughter from the synagogue.

****

In her book *The Hidden Beauty of the Shema*, the most sacred of all Jewish prayers, Lisa Aiken wrote: *People tend to be drawn to materialism and give in to their lusts by following foolish, worldly pleasures. We need constant reminders that we are part of God's Cabinet and have responsibilities to Him.*

Without these reminders we can't keep focused on what God put us here to do. His loving-kindness determined that we should say the Shema twice a day to help us stay on track spiritually.

The general purpose of any mitzvah is to preserve and heighten our spiritual wholesomeness and to attach us to God. Saying that Shema reminds us that our thoughts, speech and actions affect the entire universe.

An extract from the Shema reads as follows:

God is a faithful King.

Hear, O' Israel, the Lord is our God, the Lord is One.

Blessed is the Name of His glorious kingdom forever and ever.

And you shall love the Lord your God with all of your heart, and with all of your soul, and with all of your resources.

And these words that I command you today should be on your heart. And you should teach them to your children, and speak of them when you sit in your house, and when you go on your way, and when you lie down, and when you rise up. And you should bind them as a sign on your hand, and they should be tefillin between your eyes. And write them on the doorposts of your house and your gates.

On many nights Andrew would go into Frankie's room and say the Shema over his sleeping daughter's cot.

"Remember, my angel, God is always watching over you," he whispered.

****

In 2004, for the December holidays Joanne, Andrew and seventeen-month-old Frankie set off for a dream holiday in Thailand, accompanied by a professional child-minder and nurse — Vicky Nwayo, a nurturing African woman who had looked after the baby following her troubled arrival into this world and with whom the Browns had remained in contact.

As keen divers and snorkelers, Joanne and Andrew were looking forward to pursuing their sporting activities, secure in the knowledge that Frankie would be in the best possible hands.

After spending eight glorious days in Phuket, on the 26th of December the family had booked to go to Hong Island, a deserted island known for its magnificent snorkelling and magical nature trails. Andrew decided that they would not go on an organised tour, preferring to hire a speedboat with its own skipper. As the family was having breakfast in their hotel that morning, some friends asked them "Did you feel that earthquake?"

Joanne shook her head. "No, everything seems OK to me."

After they boarded the boat, as an enthusiastic photographer, Andrew took video footage of Joanne, Frankie and a somewhat apprehensive Vicky, who had never been on a speedboat before. When Vicky's nerves settled, turning to the Browns she said: "This must be as close to heaven as one can get."

Hong Island boasted two coves for the visiting boats to berth. Having docked in the first cove with all the other boats, for no apparent reason, once they were settled, Andrew and Joanne decided to gather up all their beach paraphernalia and move to the other cove.

Being the height of the holiday season, the pristine beach was soon packed with tourists from all over the world. About half an hour after their arrival, Frankie, who had been happily playing on the beach, grew tired.

"Let's put her to sleep in the shade and then Andrew and I can go snorkelling, while you sit with her," Joanne told Vicky." However, in their haste to get ready for the outing that morning, they had forgot to pack in the toddler's comforter, her much loved 'doodoo' blanket, with the result that a fractious Frankie declined to go to sleep.

Joanne and Vicky were sitting on the beach together with Frankie, with Andrew cleaning his goggles ten metres in front of them, when Vicki suddenly cried out: "What's everybody screaming about?"

Turning around they saw a fifteen metre high wall of water coming towards them.

****

The 2004 Indian Ocean undersea earthquake which occurred at 00.58.53 UTC (07:58:53 local time) on December 26th 2004, generated a tsunami, or giant tidal wave, that is undoubtedly one of the deadliest natural disasters in modern history.

The earthquake originated in the Indian Ocean just north of Simeulue Island, off the western coast of northern Sumatra, Indonesia. The resulting tsunami devastated the shores of Indonesia, Sri Lanka, South India, Thailand and other countries with waves up to 30 m (100 feet) high, causing serious damage and deaths as far as the east coast of Africa, with the furthest recorded death due to the tsunami occurring at Port Elizabeth in South Africa, 8 000 km (5 000 miles) away from the epicentre.

Anywhere from 228, 000 to 310, 000 people are thought to have died as the result of this underwater earthquake. In Indonesia, in particular, 500 bodies a day were still being found in February 2005 and the count would continue until after June of that year.

Joanne swirled around in the avalanche of muddy water.

"I was swept around like a rag doll ... it really didn't matter whether or not you could swim ... the brutal force of the water was far too great ... Frankie was wrenched from my arms and I thought at that time that it didn't matter if I died for I knew that my baby must be dead. What chance did a baby of seventeen months have against one of the most powerful tsunamis ever recorded? At that moment my heart felt as if it was completely broken."

****

After being buffeted around in the swirling muddy waters for what seemed an eternity, Joanne found herself approximately eighty metres away from where her traumatic journey had begun.

"Hong Island is only a small island and the wave had flattened the entire place. I knew that I was severely injured. I had fallen, which had taken skin off my back and arms. I was bleeding with broken bones, but most significantly, I had broken my back."

"Somehow I found myself in a hut that, miraculously, was still standing. There was chaos within this small shelter. Everyone was screaming and crying and this is where the injured were being gathered. It looked as if the people there had been skinned alive. Blood was everywhere. In excruciating pain, I lay flat on the hut's sodden floor."

Despite having grown up in Kwazulu Natal, a region known for its glorious beaches, as a child, Vicky had never learnt to swim. Although this was a working holiday for her, it was also a dream come true — a unique opportunity for her to travel to exotic destinations, perhaps even to swim in the water if she could pluck up the courage. Now her dream had turned into a nightmare beyond her wildest imaginings.

The tsunami had carried her off in a different direction from Joanne and she was terrified. As she tried to battle the angry swell of water, she felt something brush against her. Her first thoughts were that it must be a fallen log, but on looking down, she saw that it was a baby, covered in mud. Gathering the small creature in her arms, she somehow managed to get to a patch of dry land.

Thankfully, Vicky wiped the blood from the baby's face and when she could distinguish its features, she gasped. For, in what must be recorded as one of the most extraordinary miracles of the tsunami disaster, Vicky discovered that the child she held in her arms was her charge, Frankie.

****

I sat talking to Joanne in her beautiful suburban home a month after the tsunami disaster. Still recovering from major back surgery and walking slowly, but with tremendous determination and resilience, she told me about the aftermath of the killer tidal wave. Frankie, diligently watched by her nursemaid, played nearby — a most sweet and beautiful child who showed no after effects of her ordeal. I thought to myself how difficult it must before Joanne, still in the early stages of recovery, not to be able to lift her daughter or seat her on her lap or take the active toddler for a walk.

"What happened to Andrew during the tsunami?"

"My husband suffered from concussion. When he came around there were huge blanks in his memory. He remembers seeing certain people.

"Then suddenly they weren't there — he couldn't quite fathom out why. He recalls screaming for me and Frankie and staggered around the destroyed island endless repeating the Shema. "Help me, help me, Lord. I need to find my wife and my baby daughter.

"He made his way to the cove where our skipper had originally moored our boat. Of the thirty-five boats that were in the cove, not one remained. They had all been smashed. Completely destroyed. Some of the falling parts had dismembered people — they were lying there with their limbs cut off. Our boat, in the second cove, was unharmed."

As Andrew walked along the beach in blind despair, he suddenly saw a severely traumatised Vicky carrying Frankie in her arms. "Oh thank God!" he rejoiced. "But where is Joanne?"

Fearing the worst, Andrew walked through the death and destruction, frantically searching for his wife. A German woman, who had earlier observed the family on the beach came up to him. "I know where your wife is," she told Andrew, leading him towards the hut where Joanne lay.

With trepidation Andrew walked into the small shelter. He had no idea whether Joanne was dead or alive. When he saw her on the floor, he felt enormous relief until she softly said to him, "Andrew, I can't stand up. I can't walk."

"You must get out of here," someone yelled. "There's another wave coming."

Seeing two British guys nearby who seemed to be in reasonably good shape, Andrew said to them "Please take our baby and get her to the top of the mountain. Then get her off the island."

"You know, those two guys were absolute angels. They took Frankie up the mountain and later they took her back to our hotel," recalled Joanne.

Somehow Andrew managed to get Joanne to stand and slowly, painfully, she walked up the mountain. A miracle of courage when one learns of the extent of her injuries — six broken ribs, seven broken vertebra, a pierced lung, blood on one kidney, a burst eardrum and a myriad of superficial injuries.

"We stayed on that mountain for eight hours. There was the constant threat of another tsunami. The rocks were craggy, red ants were everywhere. No one said a word."

Finally the rescue boats arrived, but the stretcher they were hoping for that would carry Joanne down the mountain, did not materialise. "I can't get down," she moaned.

A slight Thai man — "There are simply no words to describe the kindness and compassion of the Thai people," somehow managed to carry her gently down the muddy incline.

As the angry sea calmed, Andrew concerned himself with trying to find a kayak that could take the ailing Joanne to a speedboat and hence transport her from the island. "My wife is severely injured. She is urgently in need of professional medical care," he called out, as all the rescue boats appeared to be leaving the island.

"While we were leaving, despite everything that happened, I noticed one thing for which I have no explanation. When we arrived on the island, it was like paradise. The colours were astonishingly vivid. The sky was bluer than blue; the sand was whiter than white. Even the costumes the people were wearing appeared more brightly coloured. Yet after the incident, all colour seemed to leave the island. To me everything, including the sky appeared to be black. In one second it went from heaven to hell.

"When I left the hospital I was still worrying about this phenomenon. I kept asking Andrew over and over again 'Was the sky black?' On his return to South Africa, as a tsunami survivor, Andrew gave a talk to over three hundred people at Chabad House. Another of the speakers at this meeting, who had also been in Thailand, had taken a myriad of photographs from his hotel window, before and after the tsunami struck.

"There's something very strange about these photos," he told the audience. Before the tidal wave, all the pictures came out in brilliant colour. After the tsunami, all the photographs I had developed came out in black and white."

When Joanne and Andrew landed back on the mainland, she was taken to the Krabi Hospital. "There was absolute chaos and pandemonium in this small provincial hospital. There weren't enough beds to accommodate all the injured. People were lying on the floor. There was blood everywhere. It was like something out of the worst imaginable horror movie.

"I was put in the children's ward and there was a Thai woman there called Pob, whose child had malaria, who looked after me like an angel. I'm not sure what the nurses do in these hospitals — perhaps they help administer drugs — but it was Pob, who even brought in her family from rural areas to assist, who bathed and fed me for the three nights I was in that hospital. I am totally indebted to her."

While she was still in the children's ward, which was overflowing with victims — a makeshift morgue had been established in the hospital basement to cope with the ever increasing number of corpses — Joanne heard a woman talking in a South African accent.

"Please go and see if she's OK," she asked Andrew.

Andrew found the woman, named Riekie, with a huge gash across her face. There was a small television set in the hospital ward with details of the tsunami, all in Thai. Riekie was glued to the television. It transpired that she was looking for her missing husband, her four children and a sister.

The family had lost all their possessions in the disaster and it now seemed that the remaining family members might well have lost their lives.

Blessed with a generous heart, Andrew immediately booked Riekie into a nearby luxury hotel saying that he she was to have twenty-four hour access to the hotel's telephone and Internet services. He ensured that she had sufficient clothing and toiletries for the duration of her stay.

Joanne was airlifted from the Krabi Hospital to ICU in the Bangkok Hospital. On the third night of her stay there she received a call from a jubilant Riekie.

"They've found my husband and all of my children. Everybody's fine." She rejoiced. The phone line then went quiet for a moment.

"Only my sister is dead."

"It subsequently transpired that Riekie's husband had seen a documentary on National Geographic about what measures to adopt should one be unfortunate enough to be caught in a tsunami.

He knew that you had to make for high ground. So he took his four children and helped them climb to the top of the tallest tree. When his smallest child fell from the tree, a passer-by lifted her back up. Heaven knows how long they were there. You know, in the midst of all the disasters, there were a few stories with reasonably happy endings like this one," reflected Joanne.

****

The South African Jewish Board of Deputies, SOS, Discovery Health and Netcare were the four organisations involved in assisting tsunami victims back to South Africa. From all accounts they did a magnificent job. From the Bangkok Hospital, Joanne, together with other injured South African survivors, were flown back home through the auspices of SOS and Discovery Health. She has nothing but praise for these organisations.

"Locating the different hospitals we were in, then getting the six of us from the Bangkok Hospital back to South Africa together with a team of doctors, qualified nurses and all our medications, was a logistical nightmare.

"From Lanseria Airport, which is where we landed, the other injured patients were taken on stretchers by ambulance to various different hospitals. This difficult manoeuvre was complicated by the fact that I had to be taken by helicopter to Milpark Hospital as the doctors feared that an ambulance ride might further injure my back.

"The efficiency, care and compassion of these four organisations was unbelievable. Probably the South African survivors had better care from these dedicated relief workers than the survivors of any other country in the world."

"You have been through so much, particularly with regard to Frankie ... where in this equation is God for you?"

"Lying in my hospital bed I had so much time to think. At first I was angry with God. Why did so many people have to die? Then I thought how can I be cross with God who has shown me so much mercy by sparing my family? The fact that my little daughter survived is particularly miraculous ... perhaps the whole tsunami had nothing to do with God.

"Maybe it was Mother Earth venting her rage at our human mistreatment of her beautiful bounty. It is an interesting fact that in the tsunami not a single animal was killed. From a spiritual point of view, perhaps it was a karmic occurrence ... maybe these souls all made a contract to leave this earth together. We will never know the answers."

"All I can say with certainty is that my child must have been saved for a purpose. I intend reading up about The Crystal and The Indigo children ... perhaps then I will better understand this great gift that God has given me."

As for Andrew, he continues to go into his sleeping daughter's nursery to gaze in wonderment at his little angel who was so miraculously saved.

If he finds that Frankie is fretful in any way, Andrew will gently lay his hand on her forehead and recites the most powerful prayer that he knows: "Hear, O' Israel, The Lord is our God, The Lord is One. Blessed is the Name of His glorious kingdom forever and ever." Amen.

Postscript: Following the horror of the tsunami, Joanne and Andrew, who have relocated to Israel, have been blessed with two additional miracles — another girl, Georgia, and a boy, Jamie (James).

RENÉ COETZEE

WIFE, MOTHER, SCHOOL PRINCIPAL, CANCER SURVIVOR

COLOURFUL, CLAIRVOYANT, COMMITTED & COURAGEOUS

We are never given a hope, wish or a dream without given opportunities to make them a reality. Some of the most exciting opportunities in my life came clearly disguised as insoluble difficulties! Miracles do happen. I have established my own opinion about magic and miracles. To me it really means to discover one's own inner power and then control events, so creating one's own reality ... go within or go without ... let go and let in God, the God within oneself.
Dimakatso! Izimanga! Miracles! They transcend both time and space; you just have to believe in them and then add faith!
Together we are going to conquer ... God help me not to disappoint you.

René Coetzee

"You're not good enough," was the mantra constantly ringing in René's ears. Not that she didn't try very hard to please everybody. Born into a conservative Afrikaans family, the eldest of four children, she dutifully followed all the doctrines of the Dutch Reformed Church. Together with her parents and siblings, she always said prayers before meals and her attendance at Sunday school was regular. She believed in Jesus and tried to conform to what she thought was expected of her.

Yet inside the young girl was in turmoil. She *knew* that she was different. She asked her dominee (priest) a thousand questions. "If the Blacks are God's people, why can't they go to school with us?"

"Because it's the law," replied the priest.

Dimakatso! Sotho for "miracle." Izimanga! Zulu for "miracle."

"God wouldn't create such a stupid law. I hate the way the Blacks are treated. And why do we call them all these different names? Bantu? Plural? Kaffir? Why can't people see that they've been created by God just like us? Why do they have to walk in the pouring rain when we go to places in our nice cars?"

The priest replied that René must read her Bible and that she would find the answer to all her questions. "But I didn't," the adult René told me, as we sat talking in the sun on my veranda. Her bright red hair, adorned with a single string of hanging beads with a feather at the tip, glistened in the sunlight as she spoke as did the tiny jewel pierced into her left nostril. "I read the Bible and found it to be abstract. I'm a Libra you know and we like things to be balanced."

In order to get pocket money, I used to write short stories for a youth magazine called *Tina*. The editor was happy to publish my stories, so why I wondered, did I get such average marks for my school compositions? It must be because I'm not good enough," concluded René.

It was during this period of her life that René began to 'see' psychic phenomena. I used to see people, either as shadows or else in complete human form and they'd talk to me, telling me about life."

"Dad," demanded René of her father, Piet, "these people I'm seeing ... who do you think they could be?"

"Perhaps somebody has died," replied her father stiffly, "but we don't like to talk about such things in this house."

On occasions when her parents went out, leaving René to babysit her younger siblings, she kept them amused by reading them stories she had written, or if this failed to keep their attention, she'd play the piano for them.

To her surprise, René found that, although she'd never had a piano lesson, she could play almost anything — popular tunes, jazz or classical music.

"Ma, how come I can play the piano?" René asked.

"I can also play the piano," her mother replied.

"Then why don't you?" asked her ever curious daughter.

"Too busy," her mother mumbled.

"I know now that this gift, my ability to play the piano, came from a past life. Perhaps the same was true of my mother, although she never discussed things like that. Not that she isn't extremely wise. She knew the answer to any question I cared to ask her. However, she never dared to speak her truth. She was afraid of what my dad might say."

When Piet bought an organ as a present for the family, he sent his wife for lessons. René, with her obvious talent for music, wondered why she wasn't offered these lessons as well. "Although I try my best, I'm obviously not good enough," she concluded, her self-esteem at a pretty low level.

Thus René was to graduate from high school with her shining light still hid very much under a bushel.

****

Things changed pretty dramatically for René when she entered Teachers' Training College. Suddenly she found her creative side coming to the fore and her story writing talents and unorthodox practical teaching methods gained her much recognition. She also blossomed socially and the boyfriends that had eluded her during her high school career now began to clamber for her attention.

In love with colour, René began to experiment with her appearance and she would appear at the college with brightly coloured clothes and exotically painted nails. "It's a phase she's going through," her worried father decided. He hid his concern that, not finding the answers she sought in the doctrines of the Dutch Reformed Church, his daughter was also studying the teachings of other religions.

The best pupils in the college were invited to apply to do the pre-primary teaching course. The practical examination for this was pretty stringent. Not only was there an oral exam, which involved storytelling, the candidates were required to paint, to play the piano and to sing.

To her surprise and delight, René passed the examination with flying colours. "So I am creative after all," she told herself proudly.

****

Having graduated from Teachers' Training College with distinction, René embarked on her teaching career. Without a permanent post, she taught both young pupils and high school learners; she even taught English, although, coming from an Afrikaans background, her old fears of 'not being good enough' surfaced once again. She was delighted when, that year, her Grade 8 English students all passed their examinations.

While her teaching career was steadily gaining ground, René was experiencing difficulties in her personal life. Married in her early twenties, her life was seemingly perfect. Her husband bought her a beautiful home and the couple associated with high society.

Always aware of her appearance, René did her best to look good. "You're dressing that way for other men," snarled her jealous husband and his emotional abuse soon led to physical abuse. His wife decided to keep this dark secret to herself. "Perhaps if I have a baby, things will change," she thought to herself.

Much to her joy, René was able to fall pregnant. To her great sorrow she miscarried at around sixteen weeks. "How can there be a God if he allows me to lose my child? How can there be a God if he allows Black people to suffer so?" she cried bitterly.

After four years, the couple divorced and René kept herself pretty busy. She started reading the teachings of the great spiritual teachers like Buddha and the Dalai Lama, searching for some meaning to her life. The more she studied, the more she rejected Christianity. "How could the Christians kill so many people in the name of religion?" she asked herself. She also threw herself into her teaching career, convinced that she would never marry again.

However the minute René set eyes on Christo, she fell head over heels in love. Her second marriage only served to make her more ambitious.

"They thought I wasn't good enough when I was at school. They never gave me the merit mark. Well, I'll show them. I don't just want to be a teacher. I want to be the principal of a school," she decided.

Three months after her marriage, to her delight, René found that she was pregnant but had to spend time in hospital to keep the baby. When her daughter was born, René christened her Doreen after her mother.

"The name means 'gift from God' and she is exactly that," beamed René. Little Doreen was a colicky baby. "It was my fault that she had colic," remarked her mother. "Our children are here to reflect who and what we are and I was pretty colicky in my outlook." Soon her daughter was suffering from a more serious problem — a virus in the vessel of her heart, coupled with continual diarrhoea. In order to look after her daughter, René was obliged to give up teaching.

"A teacher. That is what I am. I love it so much. Precious as my daughter is to me, it was not enough for me to simply be a mother. My old feelings of not being good enough began to resurface," remarked René, of her period of being a stay-at-home mother.

When Doreen eventually recovered, it was not easy for René to find a teaching post. "You're a married woman," the Department of Education told her. "It is our policy to employ single women."

Eventually, René found herself as acting head of a pre-primary school in Jeppestown in south Johannesburg. "It was a beautiful school, with wonderful classrooms. However, the school was dying. The White kids were moving away from the area and Black children were not permitted to join the school. They used to hang around the gate asking me if I didn't have a place for them. This broke my heart. It was around this time that the Government introduced Model B schools into the system."

"What were Model B schools?"

"Children of colour could be admitted, provided that they spoke the same language as the lessons were conducted in and they had to fit in with the ethos of the school. Also, the parents had to agree.

"At this time, I had one Coloured child at the school. Her name was Marianne. A school inspector took one look at this little girl and told me 'If I come here again, she'd better not be here.'"

Anger welled up in René. "Next time you come here, I'm going to have a whole school full of children of colour," she promised herself.

Christo had been employed as a policeman during the Apartheid regime. Schools with children of mixed colour were against everything that he had ever been taught. Yet he supported his wife wholly in her endeavour to create a school that admitted pupils irrespective of their race.

It was around this time that the Government, amidst talk of the imminent release of Nelson Mandela from jail, introduced Model C schools — the governing body of the school could decide which pupils to admit.

Soon René's school was filled with all the children of the rainbow nation. Aged between three and six years old, the majority of these youngsters spoke no English or Afrikaans.

"How did you communicate?"

"I did some research and I found ways and means of talking to these children. I noticed that they were extremely shy. So I built a stage and we held mini eisteddfods and I got them to start public speaking. I also noticed that they were scared of dogs, probably because their families couldn't afford to keep pets, and they were terrified of water."

"How did you tackle these problems?"

"I bought an enormous dog into the school. We called it Lollipop and I taught the kids to pet it and play with it. As for the water, Christo had left the police force and he now had a fibre glass company. I asked him to make me a little bench and we put it in the pool and then I and the other teachers would sit with the children on this bench in the water.

"When I saw my beautiful school filled with all these children, I felt such gratitude for this miracle that occurred. As a child I had always dreamed of being a leader, a minister."

"The Minister of Education?"

"No, I always dreamed of being the Minister of Children. Now my dream had come true — I believe implicitly in dreams — and with all these blessing my faith in God was restored."

****

It was around this time, when René, still in her mid-thirties, began experiencing abdominal pain. She had to undergo a hysterectomy — "Only now do I realise that there must have been a malignant growth there" — and, following the operation, she was given a clean bill of health.

In 1997 René, accompanied by the then principal of Malvern Primary, went to a principal's conference in Boston. The dedication and drive of the educators there was an inspiration to René and she came back bursting with new ideas about how to run a successful school.

The principal of Malvern Primary informed René that she was leaving the school. "Why don't you apply for the position?" she asked.

After some hesitation, René moved to Malvern Primary in 1997 as the school's headmistress and was immediately faced with a lot of stress. The school was financially in the red and there was a tremendous staff shortage as many of the teachers had been promoted to higher positions in other schools.

Some of the remaining staff were openly critical of René. "She's come from a pre-primary background," they whispered among themselves. "What does she know about running a primary school?"

Already suffering from a spastic colon, René worked tirelessly to raise the standard of the school, despite being in constant pain. She suffered from back pain and her colon seemed to bloat. Doing her best to ignore this excruciating agony, which sometimes threatened to overwhelm her. Nevertheless, not only was she able, through endless fund raising, to turn the school's financial position around, she also embarked on a staff motivational programme.

"There's no 'I' in team," she told her teachers repeatedly. "We all need to work together."

By 1998, unable to ignore her pain any longer, René finally consulted a doctor. He told her that some of the tissue had remained behind after her hysterectomy operation and that this had formed a band over the colon. "We have to remove this as a matter of urgency and you have to start a course of chemotherapy immediately," he informed her.

Her hair fell out, but her courage did not falter as she soldiered on throughout her illness. With the change in educational policy, René embraced the Black pupils, many from disadvantaged backgrounds, who streamed into the previously all-White Afrikaans-speaking school.

Not that her radical new approach met with unanimous approval. Sometimes, as she sat in the empty school hall, with her psychic ability kicking in, René heard a man talking to her.

"I don't like all these Blacks coming into the school. I don't like the way you line them up." His criticism of her liberal educational policy was endless. It was only some years later that René was able to identify him as an ex staunchly pro-Nationalist Government headmaster of the school who had subsequently died.

At this time, René still worshipped at the Dutch Reformed Church. "This helped heal any rift that I had had with my father and it was also the church that my husband was accustomed to. Of course, my parents were pleased to have their precious granddaughter, Doreen, praying with them in their church."

"What happened to change your spiritual beliefs?"

"I found a book by the metaphysical teacher Louise Hay called *You Can Heal Yourself*. This made a great impression on me. I tried to think myself healthy. I prayed a lot and said many positive affirmations, but finally, I had to admit that I was still ill. When I visited the doctor he told me that my cancer of the colon had reoccurred and that I had only six months to live."

"How did you react to this dreadful news?"

"I went dead. I heard nothing more that he said to me. In order to try and relax, I had taken up golf. Now I drove to the golf course and sat there in my car. I don't know how many hours I sat there just staring into space, but when I became aware of my surroundings, I realised that it was dark.

"I drove home to be greeted by my frantic family. I was not answering my mobile phone and no-one knew what had happened to me. Excusing myself, I went upstairs and, for the first time in a long time, I read the Bible.

"I heard a voice telling me to read Isaiah 38:1-5. Suddenly my room was flooded with wonderful white light and I heard a voice say: 'Wherever you read Hezekiah, substitute your name, René.'

"What I read was that God was going to save me for a prescribed number of years as I still had so much work to do on this planet. With tears streaming down my face, I looked up and whispered 'Thank you, God.'"

****

Aware that she needed to stop the chemotherapy, which was making her sick, thin and listless, René went next morning to The District Office. "I know that when you want long leave, you need to apply three months in advance. But, I need long leave and I need it *now.*"

Once the matter of leave was settled, René decided, on the advice of the doctor's receptionist, to see Hospice. One of the recently appointed teachers at the school told René about a particularly enlightened Hospice counsellor, so that is where she went.

"I can honestly say that it is with Hospice that my real spiritual journey began. I was supposed to go for counselling, but when I got there, I saw a poster on the wall which said *Become A Hospice Counsellor.* The cost of the course was written at the bottom. I looked in my bag and I had the exact amount. I heard a voice in my head saying 'Enrol.'

"This course was the best healing that I could have. Because when the lecturer spoke about the patients and the pain and suffering they were going through, I was able to process the patient's feelings, for I had been there as a patient.

"I was able to relive all my old thought processes and then I was able to re-pattern my thinking. I also started reading all the spiritual books I could find — Diana Cooper, Doreen Virtue, Brandon Bays, Deepak Chopra. What I now learned threw all my childhood religious indoctrination out of the window."

"Explain what you learned."

"Instead of seeing God as some remote distant figure, I came to realise that God is within each one of us. With this self-awareness that God was part of me, my self-esteem increased. I also came to believe in past lives.

"While I was on long leave and healing myself spiritually, I went to a health fair in Cape Town and I picked up a pamphlet from Melissie Jolly about colour therapy."

"What is colour therapy?"

"Colourworks, which works through bottles of rainbow coloured oils, is a therapy which enables one to discover for oneself what is at the root of any physical, emotional, mental or spiritual imbalance."

"What was Melissie able to discover?"

"That through all the questions that I had asked as a child about God that had not been satisfactorily answered, because I was unable to find my God, I had a bitterness in me that had created this disease."

So impressed was René with all she learned about Colourworks, while still doing counselling work for Hospice, she studied Aura Soma Therapy, Levels One and Two.

With spiritual healer Penni du Plessis, René learnt about the Antaneea Technique as she underwent therapy.

"What is the Antaneea Technique?"

"It is vibrational medicine that combines the entire spectrum of healing possibilities using only natural elements. Movement, sound, touch and colour are used to nourish the human energy system and to aid the body in recovering its own balance of health. True healing is only completed when the cause of the condition or illness is addressed and transformed."

Within her six months of long leave, René not only became a Hospice Counsellor, a qualified teacher of colour therapy, expert in her understanding of Antaneea, she also studied various other spiritual practices such as numerology and astrology.

To the amazement of her doctors, Rene's cancer was found to be in remission, but her steely resolve went into action. She was going to take her school, Malvern Primary and introduce spirituality into the school as part of the student's daily curriculum."

She knew that she would cross swords with some of her more conservative staff and that the children might have difficulty in comprehending the spiritual practices that she intended to put into operation, but this did not daunt René. She was on a Divine Mission!

****

A visit to Malvern Primary School is an extraordinary, yet totally uplifting experience. With René at the helm as headmistress, through her devotion and dedication, she has lifted her school, with its almost one thousand Black pupils aged between six and fifteen years, from being a thoroughly average institution to one crowned with awards for outstanding achievement.

"When I was diagnosed with cancer, I went on to pretend that everything was OK. Yet I still went through anger, guilt and bitterness. Through Hospice, I learnt to be a whole person. How do you heal if you don't know how you feel?"

Thus mornings at Malvern Primary start with a feeling check for both pupils and staff. A pre-school visit to the staff room reveals all the school staff, everyone from gardeners and cleaners, to teachers to the headmistress, herself sitting around tables, filled with angel cards. Incense is burning and candles are lit.

Then a feeling check is done on all the staff. "How are you feeling today?" The answers range from "Focused, excited, enthusiastic, energetic to scared, worried, fearful."

"When I started doing these feeling checks with the pupils, at first they were unable to express their feelings. So I only started with five simple emotions like happy, joyful, sad, cross, unhappy.

"Today, my learners are able to express all the emotions that are in their heart. I want all my staff and pupils to know that they are unique and important. They must never feel alone. My door is always open for either staff or pupils to come and discuss their problems with me," commented René."

Everything positive that René has learnt in her years of doing spiritual courses are incorporated into the school's daily routine and, whenever possible, she sends her staff on these courses, so that they will have first-hand knowledge of what she is trying to achieve.

Thus both staff and all the pupils will do Brain Gym exercises before academic learning starts. "It is important that real needs are met for balance in life. The Brain Gym is a series of fun and energising activities that are effective in preparing any learner for specific and co-ordination skills," explained René.

"What I have learnt is that lack of water, nutrition, emotions, environment, pollution, electromagnetic fields, lack of movement and structured learning is what contributes to stress.

"Many of my pupils come from dysfunctional backgrounds and when I began as head of the school, there were many problems with delinquency and drugs. With the spiritual practices I have incorporated, these problems have been reduced to a minimum. For example, I invite glue sniffers to come into my office and try my healing coloured oils. They soon get to know that the yellow oil will calm them."

A visit to a classroom revealed bright-eyed happy children, with a bottle of filtered water on every desk, happily doing the simple Brain Gym exercises with their teacher.

"These exercises may look basic," said René, immediately joining in with the class, "but they have been designed to develop the brain's three dimensions — the lateral dimension, the focus dimension and the centring dimension, so that my learners are empowered by the balance of left and right brain activities, the development of self-image, emotional intelligence and learning skills."

"Don't all these exercises take away from their conventional learning time?"

"That's what teachers from other schools say. However, all it takes is half an hour a day and my pupils' academic and sporting results have improved dramatically," remarked René with obvious pride.

In order to ensure each and every pupil performs to the best of his or her ability, René has also, with the assistance of numerology and astrology worked out an individual chart for each leaner. "Some of the mothers say that I know their children better than they do themselves," she smiles.

"There are almost one thousand pupils in the school. How do you find time for all this?"

"I need very little sleep. And, although my cancer is in remission, who knows how much time I have left? I cannot waste a single moment."

"Have you seen the new project that our headmistress is developing for the teachers?" asked the vice-head, Cobus Barnard, with obvious pride. (A private chat with him later revealed that coming from an All-White Afrikaans School, he initially experienced some difficulty in working under this unconventional new regime.)

René had decided to give each teacher a simple exercise book — the school's budget may be tight but her vision is seemingly endless — which she had covered and decoratedherself and inscribed it with the following message:

Your soul longs for creative expression. Honour nudges within to guide you how to express it. Write it down. Writing may be for your own enjoyment, or may be a cathartic experience of self-expression in this private journal.

As you work with your connection to the written word, you may receive Divine Guidance.
God bless.

"René, why are you so driven? Is it simply that as a child you felt that you were not good enough?"

"Rosemary," asked the headmistress of her spirit guide who is always with her, "may I tell Alexandra the whole truth about my ambition to succeed?" René grew uncharacteristically quiet for a moment and she appeared to be listening intently.

"Rosemary says that I may tell you this. When I was doing Colourworks with Melissie Jolly, I went back to one of my previous lives. I have had many lives. In one life I was a writer who was deaf and dumb. But I also found that I had been Dingaan."

"Dingaan, the Zulu chief who became king after assassinating his half-brother, Shaka, the founder of the Zulu nation?"

"Yes. Dingaan thought he was a great man, but in truth he was very cruel. Not only did he ambush and kill about 500 Boers (White farmers) in 1838, he also treated many of his own people extremely harshly. He pretended to be high and mighty, yet when he went to bed, he felt so small. Now, it is time for me to redress the wrongs of my Dingaan energy."

In other words, you present life is payback time?"

"Yes. It is time for me to fully regain my self-respect and self-esteem."

When I see the messages of adoration and love that were sent to René by both pupils and staff, when she underwent a recent colon operation (to ensure that there was no recurrence of her cancer), I would say that she has more than succeeded!

As one of her pupils wrote:

THIS IS HOW I SEE MY PRINCIPLE (PRINCIPAL) FROM A MALVERN LEARNER:

*P is for the PEACE you brought to our school.
R for the RESPECT you gave us.
I for really IMPRESSING us.
N for changing our NEGATIVES to positives.
C for CARING for us so much.
I for being INTELLIGENT as a principle.
P for PREPARING fun and games.
L for staying LATE to prepare our things.
E for letting out your ENERGY.*

PETER FELDMAN

JOURNALIST, MOVIE CRITIC, HIJACK SURVIVOR

SAVED BY A HOST OF SAVIOURS

THE GATHERING

Gather around my children hear what I have to say
My work is done now, I must move away
Distant thunder calling, spirits in the sky
Reach out for someone that is my cry
You're the only hope now, to stem the rising pain
Cleansed by the running waters of a fierce African rain
Children of Africa, fingers in virgin soil
Learn to love they neighbour, away from all this toil
The future's in your hands now
You will have to pray
Don't forget your heritage
And what I have to say
Hold hands with your brothers
Let's sing a song of love
Hold hands with your brothers
Look for the white dove above
Hold hands with your brothers
Look for a road to peace
Hold hands with your brothers
Let all this hatred cease
Gather around my children, hear what I have to say
Ancient wisdom glowing, each and every day
Smiles across a nation, light a thousand fires
Feelings deep inside me, these will never expire
Hold hands with your brothers
Let us all rejoice
Hold hands with your brothers
We have made a choice.

Peter Feldman

When the pogroms started in Russia, young Ben Feldman, a mere boy of thirteen, left the shelter together with his two brothers and came to South Africa. Their boat landed in the Cape and that is where Ben's two brothers remained. Benjamin came to Johannesburg to settle and here he met and married his wife, Mary.

Their much longed for son, Peter, was born in 1944 after the couple had been married for seven years. Ben had been called up to fight in El-Alamein, but he returned shortly before the birth of his son. Young Peter suffered from asthma and severe eczema. In order to prevent him from scratching his inflamed skin, he was forced to wear special gloves. The doctor assured his concerned mother that Peter would be all right — "Just as soon as his teeth come out."

Ben opened a furniture shop in the smallish town of Alberton. Peter who had, as the doctor predicted, overcome his childhood ailments, went to school there. As an only child, Peter was a little reserved. Although he enjoyed his own company, he was not adverse to participating in games with his schoolmates. Despite being fairly solitary, Peter was seldom alone. From a young age he was aware of the presence of the spirit world. He didn't see spirits, but he could feel them touching him — running their fingers through his hair, gently touching his arms. He also used to hear tapping sounds against the window.

"Mom, can you hear those tapping noises?" he enquired.

"No, Peter, don't be silly," replied Mary. "It's just some birds or the branches brushing the window panes."

"But I don't see any birds and there are no branches," protested the young boy.

Peter also knew instinctively when he entered a room if there was negative energy, if something bad had previously happened there. "Ma, I don't like it here. It just doesn't feel right."

Worried by their son's isolation, when the time came for Peter to go to high school, his parents made the wise decision to send him to boarding school. "I spent my formative years away from home and that gave me the structures for life. I learnt to cope on my own."

On a Saturday night the schoolboys got the chance to go to the regular dance and meet with the hostel girls. Reserved and shy with the opposite sex, Peter preferred to stay in the school dormitory along with four of his friends. The guys were playing with the Oui-ja board, trying to call up the spirits when a prefect, a deeply religious boy, walked in unexpectedly.

"What the hell do you think you guys are doing?" he asked them angrily.

"That really frightened me. Closing the Oui-ja board, I decided that the time was not right for me to continue my search for contact with the spirit world," remarked Peter.

****

At school Peter was pretty much an average student, but he loved writing.

His first article, the story of a little boy and his horse, was published when he was only seven years old. When visitors came around, Peter did not socialize very much with their children — he preferred to closet himself away in the study and write his stories.

One of his most prized possessions was and still is — a well-thumbed Collins English Gem Dictionary, which his admiring aunt gave him as a present. The inscription read: *Dear Peter: to help you with your stories. Love from Aunt Leigh.* In the fullness of time when Peter became a well-known journalist for *The Star* newspaper he still took this dictionary to work until one day it suddenly occurred to him that this most prized book might be nicked by a fellow journalist who didn't realise its sentimental worth.

A neighbour's child was a member of the *Junior Sunday Times Club,* the children's section *The Sunday Times* newspaper. "Why don't you become a member?" suggested the neighbour to Peter.

So Peter duly became a member and was given a little badge to prove his membership. The young scribe started submitting his stories and soon found himself winning prizes. The editor of the junior club was intrigued by the diligence, enthusiasm and talent of this youngster as well as being impressed by the sheer volume of work that Peter tirelessly submitted. She arranged to meet Peter and a firm friendship quickly developed.

"What do you want to be when you grow up?" she asked Peter.

Peter grew solemn and then looked her straight in the eye. "I want to be a journalist like you," he solemnly declared.

****

During his high school years, Peter continued writing his stories. He was the unanimous choice for editor of the school magazine. He also excelled at sport, playing rugby for the school team and becoming an accomplished runner. Writing, however, remained his first love and he continued to submit his stories to various publications. Peter even managed to get a story published in *The Irish Times* — quite an achievement for a South African schoolboy.

Sixteen-year-old Peter had a friend named Barry who had a difficult home life. One day Barry, sick of all the disharmony in his home, turned to Peter and said: "You know what? We ought to write a book telling parents how to bring up their kids."

"Great idea", enthused Peter. This book entitled *Is Life a Bed of Roses?* dealt with a variety of teenage issues such as promiscuity, drugs, drinking and relationships. Barry, through the angst of his difficult home life, was able to supply most of the psychological insights for the book and Peter was the writer. Once the work was finished, Peter and Barry received an enormous amount of publicity in the press ... the only thing they couldn't find was a publisher who believed enough in two sixteen year olds to actually publish the book.

Not phased, Peter decided to submit individual chapters from the book to *The Star* newspaper's *Teen Beat* section. Soon *The Star* was publishing instalments from *Is Life a Bed of Roses?* on a weekly basis, complete with pictures of its budding authors, Peter and Barry.

A visit was arranged between Peter and the Teen Beat editor, Peter Hawthorne. When Peter told him of his journalistic aspirations, Hawthorne replied: "Then come and see me when you've finished school and you've got your matriculation certificate."

After completing his schooling, Peter, who knew that *The Star* had a cadet training school for would-be journalists, went to their offices armed with his scrapbook filled with his many published articles. He applied and was accepted as a trainee journalist. The only fly in the ointment being that Peter had already been called up to do his compulsory military training.

On his return to civilian life, Peter found himself working as a journalist.

Despite his youth, he had to file some pretty grim reports — about a man whose wife and two children were burnt to death in a caravan as well as other heart rending accounts of loss of life.

Peter soon discovered that he was a good listener — that he empathised with the people that he interviewed and he was able to give them some pretty sensible advice. "You know, I was picking up things that I couldn't understand. I somehow knew what to say to these people to comfort them. I had a sense of knowing when certain things were going to happen and I also used to hear things ... the spirits were sending me messages."

Besides his desire to be a journalist, Peter had a great love of the movies. As a young boy, he knew the manager of the local cinema and he used to sneak out at night and watch films whenever he could. He knew that he was going to make a living out of writing as well as from the movies, something that made no sense to Peter's father.

"'My boy, you need to get a decent job, something that pays," Benjamin urged his only son.

"Dad, I'm going to prove you wrong," Peter muttered, filled with stubborn determination.

****

In 1976, Peter married his wife, Carla, a speech and drama teacher, and the union produced a daughter, Janna, whom her doting father describes as 'the light of my life.'

By 1978, Peter was making his mark both as a journalist and as a movie critic. By this time, his beloved father was ailing and Peter visited him every Sunday. One Sunday however, Peter had a break from this routine. Having spent the day with a friend, he had been invited that evening by well-known local deejay Lance James to come onto his show *Keep it Country*. Celebrity guests to the show would take a collection of their favourite records to the studio, talk about the music they liked and then play their chosen discs over the air. Peter told Carla that he would visit his father once the show was over.

During the course of the show Lance asked Peter if he'd ever played a musical instrument. "No," Peter replied, "although my dad always wanted me to play the trumpet."

As the show ended, the studio phone rang.

"It's for you, Peter. And it's urgent."

Peter turned to Carla who had been waiting for him during the hour-long show. "It's Dad. I know that he's passed away."

"How do you know that?" asked Carla in genuine surprise.

"I just do," replied Peter.

Peter and Carla arrived at his parents' apartment to find it in darkness.

Then Peter's mother appeared through the doorway. "He's gone," she said, sobbing. Feeling guilty that he had not been with his dad, Peter went into the bedroom. He found his father lying peacefully in his bed.

He sat next to him on the bed for an hour and Peter told his dead father that he was sorry that he hadn't been there for him but that he loved him. "I had the eerie feeling that he was still with me ... that he heard every word I said to him."

Peter's uncle came into the room. "Your dad heard you when you spoke on the radio. He was very proud of you."

Some years later, while he was working for *The Star* newspaper, his editor knowing Peter's interest in spirituality, suggested that he interview a number of psychics, including Beverley Rhodes, who was doing a show at Sun City.

"Your father is with you," she told Peter. To prove her point, she drew a quick sketch of Ben for Peter, even including his birthmark. Beverley grew silent for a moment. "Your dad wants me to tell you something. He wants you to know that he was with you that night in the studio. That he's with you all the time. He wants to prove to you that the spirit world exists and that there is life on the other side."

Peter paused for a moment. "My dad was a little Jewish guy from Eastern European stock. He lived for his family and his work. He went to synagogue only on the High Holy Days. Yet here he was, through Beverley, telling me about the spirit world."

"Would you say that Beverley was accurate as a channel?"

"She described the pattern of the bedroom carpet of the room in which my dad died exactly. I know that my late father was with us that day."

****

One evening, Carla came home with the news that a friend of hers who belonged to a spiritual group had invited them to one of the group's meetings. Although Peter wasn't able to attend this meeting, he expressed his interest in attending a séance. He later got into contact with the people involved and decided to do an interview with them.

"When I met them, I felt such a vibe, an energy within this circle of four people."

The group likewise felt Peter's energy. "We pick up that you having amazing spiritual powers. We'd like to develop you as a medium," they told him.

Peter immediately decided to join the group. It was a relationship that was to last for four years. "During this time we worked on rescue missions of lost spirits. I cannot tell you what amazing things I saw."

"What exactly did your rescue missions entail?"

"The medium would call in the spirits. They were souls in limbo. Children who had been raped and murdered. People who had died, but who were unable to pass over. The group members would hold hands and we would chant prayers and we were able to direct these unfortunate souls towards The Light or the Godhead.

"The work was exhausting and frightening. I can still hear their anguished screams. Let me tell you we heard and saw horrible sights. Despite being totally draining, we were able to do a great deal of healing work.

"When I was in the circle all the pieces of the jigsaw of my life began to fit together. I came to realise why I was here; why I was a writer; why I was able to talk to people when I was young and had little life experience. I understood about spirits and people's guides. I knew that dad was with me and I was able to tell my mother that even though he'd passed on, that my father was fine.

"My mother got ill and she died of cancer in 1991. Before she passed on I was able to tell her with certainty that she must not worry ... that Dad would be there to meet her and help her in the spirit world."

Finding it difficult to cope with his day job and his work within the circle, Peter left the group. Some years later he was to join a second spiritual circle. "Our teachers were incredible — amazingly powerful mediums. I learnt so much. Although we both wanted children, it was only after we had been married for a number of years that Carla fell pregnant.

"Through the group I was told the reasons for our problems and then we had this amazing, gifted child, Janna. Our daughter has these incredible green eyes and she is highly spiritual. She is truly a gift from God."

When this circle broke up after about six years, Peter experienced a spiritual shutdown — depressed at work, he thought that he could ignore the spirit world while he got his earthly life in order. Little did he know what a dramatic wake-up call the spirits had in store for him!

****

One rainy Thursday night in 1991, Peter was travelling down The Munro Drive, a road that winds down the mountainside at a pretty steep gradient.

Peter was travelling fast and as he descended the hill he slammed on his brakes in order to avoid the long traffic build-up at the stop street. His car skidded out of control into a stream of traffic coming towards him. Terrified, he realised that he was in danger of killing himself. Calling out to his angel he said: "What am I going to do?"

As if by magic a gap appeared between the two cars in front of him and he skidded through this gap and his car came to rest on the curb, almost as if he had parked it there. Peter broke down in tears and he cried out to his angels: "Thank you. You were with me. You are telling me something. You are there!"

The driver of one of the oncoming cars stopped. "Are you OK?"

Peter nodded and drove home, very grateful that the only damage was a slight dent to the car.

The very next Tuesday morning, Peter was to receive further proof that his guardian angels were truly looking after him. He dropped Janna off at primary school and he then returned to the house.

The garage doors had to be operated manually and so, as he slowed down his car and climbed out to close them, a man materialised from behind a tall tree. With mounting trepidation, Peter noticed that the man was stocky and well-built with disproportionately large hands, which made the gun he was holding look like a toy.

His assailant grabbed Peter and indicated that he wanted the car.

"Take the car," replied Peter. "But don't shoot me." The man simply stood there menacing him until Peter panicked and shouted. Then he heard a shot ringing out, although he didn't feel anything. It was only when Peter looked down at his shirt and saw the growing bloodstain that he realised that he had been shot in the stomach. His attacker was able to get into the car — the engine was still running — and he reversed out of the garage at breakneck speed.

Peter pressed the panic button and, alerted by his screams, Carla and the domestic helper, Lizzie, came to see what the commotion was about.

"I've been shot," cried Peter. The two women were able to pull him into the house and as he lay on the landing, he felt a fire inside him.

He closed his eyes and said: "Dear God, am I going to die?" Suddenly he felt a wonderful warmth surrounding him. It seemed as if someone was cradling his head. From his sitting in spiritual circles, Peter knew how his guides worked. "I know you're with me," he said. Then he heard a voice in his head saying: "No, you will be alright. You've still got too much work to do."

By this time, the paramedics had arrived with an ambulance. Peter heard Carla giving them the number of his car. Peter quickly called out the correct registration.

"He's going to be fine," the paramedic consoled Carla.

Peter was rushed by ambulance to the hospital. "It was like a movie," he recalled. "The sirens were blaring as the ambulance sped through the streets. Once I was in the trauma section of the hospital, one of the women working there recognised me: "It's the journalist Peter Feldman," she said.

News of the hijacking of a well-known newspaperman quickly reached the media and as soon as he was well enough, Peter had to hold a press conference to assure everyone that he had survived his ordeal.

The surgeon who operated on Peter was able to dislodge the small calibre bullet that had entered at the stomach, miraculously missing all the vital organs.

"Luckily the shooting occurred at a time when I was writing restaurant reviews for the newspaper."

"What are you getting at?"

"It's a polite way of saying that I was fatter then than I am now — the doctor said that it was this layer of fat that saved me," smiled Peter.

****

It was these two incidents that gave Peter the certain knowledge that we all have our guardian angels looking after us. With his strengthened belief in the angelic realm, he one day got a call from music producer, Patric Van Blerk.

"My sister, Cheryl, is bringing out Diana Cooper from the UK. She's very well-known there for the work she does ... through her books and her lectures Diana teaches people all about angels. I would like you to meet her and do an interview. I know that you two would get along like a house on fire."

Patric's words proved to be prophetic. For not only was this introduction the start of a great friendship between Diana and Peter. Diana also told Peter that he had a deep spiritual core that very few people were lucky enough to be blessed with.

"You are already connected to the angels. Try to develop this connection even further," Diana urged him.

As if in answer to her entreaty, a shower of small white feathers fell to the ground as they spoke.

"Peter, these are the angels' calling cards. I hope that you will embrace these signs and make the angels part of your everyday life," counselled Diana.

****

Today Peter is in a very good place. Through Diana Cooper's books, tapes and angel workshops, he feels that he has acquired a real knowledge of the angel hierarchy. This aligned with his previous knowledge and understanding of the spirits of the departed, enables him to say with great feeling: "Every day I thank God for another day. There's so much I still want to do. Whether we understand it or not, there is a reason for everything that happens on this earth.

"For the past five years, my focus has been on angels. Through my writing, through my counselling I am able to bring people into contact with angels. In my office I do angel readings."

"Do you see angels?"

"I don't see them. But I feel them. I know when they're with me. When they want me to do something. Every morning I wake up, I shower so that I'm clean. Then I meditate, thinking on my angels. I speak to them and ask them what they want me to do. I ask them to bring healing to people whom I know are suffering ..."

"Do you have a special angel?"

"Well, I know that Archangel Michael is here looking after this house. I feel his presence. I believe that he looks down on us each evening ... and you know that he is not alone when it comes to protecting the house. He has an assistant."

"And who may that be?"

"It's my little Maltese, Cassie. You won't believe this ... this tiny ball of fluff climbs onto the roof and watches out to see that no harm comes to me or any member of my family."

Peter Feldman was saved by angels twice in one week. He might have kept this knowledge to himself. But as his friend Diana Cooper writes in her famous book *Angel Inspiration*: "He is one of the most genuine and gifted journalists I know and he has the courage to talk and write about angels."

RODNEY & HEILA DOWNEY

ZEN BUDDHISTS

CREATING PRISONERS OF PEACE

All evil actions committed by me, since time immemorial, stemming from greed, anger and ignorance, arising from body, speech and mind, I now repent having committed.

FOUR GREAT VOWS

Sentient beings are numberless —
We vow to save them all;
Delusions are endless —
We vow to cut through them all;
The teachings are infinite —
We vow to learn them all;
The Buddha way is inconceivable —
We vow to attain it.

Rodney Downey grew up in England and came to South Africa with his family when he was twelve years old. An outsider at school, he began to explore Western and Oriental philosophies and mystic paths at a young age. He was later to return to England where he commenced a career in the rag trade.

On his return to South Africa, he put his search for answers into the meaning of life on hold as he concentrated in building up a successful career in the fashion industry. He married and had three daughters. His subsequent divorce resulted in him gaining custody of his young girls. A demanding career plus the responsibility of rearing his children left him little time for spirituality in his busy life.

A year after his divorce, he met Heila. A statuesque red-haired, she was also involved in the fashion industry, working as a ramp model and doing choreography for fashion shows.

Following their marriage, life seemed rich with material promise.

Rodney was by this time a director of the prosperous Foschini fashion chain and Heila's career was also flourishing. The Downeys were living a dream existence — a beautiful home, acres of garden, a swimming pool, luxury cars. And yet they both felt, that in spite of this material abundance, there was something lacking in their lives.

In 1980 they came to hear that the Buddhist retreat, in Ixopo Natal were holding a Zen Buddhist retreat for business executives and they decided that they would like to attend.

At this stage they had little knowledge of the Buddhist philosophy and practices and had they known that during the five day retreat they had to sleep in separate rooms, practice endless meditation and commit themselves to silence, they probably would not have stayed for the duration of the course.

"It was the silence that did it," said Heila with a laugh. "I couldn't ask Rodney if he wanted to leave and he likewise couldn't ask me if I was enjoying myself or not."

For both of them, this retreat was life changing. They instinctively knew that their journey through this world would henceforth lead them down a deeply spiritual pathway.

"What is Zen?" I asked.

"Zen is very simple. It is about the true essence of all things, without attachments or opinions. It is not a belief system, nor is it a dogma. Zen is a system of doing, which imbues a rare sense of dignity — free from attachments, balanced, self-reliant and open. Zen enables us to wake up to the delusions and attachments of human existence," explained Rodney.

In 1981 Rodney and Heila started the Dharma Centre in Somerset West. For some years the Centre based its activities and teachings on the Rochester Zen Centre, led by Philip Kapleau Roshi, who after many years of formal training in Japanese temples became one of the pioneers of American Zen.

In 1991, inspired by the teachings of Zen Master Seung Sahn, who established Korean Zen on American soil in the early '70's, they changed direction and formally adopted the teaching and practice style of the Kwan Um School of Zen, while still drawing on their insights and experiences gleaned whilst practising at the Rochester Zen Centre.

It was during this year that Rodney and Heila's Dharma Centre was officially appointed as the Head Temple of the school in Africa under the guidance of Su Bong Zen Master, who played a pivotal role in the further development of the Centre and school until his death in 1994. At the end of 1995, the Downeys relocated their Centre to the beautiful country town of Robertson in the Cape, while establishing a new urban Centre in Rondebosch. The Robertson centre is today the only full-time residential Zen centre in Africa, offering a daily practice schedule with teaching support. Situated in a valley of wine and roses, with cool, crisp mountain air — "There's zero pollution in Robertson," Heila was quick to inform me — the Robertson retreat, complete with its own in-house master chef, offering the best in vegetarian food, is a place that could aptly be described as heaven on earth.

In April 1996 Heila became the first African Ji Do Poep Sa Nim (Master Dharma Teacher) in Africa, officially authorised to lead retreats and teach Kong-an practice. In the same year Rodney was appointed as the Abbot of the Dharma Centre, at the same time becoming Senior Dharma teacher.

Not forsaking his links with the secular world completely, Rodney, together with Heila, have pioneered a series of lectures, combining both business and meditation practice, which they delivered at The University of Cape Town's Graduate School of Business Executive M.B.A. Course.

Heila served for many years on the Executive Committee of Lifeline crisis counselling service and also became involved in HIV/AIDS counselling. An involvement that was to stand her in good stead when Poep Am, a maximum security prisoner in Malmesbury Prison, wrote to the Dharma Centre requesting help and assistance in learning meditation.

"Inspired by Poep Am, a prisoner serving time for the murder of a prominent businessman, who had the sincere desire to transform his life of crime into something more meaningful, we started our present programme in Malmesbury New Prison in the middle of 1998. The first precepts ceremony in the history of the South African Correctional Services was held in the year 2000. There have subsequently been other precepts ceremonies.

"In March 2002 we held our first mediation retreat of three days and we now have ongoing intensive retreats based on our MAIA (Mindful Awareness in Action) Programme. These retreats are interdenominational and offer a workable approach to mindful awareness. We have up to forty inmates participating in this programme at one time.

"Our other approach is traditional Zen teaching, which is identical to what we offer at our centres in Cape Town and Robertson," Heila explained.

Their MAIA Programme with the inmates of Malmesbury Prison who have chosen, often to the scorn and derision of their fellow prisoners, to follow a more spiritual path has been highly successful. So much so, that there have been requests by the prison authorities to extend this programme to other maximum security prisons in the Cape.

The day I went to Malmesbury Prison to watch the Prison Programme in action, was the day that Rodney and Heila arrived in the hall to an enthusiastic reception from the twenty prisoners who had come for Zen Practice. The Downeys had recently returned from Brazil where they had been conducting retreats and they arrived with small presents for the prisoners.

"We've got something for you from Brazil," smiled Heila.

The gifts of wooden spoons — "We could have had problems with the prison authorities if we'd brought in metal spoons," laughed Heila to me. The spoons were enthusiastically received by the men.

"I don't know when anyone last bought me a present," one of the prisoners told Heila.

Another prisoner interjected here. "The other priceless gift you gave us was the five day retreat. "When did I last see the sun without bars?"

The prisoners then put on the simple robes of the Zen Buddhists and they went to sit cross-legged on cushions on the floor. Lean from their Spartan prison diet — "they give us enough to keep us alive" one of the prisoners told me, "not a morsel more," and with the majority of the men sporting closely shaved skulls, these unlikely spiritual seekers looked not at all like the serious offenders they were, but rather like devout Buddhists.

The room we were sitting in was a large, but simple prison hall.

An altar had been fashioned from an everyday table and the prisoner, Poep Am, as founder of the group had the honour to sit in front of this altar. The other prisoners sat in a semi-circle, with Rodney and Heila sitting opposite Poep Am, also cross-legged on the floor.

Bowing is very sacred to the Buddhists. Bows are a gesture of humility. We do not bow to another, but rather in the face of the 'other.' On the Buddhist altar is a figure of Buddha, this is the other. Bowing acknowledges the other, but not as something separate. The bow, and prostration comes from the most profound depths of our aliveness.

The prisoners are today going to start their Zen session with acknowledgement of their repentance. Heila tells them that repentance will help with their healing. She asks them to be honest and humble and tells them that what they share belongs to the group.

"Your confession needs to be as specific as possible. You can start your confession with the words I am sorry about … If you wish to address the group, hold this bowl which is filled with incense, talk, then bow again when you are finished and pass it on to the next person.

"However, if this is too difficult for you, then simply take the bowl of incense that is being passed from one person to the next, take it to your eye level and pass it on. Then bow," Heila instructs the men. Her manner is firm, yet gentle.

The men then chant the following words three times: "All evil actions committed by me, since time immemorial, stemming from greed, anger and ignorance, arising from body, speech and mind, I now repent having committed."

"Recognise and acknowledge the evil of past deeds. Genuine repentance must put an end to thoughts and actions that cause distress to others," continued Heila.

For some of the prisoners repentance is easy: "I ask forgiveness from my brothers for everything I did wrong. For my family outside I want to be a better person. I ask forgiveness for all the vows I have broken, for all the suffering that I have caused."

For others there is still anger and resentment: "I'm no angel. Far from it. At this point I don't see myself as a good person, no matter how hard I try. There is no one within this group that I trust enough to want to share anything with. When I walk passed you brothers, you don't have the decency to greet me. If you can't even do that simple thing, then how can we talk about sincerity and honesty?"

One of the prisoners called Hyon Kwang says: "I always think that I am justified in saying harsh things. I am always looking for faults in others; I never look for faults in myself. Anger and disappointment are weighing me down. Be patient with me, my brothers and I will try to be patient with you."

Only one of the prisoners declines to talk. The others are only too willing to unburden their souls. I am struck by the fluency of their words; the intelligence of their observations. Many of them come from poor homes and lack education. Within the prison, they are permitted to study. One of the men has just gained his Matriculation Certificate. Another is studying Information Technology. All the men within this room are committed to learning about spirituality and meditation.

I think of the words of Robert W Gebka, a holistic counsellor, a traditional complementary healer, and a metaphysical practitioner with the International Metaphysical Ministry in the USA: "The lotus or water lily is a flower that grows out of the dirt and mud and struggles through until it emerges on top above the water, beautiful, clean and pure. It is really an extraordinary flower. It is also a symbol used among many religions. It symbolises purity and enlightenment, transcendence — transcending the destructive habits, thoughts and feelings and entering the highest bliss of Enlightenment."

Helia pauses to reflect.

"This is exactly what is happening to the prisoners. Some of them never grow out of the mud ... either because they don't want to or they are used to staying in the state of criminal mind. But some of them do want to grow, to move through the pain and misery of rehabilitation, finally emerging on top, being mentally balanced and having the life skills to live a life free of crime with a more peaceful mind.

"Therefore, do we give them a chance or do we let them stay at the bottom of the deep and dirty lake of criminal life style? I say we give them a chance. I think that there is nothing more worthy than to invest in a human being who will one day become part of society and who will once again be a balanced person rather than a criminal."

****

Heila and Rodney, with the permission of the prison authorities, have arranged for me to talk to some of the prisoners. Here are extracts of some of the interviews I conducted with these men. These are murderers, rapists and thieves, violent men, who are all serving long-term prison sentences.

I am humbled by listening to them. I come to understand Heila's words: "I regard these men not as criminals; but as human beings with expectations of upliftment. Rodney and I support them; we give them the chance to be who they truly are."

This is what Poep Am, the prisoner who first requested Heila and Rodney, to provide a meditation programme for the prisoners, said:

"I became connected with the Chinese mafia. We kidnapped a guy, who was then murdered. For my part in this, I was given a twenty-six year sentence.

"Now there is a possibility of me being released. Should this happen, it will be a culture shock for me. I have become set in the ways of the institution. My family life has disintegrated and I am divorced. Yet I have grown immeasurably in prison. I am studying Information Technology and I am now in my fourth year of study.

"I seemed to spend my whole life searching for something. I read books on meditation and psychology. I could never find anything to satisfy my inner quest. I committed crimes and ended up in prison. I want to change this person. This bad guy is not the person that I truly am. I wanted to know why I behaved so badly, when at heart I've always been a good guy.

"Frustrated by my lack of direction in life I wrote to Heila. I asked her and Rodney to come to the prison. Since its inception the MAIA and Zen prison programme has grown immeasurably. We even do three and five-day retreats based on the principles of Zen Buddhism. Usually we have at least forty prisoners at these retreats … sometimes a translator in the African language, Xhosa, is introduced, because some of the prisoners have a poor grasp of English.

"Last year I asked the prison authorities if I and one or two of the other prisoners could be kept in isolation. For thirty days we took a vow of silence. We fasted to a certain degree. It was hard. Very hard. I had no alternative but to look within. To open many doors that I had kept closed for so long. I reached a level of peace and tranquillity that I would never have believed possible.

"Today when my family visits me, they can't believe that I am the same man. I have asked for their forgiveness and they love me unconditionally. I have a child who visits the prison and who also loves me unconditionally. Every time I feel that I am about to stumble and fall, I write a letter or I phone Rodney and Heila.

"They are amazing people. They don't judge. They give guidance and support, coupled with unconditional love. They have unlocked my mind and I find deeper meaning in things, away from the trivial. I never fail to do my meditation and I get up at 2.45 each day to say the five precepts.

"Taking precepts is a strong statement of an intention that right now I will cut through my ambivalence in order to live with clarity and generosity. As such, the precepts are not strict moral rules, but signs pointing toward how to keep the just-now in mind."

The five precepts are:

* I vow to abstain from taking life.

* I vow to abstain from taking things not given.

* I vow to abstain from misconduct done in lust.

* I vow to abstain from lying.

* I vow to abstain from intoxicants, taken to induce heedlessness.

The next prisoner I spoke to was Chong Kwang who was sentenced in 1997 to eleven years for murder. "I was eighteen when I committed the crime. It was a person that I knew ... not very well. We had a fight and I was very violent at that time.

"I grew up in the township of Guguletu here in Cape Town. My mother, a freelance nursing sister, a very good woman, was a single parent. I had a big brother and a younger sister. Without a parent at home, I learnt crime on the streets. I was a wild, violent fighter and I used to steal cars.

"I came to prison very young. You had to be strong to survive. There was a distance between the wardens and the prisoners — the wardens were only interested in doing their duty ... they barely saw us as human.

"I went to other prisons before I came to Malmesbury. I came from a Christian home. I always had a lot of questions in my mind. I needed something to believe in. I noticed Poep Am. He wasn't like the other prisoners ... many of whom are restless and angry. He always seemed so calm. I heard that he was a Buddhist.

"One day we got talking and he told me about meditation. I began to meditate in 2001 and it totally changed my life; I'm no longer the person that I used to be. Meditation brought up all kinds of things. My art for example. As a child I was always good at art. I got compliments for my drawing from a young age. But I certainly didn't grow up in the sort of environment where you take that kind of thing seriously.

"Now, thanks to the meditation, it all came back to me. Malmesbury is a better prison than some of the others I've been in. I'm in a single cell and since I've been following a spiritual practice, my interest in art has been reawakened. I just began drawing and painting and I can't stop."

"What do you paint?"

"Anything from nature to people. The ideas come pouring out.

"Nothing is ever going to separate me from my art again. Also in prison I repeated my matriculation exam. My grades were low and I want to go to university when I get out of here. My subjects were English, Xhosa, History, Criminology and Biblical Studies."

"When are you due for parole?"

"Towards the end of this year. But I'm scared of life outside these prison walls. My brother died. We had different fathers. He was shot. His passing brought out a lot of things. I feel that I have to take on his role as the eldest.

"My mom loves me and she's very proud of me. She's retired now and I want to take care of her. That's why I've started to do pottery. It's not easy to make a living from art, but I know that I'll be able to sell the pottery I produce. I'm going to need a kiln ..."

"The township is a violent place. Will the people there accept you as an artist and a potter?"

Chong Kwang shakes his head. "I know it's going to be rough out there. That's why I'm first going to stay at the Dharma Centre in Robertson with Rodney and Heila. They'll support me and give me the strength to face up to life in the community."

"How long do you thing you'll be in Robertson?"

"Let's say six months."

"Hey, Chong Kwang. Let's say three months," smiled Heila putting an affectionate arm around the young man. "I've already started to find homes for his paintings. People love them. They're so full of optimism and hope. Soon he won't be able to keep up with the demand."

I also spoke to a prisoner named Hyon Kwang, who received a twenty-three year sentence for murder and armed robbery.

"A number of factors contributed to my violence and anger. I believe that I was over trained by the military. After serving in the army I was given intensive training for the navy. Following all this discipline I wasn't equipped with the tools for everyday civilian life. My anger intensified and my wife divorced me in Zambia. I still miss her and cry for her.

"When I first went to prison I joined a prison gang. All you want to do is to get out. For five years I plotted a way to escape. Having managed to get away I was caught and arrested and given a longer prison sentence. The length of time that I was now going to stay in prison made my wife divorce me.

"I was in a pretty bad space when Johan got me interested in the work that Rodney and Heila were doing at the prison. I joined the group and I've been with the prison programme for six years. I have much more control of my temper. I know who I am and why I am here. If I seem in control today, it's all thanks to Rodney and Heila. What helps me particularly is the practice of zazen."

"What is zazen?"

"Sitting meditation or zazen forms an important part of Zen practice. Zen means meditation and meditation means keeping a not-moving mind from moment to moment. If your mind doesn't move, your anger dissipates."

The MAIA and Zen programme that Heila and Rodney do for the prisoners is done with no subsidy from The Correctional Services Department. Their work is done entirely from donations from the public. Yet for both of them the rewards go well belong monetary considerations.

"My dad was stabbed thirty-four times by two women in Kroonstad who were under the influence of drugs and alcohol. He was not well and they overpowered him and did terrible things to him," said Heila softly.

"I never felt anger about his murder, only pain and sadness. But you know what? Our Group got me through this difficult time. They understood the minds of the murderers and they gave me so much love and support."

Through their vision and guidance Rodney and Heila have been able to transform the negative attitude of prisoners who are used to seeing the prison as a place for punishment and degradation into a positive attitude where they see the prison as a personal development centre. For those prisoners who have the courage to embrace this spiritual path, choosing to ignore the spiteful barbs of the majority of their fellow inmates, their rehabilitation and transformation is truly miraculous!

www.dharmacentre.org.za

SANETTE BOULTON

LEUKAEMIA SUFFERER

THE LITTLE FLOWER WHOSE LIFE WAS CUT SHORT

It's me. It's me. Oh Lord
standing in the need of prayer
Not my mother
Nor my father
But it's me Oh Lord
Not my brother
Not my sister
But it's me Oh Lord
standing in the need of prayer.

(Prayer by an anonymous author that is taught to Sunday School children)

There was much celebration when Sana married her sweetheart Paul Boulton in 1990. A worker in the aluminium industry, Paul was also a deacon in the Christian Revival Church and Sana was a Sunday school teacher. The happy couple both hoped their union would soon be blessed with children. Sana's father had twin sisters and with this family genealogy, Sana's dream was to become the proud mother of twins.

For seven and a half long years, Sana battled to fall pregnant.

She saw nine gynaecologists and underwent all sorts of fertility treatment. "We could have bought a house with the money we spent on doctors," she laughs ruefully.

Adoption was discussed, but Sana and Paul did not regard this as a viable option for them, although their heartfelt prayers to the Almighty remained unanswered. Not that her faith ever wavered. "I know that God will give us a gift," Sana told her husband.

Then in 1997 she went to speak with a pastor. "Buy nappies in faith," he said, "believing that you will fall pregnant. But buy sufficient not for one but for two babies."

The pastor's prediction came to pass for on the 8th of April 1998 Sana and Paul eventually became the proud parents of two beautiful little girls, Sanette and Paulette. The babies were born one month and two days prematurely at St Augustine's Hospital in Durban, but they were not placed in incubators, and, from the start, these perfect infants both thrived.

The birth of the twins was greeted by their family and friends with unbridled joy. Gifts for the girls poured into Sana and Paul's home. A double pram, toys, cots, clothes, substantial sums of money. "Apart from buying the girls some basic toiletries, I never had to buy a single thing," recalled Sana with a laugh. "The girls were my parents' first grandchildren and it was their pleasure to spoil them. Our whole community celebrated their birth, with presents pouring in from well-wishers all over the country."

It was hard work looking after the twins, but although she sometimes felt tired, Sana delighted in her two girls and some important milestones passed all too quickly for Sana and Paul. First there was the babies' christening — as committed Christians this was a very special and sacred occasion — then it was their first birthday, their second birthday. The girls' third and fourth birthdays were also times of happiness and celebration.

Almost before Sana knew it, the twins were five and due to start school. Paulette was the sporty one and Sanette was more gentle and feminine of the two. Both girls were bright as buttons and so they were eagerly looking forward to the new school year that got underway in January. Sana, too, was eagerly anticipating having her beloved progeny off her hands for a few hours each day — not that she was complaining, but the two lively girls were a handful sometimes.

By mid-February Sanette suddenly started complaining of bodily pains. She ached from head to toe. Bruises began to appear on her body. "The first bruise I saw appeared on her hip. So I thought, well, perhaps she got hurt on the jungle gym," reflected Sana.

Soon Sanette could barely walk and Sana was forced to carry her ailing daughter around the house like a limp doll. In desperation, in an effort to ease the pain, Paul rubbed a light Voltaren solution over his child's aching limbs, but nothing brought relief.

The Boulton's general practitioner detected a spot of blood in the child's urine and antibiotics were prescribed. "I am a very restless mother, because I know how my children should be," stated Sana. "So when there was no improvement in Sanette's condition, we immediately took her back to the doctor. Stronger medication was prescribed, but this, too, had no effect."

"By the third week, Sanette started haemorrhaging and she was very pale — I remember that week we had a family function — and she was getting extremely high temperatures of around 39 or 40 °C. She also had a very small clot on her tongue. By the Monday morning it was the size of a ten-cent piece and it was jutting out. Paul said to me that I must take Sanette straight to the doctor.

"Our GP took one look at the ailing child. 'Mrs Boulton, I can't do anything' he said. I'm going to give you an emergency letter to Dr Kitch the paediatrician at the hospital,'" recalled Sana.

"Dr Kitch only gets to the hospital at around ten o'clock and I was there at about quarter to nine. When the doctor arrived — and here, once again, God has been so good — you normally can't show up without an appointment — but, for once, the doctor had her first appointment of the day free and was able to see us immediately.

"She laid Sanette on the bed and she checked her spleen and her liver, which was already enlarged by 4cm. My little girl was haemorrhaging. Dr Kitch told me that my daughter was extremely ill and that I was to go upstairs to the hospital — she said that I shouldn't even bother to worry about having Sanette admitted — but that I should go straight to the isolation ward.

"We took her upstairs and, after having a blood sample taken in the lab, we went into the ward. Seeing that Sanette had a high temperature, the nurses immediately turned the air conditioning up and switched the fans on in an effort to cool her down — they even put my little girl in a cool tub, but nothing helped.

"I remember her results came at quarter-past-eleven. Dr. Kitch told me that they were not good. All I can recall that her platelets were five. The doctor informed me that she was almost one hundred per cent sure that my daughter had leukaemia ALL.

"Then she told me that she was going to send Sanette to Dr. Janet Poole who works at the Johannesburg General Hospital. When it comes to childhood cancers, she's the best in Africa," Dr. Kitch assured me.

Trying to pull herself together, Sana phoned Paul. When she gave her husband the bad news, in a state of shock, Paul did not get a taxi or drive himself to the hospital. He walked the entire ten kilometre distance.

****

Statistics supplied by CHOC reveal:

- The incidence of childhood cancer is about 1 in 600 children.

- It is estimated that in Third World countries only half of the children are diagnosed and reach a treatment centre in time.

- The good news is that if diagnosed early and treated correctly, the majority of children (about 70%) can be cured.

- The cancers that occur in childhood are generally different to those of adults and most often occur in developing cells, like bone marrow, blood, kidneys and tissues of the nervous system.

- The most common childhood cancer is leukaemia, followed by tumours of the brain, and by a wide variety of other tumours.

- Life threatening blood disorders include: a plastic anaemia, thalassaemia and ITP.

- Generally childhood cancer is treated with chemotherapy, surgery or radiation, and in some cases a combination of these treatments are used. In certain situations, bone marrow or stem cell transplantation is done.

- Childhood cancers are diseases requiring specialist paediatric treatment at a centre where there is expertise in the management and care. In most developed countries these specialist units are linked to the major academic hospitals.

- Travelling from home to attend these clinics for treatment adds another dimension of practical and emotional difficulty to an already overwhelming situation.

****

The day following her diagnosis Sanette, accompanied by her parents, boarded an emergency airlift from Richard's Bay to Lanseria Airport in Johannesburg. Owing to the gravity of Sanette's condition, a qualified doctor and nurse were also in attendance on this specially chartered Netcare flight.

A Netcare flight then took the traumatised family to the Johannesburg General Hospital. In addition to coping with the shock of Sanette's diagnosis, Sana was now faced with the daunting fact that, for an unknown period, she and her gravely ill child would be based in Johannesburg, a vast city that was almost entirely unknown to her. Understandably, she was worried, not only about Sanette, but also about Paulette. How would her other five year old fare without her mother to look after her?

The only person on board that mercy flight who could be described as cheerful was Sanette. As a child raised in a religious Christian household who was fond of her Sunday school teachings, she spent the entire hour long duration of the flight singing the following song of devotion to her beloved Lord:

If I was a butterfly
I thank you Lord for giving me wings
If I was a robin in the tree
I thank you Lord that I could sing
But I just thank you Father for making me
Me Me Me
'Cos you gave me a heart
and you gave me a smile
You gave me Jesus
And you made me his child
But I just thank you Father for making me
Me Me Me.

When the plane landed, the pilot was surprised to learn that a child in Sanette's condition should want to sing songs, especially of a devotional nature. But Sana understood this perfectly. No matter how adverse the situation, her daughter as a child created by God, had a reason and a purpose to wish to continue living.

On arrival at the hospital's oncology unit Sanette immediately underwent a lumbar puncture and a bone marrow test to confirm the diagnosis. That afternoon Janet Poole told her waiting parents that Dr. Kitch's diagnosis was correct. However, she gave Sana and Paul hope by telling them that statistically girls generally healed faster and that in the age group 0-6 years, the treatment success rate was high.

"Sanette, being five at the time of her illness, fell within this age group," said Sana. "The night before we came up to Johannesburg, we prayed together with the congregation at Rhema Church. We told God that even if he were to take our child, we would never stop loving and serving Him. To me, Sanette's illness represented a very hard test of our faith, but now, when I heard that Sanette's chances of recovery were good, I felt that, once again, God had seen us through."

The Boulton family arrived in Johannesburg on a Tuesday. A couple of days later, they received a tearful call from Paulette that almost broke Sana's already aching heart.

"Mommy, on Saturday it's the school sports and I'm going to be a drummie.* Who will come and watch me?"

As the family had flown from Natal to Johannesburg, they didn't have a car at their disposal. Immediately, Paul made a decision.

"I will take the bus home. I can't let Paulette perform without either her mom or dad being there to watch her."

For five difficult weeks Sana stayed at the hospital with Sanette while she underwent chemotherapy. The child's hair fell out and she often felt grievously ill. But the agony was worth it.

After fourteen days, Janet Poole approached Sana with the following news: "Mrs Boulton, I have just seen Sanette's test results … "

"And how are they?" queried Sana, biting her lip.

I'm pleased to tell you that your little girl has gone into remission," smiled Dr. Poole.

****

CHOC, the Childhood Cancer Foundation of South Africa, was established in Johannesburg in 1979. The goal of this dedicated group is to improve the wel-

---

* drummie — abbreviation for drum majorette

fare and quality care for children with cancer. In 2000 a new national group was formed, linking parent groups in all parts of the country.

The organisation, which is not government funded, provides direct practical help to children with cancer, from diagnosis onwards, recognising the inevitable disruption to family life when a child faces vigorous and often lengthy treatment.

CHOC House, which was at that time situated in the leafy suburb of Saxonwold in Johannesburg, is a large single-storey suburban house, where out-of-town child cancer patients and their parents can stay during the child's treatment.

Everything there, from the beds to the pots and pans to the giant television screen in the sitting room has been donated by the generosity of various benefactors. The overall impression is of a comfortable suburban house, warm, welcoming and inviting. The staff who work there are not only dedicated and very loving to the patients, they are all also parents who have had a child who suffered from a life-threatening illness. Therefore, they can empathise not only with the children, but also with the parents who accompany their offspring to their treatment.

Nothing has been spared in the effort to make CHOC House as cheerful as possible. Even the outside garden is a haven for the children, where they can run around and play in the sun — not without careful supervision to ensure that they are wearing their sunscreen and, most often, their protective sunhats — or they can climb on the jungle gym.

One might almost be misled into thinking CHOC is a crèche, most the children look so well — the success rate of patients in remission is pretty healthy — until one catches sight of a child who is obviously desperately ill and one observes that almost all the children are accompanied by a parent or care giver.

Then too there is the unobtrusive, but very private room, for a child to stay who is on the critical list and for a grieving parent whose only solace is privacy.

Following five weeks in hospital, Sana and Sanette moved into CHOC House, where the gravity of Sanette's condition necessitated them staying a long six months so that she could go for treatment as an outpatient at the Johannesburg General. Their only break was for twelve days in July when Sana and Sanette went home for a bittersweet family reunion.

"The people at CHOC are so supportive and loving, but still one misses one's family and the important milestones in one's child's life. For instance, Sanette was not there when they took her class photos," remarked a weeping Sana.

Still, very grateful for the support, both practical and on a more spiritual level, on one of the days that I was visiting, Sana showed her gratitude by cooking one of her renowned curry dishes for the twenty or so members of the CHOC committee who were to attend a meeting at the house that night.

Amongst the literature I was given to read about the work that CHOC does was this moving yet practical open letter to a parent with a child newly diagnosed with a life threatening illness, written by Julian Cutland:

You have just started into one of the periods of your life that you will always remember.

You never thought that something like this could happen to your child.

You thought that it was your right that your child would grow up to be just like you, with the occasional illness or broken limb, but you never anticipated an illness that could take their life.

Now you know differently and if you are like most of us who have been down this path ahead of you, then your outlook on life will probably be changed forever from this week onwards.

- *During the next few weeks you will go through many emotions:*
- you will feel anger at the unfairness of it.
- you will grieve that all of the dreams had for your child will come to nothing.
- you will try to bargain with God to cure your child.
- you will blame yourself for causing the illness.
- you will regret not doing things with your child that you intended to.
- you will feel lost and confused by lots of medical jargon and new words.
- you will agonise over what you should tell your children, your parents, your friends and you will wonder how you will cope with it all.

In other words, you will behave just like all the rest of us parents who have ever been in your situation.

You will have to develop your own methods for coping with things, depending on your personal situation. However, you may find a few guidelines useful as a starting point:

Be honest and open about the illness, to your relatives and friends, to the school, your employers, but most of all to yourselves and to your children. Your child will know that they are ill: don't make them hide their feelings to protect you.

Your family and friends will not at first know what to say to you, and they will be very uncomfortable with you. The more openly you talk about things, the easier it will be for them to respond to you and give you the help that you will need so much in the coming months.

Get used to saying the name of the illness out loud. Words like cancer and leukaemia are normally only spoken in hushed voices, and never in the presence of someone who has them. It will be with you for a long time, so get used to saying it, and even talk about death. It makes it much easier for all your family and friends to talk openly if you do so.

Don't be ashamed to feel or show emotion: It just shows that you are human. If you didn't feel angry, sad, confused, and many other emotions, when you learned of the diagnosis, then you are very unusual. Don't forget that your sick child, and other children, will have to cope with many new experiences and emotions. Let them see that it's all right to feel afraid, to be unsure, to cry at times.

Remember that you are in this as a family. Many families, who have a good marriage to start with, find that they are all strengthened by the experience: but it is not unusual for a marriage to be very stressed by all the extra demands that an illness like this will put on it.

Do not forget the siblings. Brothers and sisters of the sick child are also affected by the illness in the family. They see their parents giving all of their intention to the other child, and can feel very neglected and confused.

Call on all the resources that you have. Use your family and friends: if they are true friends they will be only too glad to help you now that you really need them. Use your church: get people to pray for you and your child. You will be *surprised how much and how readily people will open up and help you, if they only know how: and that is why you need to make your needs know.*

There are no guarantees. The medical staff will do their best; there may be a very good prognosis for your child: but it is still a life threatening illness, and you will have to live with this for a long time.

Don't be afraid to ask the medical staff. You will probably not take in half of what is said in the early discussions and there will be a whole new vocabulary in your life. Keep notes of the questions you want to ask.

There is a lot of literature about, and you will want to get as much knowledge as possible, so ask the staff what they recommend.

There will be times when all seems very dark, and some very happy times. The best way to get through the coming weeks and months is to take one day at a time.

May you find the strength in yourself, your family and your friends to grow through this trying time in your lives.

****

Following six months of gruelling treatment, there was good news for the Boulton family. Sanette was better. So much better in fact that she and her mother could go home. Yes, they will have to come up for periodic treatments, but Dr. Poole has given the little girl a clean bill of health. Sanette's weight had picked up. Eighteen kilos at the start of the treatment, she was now a satisfactory twenty-three kilos.

I requested permission to photograph Sanette before she left CHOC House for her home in Richard's Bay. Inadvertently, the time of the photographic session coincided with the time that the late Dr. Ivan May, a tireless fund raiser for CHOC following the death of his beloved adopted son, Xolani Dyusha, better known as 'Tunkie', had arranged to take all the children currently resident in the home to the nearby Wimpy Restaurant. The kids, wearing hats to hide their baldness, were all rearing to go.

Sanette, too, was anxious not to miss a second of this eagerly anticipated outing. It was difficult to keep her still. So many people had prayed for her and their prayers had been answered. This bright little butterfly was once again flying high!

www.choc.org

Unfortunately Sanette suffered a relapse and passed away on the 28th of October 2007. Her parents gave their consent for her story to be told.

Her parents, her doctors, her caregivers and all who met this incredible child concur that there is one more angel in heaven.

ALIYA B HAERI

INTEGRAL LIFE PSYCHOLOGIST & COACH

PEARLS OF WISDOM FROM A CULTURED TEACHER

Your remedy is within you,
But you do not perceive it,
Your illness is from you,
But you do not sense it.
You presume you are an insignificant entity,
Yet within you is enfolded
The entire universe.
You are the illumined book,
By your signs, that which was hidden
Becomes manifest.
Thus, you have no need to look beyond yourself
What you seek is within you,
If only you reflect!

Sufi saying

"It was a crisis in my personal life that sent me searching for a deeper meaning to our existence on this earth. But then I believe that from an early age I have always been a seeker. Let me start at the beginning …

"I grew up in paradise. On one of the Hawaiian Islands in the Pacific. There were three children in the family — I had an older brother and a younger sister. Although my parents were fine, upstanding and moral people, respected in the community, somehow I never felt that I belonged to this life.

"When I was about nine years of age, I had a near death experience. I was swimming in the Pacific when I was caught and pulled down into the depths by an undertow current, and in the swelling oceans of water I found myself struggling and gasping for breath. My entire life began to flash before my eyes. Then I got to a point where the struggling stopped. I felt a total peace. Beyond words could describe.

"Suddenly I found myself on the shore coughing up water. From that moment on I knew not to fear death. I also realized that there was more to life than simply growing up and going to school, more than what simply appeared on life's surface. I never told anyone, not even my parents, about what had happened to me."

From an early age Aliya had a deeply intuitive sense of what was going on with other people. This manifested in her ability to heal. She explains this as 'a natural ability, which potentially everyone possesses.'

"In truth," she continued, "no one has the power to heal. We only access the healing force of nature within, and it does the work."

Aliya discovered that she could go deeply into a meditative state and symptoms or illnesses would disappear. "I found myself going to gatherings where people would often say that because of my presence, they felt healed."

After finishing her schooling, Aliya went to university in New York. In the course of her research she studied some very powerful psychics and people who channeled and who had access to invisible realms.

"We did a great deal of spiritual healing either by prayer or by meditation. Becoming more involved with psychic research, I travelled to quite a few countries, visiting people who displayed extraordinary gifts."

"Who was the most impressive person you studied?"

"Uri Geller. After watching him at work, it became undeniably clear to me that some other reality other than our everyday three dimensional world was at play and accessible to us."

Aliya set up and conducted a study of twelve psychically gifted children in the United Kingdom, who were able to demonstrate feats of metal bending, as well as telepathy and healing. "These children ranged from the son of an Oxford professor to an impoverished teenager who grew up in very humble circumstances in Scotland. It then occurred to me that this ability to access the subtle realms was universal to all people. It didn't matter what background you came from or what beliefs you held.

"This research and other investigations brought the phenomenon of paranormal ability into the main stream, for we approached it not as a sensational project, simply as a way of getting greater society to recognise these extraordinary gifts that some seemingly ordinary people possessed."

Through the research she was doing, Aliya gained insight into an unseen world. "Undeniably there was a realm of light and phenomenology that was much more vast, luminous and inexplicable than the world we live in," she remarked. "But after a few years of studying this, I felt that I was accumulating more and more data, but that my search for deeper truth and meaning was unsatisfied. I had also ended a relationship at the same time and my work no longer held any meaning for me. I was facing a spiritual crisis.

"I fell into a state of loss and despair. I decided that I must not take the easy way out. I would not call a friend or distract myself by going out for coffee or taking a short holiday. I decided to face my problems. I closed down the house in which I was staying and I notified my friends that I would be away for the next few days. I disconnected the telephone and in the darkened room, I sat in a wide armchair and waited, not knowing what was going to happen. I had decided to accept and to face whatever arose in my heart. It was on a Thursday that this took place, for this fact would later prove significant.

"This was a terrifying time. I totally lost my sense of security and stability. If I was not this researcher known for work in this field, then who was I? If I had no sense of my own identity, did I exist?

"I had made a commitment not to leave this room, this chair, whatever might happen. It seemed like an eternity. I waited. Then I began to fall deep within myself, feeling a terrible sense of loneliness. As I fell deeper and deeper, I was overcome by despair and a sense of loss. I continued to descend into this void of absolute darkness. Then I stopped falling.

"Before me in the darkness a door appeared. I knew that if I went through that door the next day I would be discovered dead or stark raving mad. Something in me did not accept that door. In my inmost core, I was saying 'no' to negation. In that instant, I found myself slowly rising to the surface as if from the bottom of the ocean. Ascending, empty of all those feelings, I felt a growing lightness within.

"Returning to consciousness of the room, I discovered that a full day had passed and that it was now the following morning. In an intellectual sense I could not fathom what had happened, but a sense of trust in guidance had been borne.

"There *was* guidance in the Universe and although I could not understand where I was being guided or the source of this trust, I knew that whatever happened next would be the right unfolding for me. I felt as if I was being given life again."

It was now Friday morning and Aliya got herself ready to set off on a trip that had been arranged earlier in the week. Some friends had suggested that she might be working too hard. Why didn't she fly from Toronto to Washington DC to join them for a few days?

"As the plane took off, my soul began to soar. I felt that I was flying into the unknown towards a new horizon in my destiny," smiled Aliya. "When I arrived, I was met by friends who were taking me to dinner and then a symphony concert. On our way there, my friends asked if I would mind if they dropped off some books?

"We took the lift to an upper story apartment and when the door opened, the young man had a look of surprise on his face. He was a student of the spiritual master whose apartment we had come to. I had been seeking spiritual guidance and guidance had been brought to me. This spiritual master would be my first teacher."

Aliya reflected for a few moments before adding "What I didn't know until later was that this teacher followed a path in which spiritual retreat was observed on Thursday nights. When he emerged from this retreat, which happened to be at the same time that I was surfacing from my vigil, he told his student that he had a vision of a woman from the East who would be coming to meet him.

"When he began to speak I felt that I had finally come home. My life on the Sufi path of God's truth and love began at that moment."

****

Following this auspicious meeting, Aliya began to dream in foreign languages, seeing images that she had never seen in this life, all pointing to a destiny that she had not been aware of.

Going deeper into her meditation and fasting and invocation practices, Aliya gave up all her worldly possessions. With only the clothes on her back and a few personal belongings that fitted into two suitcases, she went off to live in a Sufi community. When her teacher learned that she'd given up everything, including a fine fur coat, he inquired, raising his eyebrows, 'Why on earth did you do that?' Later, of course, I would discover that simplifying your life does not mean that you own nothing, but rather, nothing owns you."

Aliya's teacher then instructed her to stop all psychic practices, saying that at this stage in her life, these were a distraction that would impede her spiritual growth.

"There are many levels of reality that manifest in this existence. In both the spheres of the seen and the unseen. The psychic realm is not the realm of higher reality," explained the master. "If you want absolute certain truth that there is an eternal Source that created out of love everything in this existence, then you have to single-mindedly make that your goal.

"Nothing was more important to me. Nevertheless," said Aliya, her eyes twinkling, "although I tried to remove all psychic phenomena from my life, it took a full year before my coffee spoons stopped bending."

****

Aliya later was married to her teacher, Shaykh Fadhlalla Haeri, who is a recognised master of the Sufi tradition.

Subsequently, Aliya underwent a spiritual retreat in which she was isolated in a darkened room. She had no contact with the outside world apart from a knock on the door three times a day, when somebody would leave a plate of food outside her door.

Otherwise she spent the entire time calling upon the divine name of God, performing her prayers and essentially remembering only God in this creation.

"The purpose of this retreat was to focus your physical body, your mind and every atom of your being on God, by invoking God's divine name." Apart from a few hours of sleep, Aliya sat in single-minded remembrance of God, stilling the body, stilling the mind, and stilling all awareness of anything other than God through His beautiful name.

"At the end of the second day, I disappeared into nothingness. There was nothing of me that existed. As I returned to my consciousness I could hear the name of God echoing in the vastness of space. It was everywhere, vast and boundless — and I was one with it.

"At that point I was overcome with awe. I knew that I knew nothing. It filled me with the unshakable certainty that there was a vast, boundless, eternal reality that was more real than anything I could experience in this life — and I was a part of it.

"A spiritual teacher once said: 'Only the one who knows that they do not exist, knows that God exists.' On reflection, what this means is that we can only come to know our true existence if we abandon our self-image and ego; then we will discover our real nature, our essence, which is the light of God within us that we call soul.

"This is what is meant by 'God is within.' Of course, God is everywhere. The source of all life; of all creation. God is transcendent, beyond creation, yet God permeates everything in creation, giving life to every single thing in this existence and then sustaining it. Everything that was, is and ever will be is God. And yet, even beyond this is God, a timeless, eternal presence. It was that reality that made itself known to me in that darkened room.

"It was a great gift to know that our soul is indeed that — eternal and ongoing — and it is simply the form of body that we are loaned in this life that is temporal and dies away, but who we are in essence continues to exist in timeless eternity. This life is simply one stage of our journey that never ends.

"Consequently, death is not an end, but a beginning. I hope that this knowledge will bring a measure of comfort to all those who mourn the loss of a loved one."

****

Aliya had spent considerable time talking to me. Yet, petite and exotic as she is, like some delicate lotus flower, she did not wilt, for it was important to her as a committed spiritual teacher to impart her vast knowledge of All That Is.

"Our world was created out of love, and this love courses through the universe, and it is this love that holds the universe together and connects us inseparably and with all existence. It is only when we are forgetful, that we become isolated and life is a struggle.

"Everything in existence is created in duality. How can you know joy unless you have suffered pain? How can you know what it is to be healthy unless you have been ill? Every experience, even the greatest suffering, leads us to knowledge. I believe that the more we open ourselves in surrender to life's moment, the more enlightened we ultimately become.

"In truth you are enlightened. The light you seek is there within you. What veils the light are its shadow qualities of the ego-self which constantly arise. Turn away from the shadow self and the light of the soul is already there. Then you will discover your original enlightenment.

"A great Sufi sage, Rumi, wrote:

> *If you could get rid*
> *Of yourself just once*
> *The secret of secrets*
> *Would open to you.*
> *The face of the unknown,*
> *Hidden beyond the universe*
> *Would appear on the*
> *Mirror or your perception."*

Aliya paused for a moment, choosing her next words with great care.

"This knowledge puts the events of this outer life into perspective. We often magnify what happens to us in life, as if our outer life is our only reality.

"When we begin to listen to the soul and act according to its light qualities, our inner illumined nature begins to radiate. We realise that we are beings of light, illumined eternal souls. That we live in a sacred universe. And we are one and inseparable with all that is. That is who we are in truth; and this knowledge enables us to deal more effectively with our outer life. We acquire a greater respect and accountability for our actions.

"There can be no freedom without responsibility. The freedom we all seek comes from being accountable for every act that we chose to undertake in this life. Whatever we do has consequences. Since we are all created from the One divine light and we all carry that sacred light within, how can I look down on anyone else? I know I am no better than anyone else, and also no one is better than I.

"We know that thought is power. Sages and saints, of course, have said this for thousands of years. The way we think creates not only how we see the world but also how we experience it. The world is but a mirror to our inner state. If we let our problems get the better of us, we will see problems everywhere.

"But if we have a good opinion of life, we will see goodness everywhere, even in adversity, because it can teach us something useful. We are constantly making choices, consciously or unconsciously, about how to respond to our experiences. In this way we are responsible for what happens in our life.

"As I have said thought is powerful. Prayer is powerful. What is prayer other than thought? Thought that comes not from the mind, but from the heart. I have been praying for most of my life, having been raised in a Christian family and then exploring spiritual traditions and paths and, subsequently, making a commitment to the Islamic faith, that are heavily indebted to spiritual practices such as prayer and meditation. For there is only One God, One Truth, behind the many spiritual traditions and paths.

"I have frequently asked God for guidance and help and since I have gained these insights I find that my prayers have turned almost wholly to expressions of gratitude. I am so overwhelmed by the generosity of this universe. I have no doubt that we live in a merciful universe. A Sufi teaching states that the grace and compassion of the One encompass everything. Not only in the bees that make the honey, but also in the wasps that sting perfectly."

"How can you say that the universe is merciful when there is so much suffering everywhere?" I asked Aliya.

"Some years ago in Bosnia, countless thousands were put to death for their religious beliefs. Where is the compassion in that? It is sometimes difficult for people to accept that, no matter how tragic or unfortunate a situation may appear, you as a human being always have the choice to use that experience as you choose.

"If you choose to use that experience as a window for your own growth, for your own expanding consciousness to the greater light within you, then you are that much closer to fulfilling your purpose, which is to awaken to your true nature and to come to know the Source within you. People of all religious backgrounds and people with no religious backgrounds have discovered this and made it a way of life.

"Many of the great Sufi Masters from the great tradition of Islam have written beautifully on this subject. They have said that if you see that at every instant

Life or the Universe is sending you the best for you, you would never be able to cease in your praise.

"Such is His generosity that if you take one step towards God, He takes ten steps towards you. But the truth is that God is always with you.

"Often, it takes something unexpected to turn our lives inside out before we awaken to this truth. Victor Frankl, survivor of the WW II camps and renowned psychiatrist, has said: 'Through suffering comes the birth of meaning in one's life and hence gives one a meaningful life.'

"There is a great truth in this. For when I look at what appeared to be the major turning points or crises in my life, out of these came not only the greatest openings into my own window of seeing this world in its true nature. My growth and development sprung from these events and I would never wish that they had not happened.

"Today I actually can't say or believe that anything is wrong or a mistake in life. We make our choices at every moment and sometimes it may seem that we did not make the best choice. But if we again look at this as a gift and a blessing, not only will we never repeat that same decision again, we will also grow in self-discovery and what we do with our lives.

"If we look on whatever happens to us not as adversity, but rather as an opportunity for us to live more consciously, in greater awareness, then we also make the choices we decide upon for our outer life to become more meaningful, useful and joyful, not just for ourselves, but for others as well.

"What prevents us from living in a state of constant awareness is the assertion of the self, or what we call the ego-self. The self is the shadow of the soul and contains the opposing qualities of light. It is filled with our desires, our expectations and it is driven primarily by fear.

"Again, fear has its usefulness. Fear of danger is life preserving. Fear of making mistakes allows us to move more effectively towards our goal. But what is even more powerful than fear is love. And love is the quality of one's soul. Love is the opposite of fear. It is the interplay of these two qualities, these two emotions that drives everything that we do in our lives.

"Psychologically these two elements are called 'the attraction/repulsion principle.' In other words we repulse away from us anything that we fear or that causes us pain. Conversely, we attract towards us what we love and that gives us pleasure. We start off by saying 'If only I had this wonderful house, then everything would be all right.'

"Well, we acquire the house and somehow it still doesn't fill that void, the emptiness within us. Each time we achieved another goal we find that we are still far removed from that state of contentment until we arrive at a point of realization that we will never find the ultimate fulfilment by seeking outer achievement and therefore we begin to turn inward.

"What are the moments that we feel totally at peace? Could it be in the arms of a loved one? Could it be when we walk along a tropical beach, the waves lapping gently at our feet? Or standing atop a mountain where the horizon stretches without end before you? Or feeling the cool soil with bare hands as you plant a new flowerbed? There is such exquisite sense of perfection in nature that you feel that nothing could add more to this sense of joy that one feels. It is in these momentary glimpses of contentment and joy and experiencing love unconditionally that we find our soul.

"It is human nature for this love and joy to vanish as the fear sets in. What if he doesn't love me? What if he finds someone else? It is the fear of the self, what I call the everyday mind, which occludes the trust and the love and the beauty of the soul to manifest at all times.

"Life has a way of jolting us out of our complacency and pulling us into higher consciousness and it always enters our life in the form of some extreme challenge. It can be the death of a loved one, or a physical challenge, a handicap or an accident that takes away the career of a sportsman; or an illness; or the loss of a great deal of money that changes one's whole sense of identity, who you are and what you are in this world."

Putting down her teacup, Aliya continued speaking quietly, but with great intensity. "You can be absolutely sure that life will at some point send you a blessing in the form of an immense challenge. Mine came with a feeling of total despair and an existential loss of identity. Out of that arose a whole new awakening; a whole new way of seeing the world and oneself in it. To be in the world, but not of it.

"When so-called misfortune occurs, I can only be grateful to God for it. Whatever the gift is that is contained in that perceived misfortune is always greater than the difficulties it caused. One has to surrender oneself completely into that moment of crisis in order to see the gift that is there. You can't bargain with the Universe."

Aliya paused contemplatively. "How can one live in this state of higher awareness? What I've found most powerful in seeing the perfection that is all around me is to withhold judgement. To go beyond saying this is good. Or this is bad. To let go of one's personal agenda.

"Not to say I want this. Therefore this must be good. I don't like this. Therefore it must be bad. What you want may actually turn out to be bad for you. And what you dislike may end up being good for you.

"To live in the state of higher consciousness is to let go of your mind-set.

To let go of the material things we feel give us a sense of balance and meaning. Simply to stand naked in your soul in the world that you face. See what is happening before you. Not with your eyes, for they interpret what you see, but *through* your eyes, which simply *witness.* Then you will see things as they are. And you will see its perfection."

"What do you mean by this?"

"For example, one should not say 'My beloved great aunt passed away and I cannot get over the loss.' If, however, one saw the perfection of all things, one rather would say, 'My beloved great aunt passed away and she is now free of the pain and suffering that she would have had to undergo on a life support system. Isn't that merciful that she went with dignity in the way that she chose to go?' That is your soul speaking and that is your soul witnessing her."

Aliya then stood up and invited me to walk with her in her immaculately manicured garden. "Sometimes, in the midst of my work, I leave my computer and walk in the garden. Everywhere I see signs of beauty and majesty."

She paused for a moment in front a fragrant rosebush, cupping one of the perfect blooms within her hands.

"Who could ever design anything as beautiful as a rose with our human mind? And how does the rose know when to bloom and when to fade and return to its origins in the soil so that a new flower can come forth?

"Not only does this rose bring joy to the heart, it also brings solace. For one begins to see signs of the perfection in this existence that point to reality, a divine intelligence, which one can trust. We are humbled, awed by the miracle of the rose. This life is far greater and far more mysterious than anything we can imagine. Yet even in its overwhelming intensity, we sense the intimate wondrousness of it all. Something in the heart calls us to trust.

"But we can only trust, if the trust is based on the knowledge that life knows more than we ever can, our soul knows more than our self, and our higher consciousness knows more than the mind can imagine.

"To become truly human is to awaken to your true nature, which is your enlightened soul. In our Sufi teachings, and it is echoed in many of the other religious traditions of the world, we accept that the soul is the abode of all Godly attributes and the potential of all that we need in this life. Everything that you need is within you. You need not look beyond yourself. You are enlightened. It is your true nature. It's your Original Face.

"Our work in this life is to awake. To wake up to who we truly are. If we live by our light attributes, we will more ably try and overcome the difficulties and adversity with which we have to deal, seeing these rather as challenges, which give us the opporatunity to fulfil our true potential and become the enlightened souls that is our birthright."

www.aliya-haeri.com
www.askonline.co.za

OTHER GREAT TITLES
BY HEART SPACE PUBLICATIONS

Dance of Light: a new way of understanding the Earth and all life forms

All is One : an extra ordinary book that teaches difficult concepts in a simple way!

Yogi, the Tails and Teachings of a Suburban Alpha Doggy: a delightful read illustrating the wisdom and humour that animals bring to our lives

Second Chance, Regain your Health with Tissue Salts: this book will help the full spectrum of users, from concerned parents, experienced pharmacists and health care workers

 ***The Art of Walking:*** a treasure trove of knowledge, practical guidance and inspiration in lyrical prose

PATRICK GRAYSON

Know Thyself: a workbook that can become a lifeline for alife that works

 ***Towards a Soulful Sexuality:*** an intelligent, thought provoking and candid new perspective of sex, age and menopause for all women.

How to Write - Right!: with this book you will become the writer you have always wanted to be

PATRICK GRAYSON

Trees, the Guardian of the Soul: a book of short stories that imparts the wisdom of the ages, appealing to all age groups

---

The Halo and the Noose: a great piece of work which stimulates one to look at life differently

Hillhairyass Poems: poems and illustrations created to entertain and support young adults

---

Guided! How to Communicate with your Spirit Guides: Discover your soul's purpose and learn techniques to communicate with your spirit guides

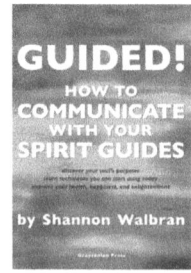

The Irritable Woman's Cookbook: "cooking is like sex; you have to be in the mood", says the humorous author of this Jewish cookbook

---

The Seasons of Our Lives: George Kouloukis shows that the alternating trends of our lives - going from good to bad and vice versa, are according to specific patterns.

The Path of Cosmic Consciousness: journey through initiation to enlightenment in the sacred Andean tradition

---

What if: an encounter of simple truth about life and spirituality

Paws and Listen to the Voices of the Animals: Read this book, then open your heart, free your mind and listen to the ancient wisdom of the animals that you love.

Spunky: Join me on my journey of becoming a cancer survivor, and against all odds a provincial badminton player.

Bleeding Heart: Bleeding Heart is a timeless fable about living life with passion. It will bring joy to your soul as you turn the pages ever faster.

Saving your life one day at a time: There are many books on improving health, and many on how to improve your life - but there are not many that include both. This book does. And every so often, perhaps once a generation, a book emerges that clearly stands above the rest. Saving your life, one day at a time is one such book.

The Power to Navigate Life: Tony Fahkry has written what is arguably the most complete and powerful teachings on the mastering of life.

Heart Space Publications

Australia: +61 450 260 348

South Africa: +27 11 431 1274

pat@heartspacebooks.com

www.heartspacebooks.com

www.ingramcontent.com/pod-product-compliance
Lightning Source LLC
Chambersburg PA
CBHW070555300426
44113CB00010B/1266